Sovereign God
For Us and Through Us

A Faith Building Revelation of
God's Power and Purpose
to Use Everything
to Mature and Empower Us

For His Use

David Eells

Faithful Publishing
Buford, Georgia

Published by
Faithful Publishing
PO Box 345
Buford, Georgia 30515
faithfulpublishing.com
888-860-5394

ISBN 10: 0-9759941-9-0
ISBN 13: 978-09759941-9-1
Fourth Printing – Large Print Edition – 2006

"Bible Code" ©1997 by Michael Drosnin, Simon & Schuster Publishers
"Theomatics" ©1977 by Jerry Lucas and Del Washburn
Stein and Day / Publishers / Scarborough

Scriptures are taken from the American Standard Version because of its faithfulness to the ancient manuscripts and Bible Numerics, a system designed by God for proving authenticity. Available from Starbible.com.

We have departed from the A.S.V. only in the name Jehovah, which we replaced with Lord. Neither represents the original YHWH but Lord is less confusing to many and we did not want this to distract from the teaching.

We desire to make this book free on our part because Jesus said, "Freely you have received, freely give," but the business of publishing does not lend itself to that. We can say that any profits made from this book will go toward promoting the message of the kingdom of God and not to any personal, fleshly gain. Free copies of the book are made available through the generous donations of His faithful servants and can be requested by email at: freebook@faithfulpublishing.com

Managing Editor: April S Fields
Copy Editor: Dwora Jawer
Proofing: Brad Moyers
Typesetting/Formatting: Jamie Hughs
Cover: April S Fields
Cover background courtesy of Hubblesite.org

This book is dedicated to our heavenly Father, Who is working all things together for our good, and to His people who should know Him as the omnipotent, omniscient lover and creator of our eternal souls.

Introduction

Sovereignty:
To exercise supreme and independent authority.

The purpose of this book is to give you confidence in an all-powerful God who lovingly works all things together for your good to the end that you will be the vessel He so desires. As a vessel of God, you will see that faith in God will work for you and through you for others. Included in this book are many exciting testimonies of God's sovereignty manifested in power and grace. The questions on page vi and many more are answered from the Word of God.

This study and experience of the sovereignty of God has born much fruit in my life in the area of rest, peace, faith, and respect for Him. Others have told me the same thing and urged me to make a book of it. This study has sharpened my fear of God and removed my fear of man's conspiracies by the devil. It has given me a strong sense of the awesomeness of God. I feel it is my commission to share this with anyone who has the eyes to see and the ears to hear. Knowing the purpose and omnipotence of God lays a foundation for faith in the promises that removes the struggle from it. We will see how to cooperate with God in the process of His plan and so be vessels for it.

When we discuss something as controversial as this we have to make sure we are based in the Scriptures, not adding or taking away. We must "contend earnestly for the <u>faith which was once</u> for all <u>delivered unto the saints</u>," not the apostate faith of our day. The reason this subject is so controversial is because Christians as a whole tend to pick and choose verses to align with what they wish to believe. But truth can only come by accepting and fitting them all together for "the <u>sum</u> of thy word is truth." Many of the Scriptures we are going to look at have been ignored because they are contrary to human sentiment and reasoning, but they are there to bring us into the full knowledge of God that sets free.

I realize that I am writing to a cross-section of Christianity and you may see some things that you cannot accept. However, I am sure that if you will not throw the baby out with the bath water, you will see things that will change your life. If you will read this book slowly and prayerfully, I am sure God will bless you.

Your servant in Christ,
David Eells

TABLE OF CONTENTS

Do we limit God in circumstances?•Catastrophes: from God or devil?• To what extent do we have authority?•Is God involved in every affair of man?•To what extent does God control evil?•From whom does evil get authority?•Can God love me in this mess?•Does God deceive some?Why?Can we change our future?How?•Can we be sure that God will use us?•Is there purpose in my circumstances?•Does the devil need permission concerning me?•Does God ever fail or repent?•Are any predestined?Who?•Can we rest in God's plan?•Is evil sometimes for good?•Does God make good and evil?•What can bring God's power to me?•Does everything serve God's purpose?•Is God into insurance or assurance?•Should I give thanks for all things?•Is it right to ask for a sign from God?•Can the devil thwart God's plan?•How and what is a free will?•Did we choose God or He, us?•Does only good come from God? •Who does God gain counsel from?•Does God desire to rule through us? •Do we have any authority over the curse?•Can our own desires deceive us?•Will God increase my faith?•Calvinism, free will, or both?•Can God give peace with enemies?•What gives angels authority over me?•Does only bad come from the devil?•Should we resist evil? In men or spirits? •Are we commanded to use God's power?•Must we reap what we have sown?•Does the Bible teach fatalism?•Will God give me His desires? •Will history always repeat?•Are Christians to rule the world? Now?•Is God still in the miracle business?•Is God not willing or wishing that any perish?•Can ignorance of God's Word destroy us?•Is it advantageous to be hated sometimes?•Can curses come for no cause?•Does God use evil spirits?•Is God really all-powerful, all-knowing, and everywhere?•Why does history repeat?•Does everything serve God's purpose?•Can He really repair my life?•How can I cooperate?•Where does God's responsibility stop and mine start?•Does everything serve God's purposes?•Is there any such thing as luck?•Can we believe God to heal, deliver and provide? What did Jesus accomplish at the cross?•Why don't we have what the Word says we have?•Is evil also for our good?•How can God tell us to be anxious for nothing?•How does God create?•What tools does He use? •Did I choose Him or did He choose me?•Does anything get by God?•Does He permit us to tie His hands?When?•Why does God allow evil people to come into positions of power?•Who really killed Jesus?•Why does God choose to use man to conquer evil and bring blessing in the earth?

Chapter 1
God's Sovereignty and Purpose in All Things

And we know that to them that love God <u>all things</u> work together for good, even to them that are called according to his <u>purpose</u> (Rom.8:28).

Do we really believe that all things work together to bring to pass the good purpose of God for His called? Our reactions to life's circumstances are a good gauge of this. Knowing God's purpose in all things gives great peace. What purpose is Paul speaking of in this verse? In the next verse we can see that he is talking about the purpose of bringing many sons into the image of Jesus Christ. *(Rom.8:29) For whom he foreknew, he also foreordained [to be] <u>conformed to the image of his Son</u>,* that he might be the firstborn among many brethren. God foreordained or pre-determined to bring His true children into the image of Jesus. This has been God's purpose since the creation of the world, even before man was created and fell, as we shall see.

All things serve God in order to manifest His sons. That is why God created this world. Some people who do not understand may see failure in God's plan. But after studying the sovereignty of God, we will see there is no failure in God's system. Sovereignty means to exercise supreme and independent authority. Even sin, evil, and the fall will serve God's purpose, as we shall see. He is going to have sons to fellowship with through eternity. Toward this purpose, He is going to make <u>all things</u> work together for good. All things are not good, but all things work together for good. As my good friend Ray Taylor was fond of saying, "What does 'all' leave out?" Applying this truth to our life takes thought.

God must be omnipotent (all-powerful) over all things to make this statement. He must also be omniscient (all-knowing) in order to make such all-encompassing statements in His

1

Word. As we shall see, the Scriptures proclaim that God has sovereign control over all things that have anything to do with your life. He never falls off the throne and as we shall see, He never shares the throne with the devil. The authority that the devil has is according to God's design and laws.

Everything serves God in the ongoing creation of sons. *(Ps.119:91) They abide this day according to thine ordinances; for <u>all things are thy servants</u>.* All things serve Him in this process, good and bad, to bring to pass His plan. God never created anything that could thwart His plan, because God never makes mistakes. God even makes the evil to bring to pass His plan. Some will argue with that. Hopefully, you will change your mind as we examine the Scriptures. Evil is a tool of God's sovereignty to bring us to purity and maturity. Without the evil, there is no one to put us on the cross, to persecute us, and to cause temptations to rise up so that we might reject them and be cleansed. God has made everything, even the wicked for the day when His people will need chastening. *(Pr.16:4) <u>The Lord hath made</u> <u>everything</u> for its own end* (Some manuscripts say: for His own purpose.) *Yea, <u>even the wicked for the day of evil</u>*. Six times in Bible history, God raised up a great beast kingdom to come against His people when they fell away, to persecute them and bring them to their cross. In every case, the Bible gives credit to God for raising up these beasts – Egyptian, Assyrian, Babylonian, Media-Persian, Grecian, and Roman – for the purpose of being used to come against His people. God will do the same for the Church soon, for Revelation declares that He will bring two more beast kingdoms (Rev.17:10,11).

The apostle Paul learned contentment. He understood that none could thwart God's good plan for him. Anxiety, fear, or impatience only comes because of our own nearsighted, immature understanding of God's master plan for us. You can imagine how valuable a great apostle and evangelist such as Paul was to the saints in his day. But, in this case, Paul was put in prison. *(Phil.1:12) Now I would have you know, brethren,* *that <u>the things which happened unto me have fallen out rather unto the progress of the Gospel</u>; (13) so that my bonds became manifest in Christ throughout the whole praetorian guard, and to all the rest; (14) and that most of the brethren in the Lord, being confident through my bonds, are more abundantly bold to speak the Word of God without fear.* Paul had an understanding that the devil was not the author of his imprisonment because of its value to God's kingdom. The kind of thinking that would be in most minds today is, "Certainly the devil did this to thwart God's plan." Paul is not saying that the devil did not have a hand in his situation, but that the devil cannot thwart God's plan. Everything is going to work together for the good, individually and corporately. Individually it was for Paul's good, and corporately it was for the brethren's good. The Gospel went out because Paul was in prison. It was from prison that Paul wrote much of the New Testament. The Word of God went more places and was spread much faster because Paul was in prison. People became bold to go out and preach the Gospel because he was in prison. In the last verses of Philippians, we find out that even some of Caesar's household were converted because Paul was in prison.

Sometimes we look at circumstances instead of the Word and think that the devil has been able to put a stop to God's plan. God would have never made the devil if he had been someone who could stop His plan. Of course, some would say that God did not make the devil but rather a good angel that fell. Since God is all-knowing as the Scriptures say He is, He knew His angel would become the devil. He is also all-powerful to stop what He knew would happen, therefore, at least by omission, He is the creator of the devil. God says, *(Isa.45:7) "I form the light, and <u>create darkness</u>; I make peace, and <u>create evil</u>. I am the Lord, that doeth <u>all</u> these things." (Isa.54:16) "I have created the waster to destroy. (17) <u>No</u> weapon that is formed against thee shall prosper ...."* Since God created the evil waster, then obviously, He has authority to say that he cannot prosper against us. Evil cannot prosper for its own purpose, only God's good purpose. Do you suppose the three Hebrews wondered why the God to whom they had been so faithful had ordained the wicked to cast them into a fiery furnace? Be patient if you believe that "ordained" is too strong a word. Those Hebrews found out this trial was to impress a heathen king with the power and saving grace of the God of Israel. He was impressed when God appeared to be walking with them through the fire and there was no harm to their bodies or clothes, <u>only their ropes were burned off</u> (Dan.3:25-27). God's purpose was to impress the heathen and to deliver them from bondage. This is a type or shadow of His purpose in our lives, too.

All of these Old Testament <u>stories</u> and <u>laws</u> are also parables (figures, types, or shadows) with deeper meanings for us. *(1 Cor.10:11) Now these things happened unto them by way of <u>example</u>* (Greek: "figure, type, or shadow")*; and <u>they were written for our admonition</u>, upon whom the ends of the ages are come. (Col.2:16) Let no man therefore judge you in meat, or in drink, or in respect of a feast day or a new moon or a sabbath day: (17) which are a <u>shadow of the things to come</u> ....*

Another reason for the Hebrews' trial, which they could not have foreseen, was that the king would preach the God of Israel to the whole kingdom of Babylon. *(Dan.3:28) Nebuchadnezzar spake and said, Blessed be the God of Shadrach, Meshach, and Abed-nego, who hath sent his angel, and <u>delivered his servants that trusted in him</u>, and have changed the king's word, and have yielded their bodies, that they might not serve nor worship any god, except their own God. (29) Therefore I make a decree, that every people, nation, and language, which speak anything amiss against the God of Shadrach, Meshach, and Abed-nego, shall be cut in pieces, and their houses shall be made a dunghill; because <u>there is no other god that is able to deliver after this sort</u>. (30) Then the king promoted Shadrach, Meshach, and Abed-nego in the province of Babylon.* Wow, there was even a promotion in it for them!

Nebuchadnezzar went on to preach and glorify our God to the whole world because of this one act of faithful obedience. *(Dan.4:1) Nebuchadnezzar the king, unto all the peoples, nations, and languages, that dwell in all the earth: Peace be multiplied unto you. (2) It hath seemed good unto me to show the signs and wonders that the Most High God hath wrought toward me. (3) How great are his signs, and how mighty are his wonders! His kingdom is an everlasting kingdom, and his dominion is from generation to generation.*

After the Medes and the Persians conquered the Babylonian kingdom, Daniel was used of God to preach Him to that generation, also. He probably did not know that being thrown in the lions' den by the wicked for his faithfulness was actually God setting the stage for this miracle that he, no doubt, had prayed for. Darius, the king, saw that Daniel was delivered from the hungry lions and that *"no manner of hurt was found upon him, because he had trusted in his God"* (Dan.6:23). He then threw Daniel's enemies in the lions' den. Their god was not able to deliver them. Then Darius decided that Daniel's God was *"the living God"* and proclaimed Him to the world. *(Dan.6:25) Then king Darius wrote unto all the peoples, nations, and languages, that dwell in all the earth: Peace be multiplied unto you. (26) I make a decree, that in all the dominion of my kingdom men tremble and fear before the <u>God of Daniel</u>; for <u>he is the living God</u>, and steadfast for ever, And his kingdom that which shall not be destroyed; and his dominion shall be even unto the end. (27) <u>He delivereth and rescueth</u>, and he worketh signs and wonders in heaven and in earth, who hath delivered Daniel from the power of the lions.*

I believe that God has shown me that there will be a fulfillment of Daniel and the three Hebrews' victories in the coming days. Are you ready to see trial and persecution by the wicked as a means to that end? These four only lost their bondage to the wicked in their fiery trial. In other words, they received sanctification and freedom. Not that all will physically be preserved, but the righteous never die: they only change addresses. The carnal mind does not understand God's use of all things to fulfill His plan. But this understanding helps us to cooperate with God in our individual trials now so that Christ's glory may be revealed in us. *(1 Pet.4:12) Beloved, <u>think it not strange</u> concerning the fiery trial among you, <u>which cometh upon you to prove you</u>, as though a strange thing happened unto you: (13) but insomuch as ye are partakers of Christ's sufferings, rejoice; that at the <u>revelation of his glory</u> also ye may rejoice with exceeding joy. (14) If ye are reproached for the name of Christ, blessed [are ye]; because the [Spirit] of <u>glory</u> and the Spirit of God resteth upon you.* Notice that God takes credit for this trial for the good purpose of proving us.

Paul's understanding of the sovereignty of God to fulfill His good plan gave him contentment that most Christians do not have. *(Phil.4:11) Not that I speak in respect of want: for I have learned, in <u>whatsoever state I am, therein to be content</u>. (12) I know how to be abased, and I know also how to abound: in everything and in all things have I learned the secret both to be filled and to be hungry, both to abound and to be in want.* What was his secret? He knew the answer to the question *"if God is for us, who is against us?" (Rom.8:31)* He knew that God could not fall off the throne and that God was not sharing it with the devil. Let us look at the secret of Paul's peace. *(Phil.4:6) <u>In nothing be anxious</u>; but in everything by prayer and supplication with thanksgiving let your requests be made known unto God. (7) And the peace of God, which passeth all understanding, shall guard your hearts and your thoughts in Christ Jesus.* Paraphrased: "Do not worry about a thing. Just ask God and thank Him, and you will be guarded by His peace." Paul understood that God would not permit any situation that he should be anxious about. He understood that by simply asking, believing, and thanking there would be no situation where God would not meet his need. That is why

6

Paul had peace and contentment in any situation. Notice that he is suggesting that we give thanks for what we have prayed for even before we receive it. That is the way faith works. *(Mk.11:24) Therefore I say unto you, <u>all things</u> whatsoever ye pray and ask for, believe that ye receive them, and ye shall have them.* Form this habit because it brings peace, contentment, and results. Many do not receive because they do not enter into the faithful rest of believing that they have received.

Fear not. How many times does the Bible command us to fear not? I have been told that it commands us not to fear 365 times, once for every day of the year. Only God Who is sovereign could say this: *(Phil.4:4) Rejoice in the Lord <u>always</u>: again I will say, Rejoice. (Epe.5:20) giving thanks <u>always for all things</u> in the name of our Lord Jesus Christ to God, even the Father.* What reason could we have for rejoicing and giving thanks for everything? We rejoice because an all-powerful God loves us and because He has all things under control always, even in the fiery trial. These verses do not give the devil any credit. Did you ever notice that in the Scriptures, the saints did not give the devil the credit that your average Christian does today? That is because modern Christians ignorantly have faith in the devil. Paul is giving all the credit to God, for the good and the evil. Paul says, *"Giving thanks always for <u>all</u> things."* I have actually heard preachers say, "Well, that is just talking about the good things which come from God." It does not say that, and it does not mean that. There is only one way to define *"always for all things."* Giving thanks to God always means that ultimately all things come from Him. To the believer, to him that is called according to His purpose, there is nothing to be anxious about. *"All things"* do not just apply to the things at hand but also to the things that we have in Christ, which are His promises. Thank God for the things that His promises say we have even though we do not see them yet.

God has put us into a controlled environment, in which He wants us to learn and grow. When the disciples were in the boat that was filling with water, I am sure that their minds perceived danger. That environment was more controlled than they understood. All they saw was the boat filling up with water, and they were fearful and ran to Jesus. What did Jesus say when He woke up? *(Mk.4:40) And he said unto them, Why are ye fearful? Have ye not yet faith?* If Jesus was in the boat, what were they worried about? Jesus is always in the boat with us. What are we worried about? Just have faith. The disciples perceived danger. Jesus did not see any danger because He had faith. Jesus was so calm that He was sleeping through the storm. Give thanks always for all things in the name of the Lord Jesus Christ. *(Epe.1:11) In whom also we were made a heritage, having been foreordained according to the purpose of him who worketh all things after the counsel of his will.* The only way that God can foreordain is for Him to work all things after the counsel of His Will. Otherwise, one rebellious free will could spoil His plan, and we could never trust Him to do what He says. He does not consider any counsel other than His own Will because He never makes mistakes. God sees the end from the beginning. God does not assimilate knowledge from senses like we do. He has all knowledge. God made a good plan from the beginning; He has never had to change it.

Everything that God is doing, He is doing according to the counsel of His own Will. There is not another completely free will in all of creation. If there were, this would be a dangerous place. A free will is a will that is able to do what it wants. Thank God that it is only His good free will, which *"worketh all things after the counsel of his will,"* that is in control.

None of us has a completely free will, <u>yet</u>. We are entering into the free will, which is God's free will. Before we came to Christ, we had less of a free will than we have now, because <u>we were bound in sin,</u> but Jesus came to set the captives free.

(Isa.61:1) The Spirit of the Lord is upon me; because the Lord hath anointed me to preach good tidings unto the meek; he hath sent me to bind up the broken-hearted, to proclaim liberty to the <u>captives</u>, and the opening [of the prison] to them that are <u>bound</u>. We were limited in every direction. Now, we are still limited in the directions in which we would like to go, but God does not want us to go. We are limited by our ability, thinking capacity, and nature from going in directions that we would like to go. The great thing is that the Son has come to set us free. *(Jn.8:36) If therefore the Son shall make you free, ye shall be free indeed.* The more that we receive His Will, the more of a free will we have because He does what He wants to do. When we have His Will, we do what we want to do. That is a free will. God is the only one, in all of the Scriptures, who can do what He wants to do consistently. The only way for us to have this free will is to have His Will in us. That is why we are studying the Scriptures and repenting, or changing our minds. If we want to be free, we have to see what God sees, which is to have His understanding and desire in us. God has the only free will, and we have proof of that because history keeps repeating itself. That means there is only one mind in control of all of history. God uses the wills of all to do what He wants to do. God has vessels of honor and vessels of dishonor.

We must understand how God uses us to fulfill His Will. *(Phil.2:13) For it is God who <u>worketh in you both to will</u> and to work, for his good pleasure.* God predestinates by using our will to do His Will. God uses all wills to do His Will. Everything, all creation, serves God in preparing His sons to face Him. All creation is the dirt into which God plants the seed that is going to bring forth fruit. Many think that if God were in control this world would be like ice cream. Ice cream is sweet, but it will not grow plants. We need corruption to grow a crop. God is using this world as a farmer uses the dirt, to bring death to the outer seed that the inner seed would have life. God created this world to be the dirt that would bring forth

His sons. God's plan is perfect and will not be thwarted. Some immaturely believe that God was caught off guard and had to go to plan "B" when Adam fell. Not a chance! That is where the dirt came in, as we shall see later. God is still using plan "A." He does not have a plan "B" because He does not make mistakes. God does not decide what He is going to do by depending upon what we do. If that were the case, we would be ruling Him. Some say that faith changes things, but faith is *"not of yourselves it is a gift of God" (Epe.2:8)*. Therefore faith that comes from Him fulfills His Will.

God is *"declaring the <u>end from the beginning</u>, and from ancient times things that are not [yet] done; saying, My counsel shall stand, and I will do all my pleasure" (Isa.46:10)*. God is actively involved in everything to do His pleasure. Since He has already spoken everything beforehand, it must come to pass. *(Jer.1:12) Then said the Lord unto me, Thou hast well seen: for <u>I watch over my word to perform it</u>*. God does not merely permit; He <u>causes</u> as we read from the Scriptures. God *"<u>worketh</u> all things after the counsel of his will."* We like to use the word "permit" because it is comfortable to our immature understanding. The Scripture teaches that He works, He does, He uses, and He causes.

(Ps.65:4) Blessed is the man whom <u>thou choosest, and causest to approach unto thee</u>, that he may dwell in thy courts. God's method of salvation to us is for Him to put His Will in us. If in any way we are missing part of His salvation, we need to go to Him and ask Him to put His Will in us. We are acknowledging that everything comes from Him, that all grace comes from Him. Our prayer should be, "God, put your desires in me, then I will do what is right." *(Ps.119:32) <u>I will run the way of thy commandments, When thou shalt enlarge my heart</u>. (35) Make me to go in the path of thy commandments; For therein do I delight. (36) <u>Incline my heart unto thy testimonies</u>, And not to covetousness.* The Bride said, *"<u>Draw me, we will run after thee</u>" (S. of Sol.1:4)*. When God draws us, we are going to

run after Him. If He does not draw us, we will not run because salvation is by His grace or favor. *(Rom.10:20) And Isaiah is very bold, and saith, <u>I was found of them that sought me not</u>; I became manifest unto them that asked not of me. (Rom.3:10) As it is written, There is none righteous, no, not one; (11) There is none that understandeth, There is none that seeketh after God; (12) They have all turned aside, they are together become unprofitable.* All were bound in sin and *"shapen in iniquity."* As we can see, a corrupt nature does not seek God. God has to make the first move. *(Jn.6:44) <u>No man can come to me, except the Father that sent me draw him</u>. (Jn.15:16) <u>Ye did not choose me, but I chose you, and appointed you</u>, that ye should go and bear fruit.*

How does God draw us? He draws us by putting in us the desire to change our mind (repent) and to come to Him. The Bible says God grants repentance. *(Acts 11:18) Then to the Gentiles also hath <u>God granted repentance</u> unto life.* If we repent, it is a gift from God, like faith. We are in God's kingdom because of His mercy and grace. To the extent we want to progress in His kingdom, we still need His mercy and grace to repent. He wants us to acknowledge His ability in our life in all things. He wants us to seek Him for the desire to do right. He works in us to <u>will</u> and to <u>do</u> of His good pleasure; if not, we would be in big trouble.

I have always admired King David because of his New Testament wisdom and knowledge among Old Testament people. *(1 Chr.29:10) Wherefore David blessed the Lord before all the assembly; and David said, Blessed be thou, O Lord, the God of Israel our father, for ever and ever. (11) Thine, O Lord, is the greatness, and the power, and the glory, and the victory, and the majesty: for all that is in the heavens* (including the second heaven where Satan's kingdom is) *and in the earth is thine; thine is the kingdom, O Lord, and <u>thou art exalted as head above all</u>.* Who or what does "all" leave out? God is the head above all, always. He would never have it any

11

other way. The idea that God is always at war with the devil and we never know who is going to win is the thinking of the immature. It allows them to not charge God with evil intent until they grow up and understand the whole wonderful plan. God always wins. God is going to get those that are His, and the devil is also going to get those that are given him. This is God's plan.

(1 Chr.29:12) Both riches and honor come of thee, and <u>thou rulest over all</u>; and in thy hand is power and might; and <u>in thy hand it is to make great, and to give strength unto all</u>. God likes to use that word "all." When we are talking about God, we have to use that word "all" a lot. Notice that God rules all and gives strength to all. *(13) Now therefore, our God, we thank thee, and praise thy glorious name. (14) But who am I, and what is my people, <u>that we should be able to offer so willingly after this sort</u>?* (Who are we that we should have this will to serve God? David understood the grace of God in giving them the will to offer to God in this way.) *For <u>all things come of thee, and of thine own have we given thee</u>.* Is it not amazing that God is giving us a reward for what He gives us in the first place? Paul said, *"What hast thou that thou didst not receive?" (1 Cor.4:6)* The correct answer is that we do not have anything that we did not receive from God, and yet, we are going to get a reward. That should really humble us to know that we do not have anything to be proud of or to brag about or that would cause us to judge or look down upon anyone else because everything that we have is from God by grace. What He gives, He can take away. We need to be careful how we walk before God. *(1 Chr.29:15) For we are strangers before thee, and sojourners, as all our fathers were: our days on the earth are as a shadow, and there is no abiding. (16) O Lord our God, all this store that we have prepared to build thee a house for thy holy name <u>cometh of thy hand, and is all thine own</u>.* Everything that God puts in our hand belongs to Him and is to serve Him. We are here to serve Him.

12

John the Baptist had rest and peace, but he warred with spirits that came against him, just as we do. These spirits tried to put competition and jealousy upon him by using his own disciples. *(Jn.3:25) There arose therefore a questioning on the part of John's disciples with a Jew about purifying. (26) And they came to John, and said to him, Rabbi, he that was with thee beyond the Jordan, to whom thou hast borne witness, behold, the same baptizeth, and all men come to him. (27) John answered and said, <u>A man can receive nothing, except it have been given him from heaven</u>.* John's understanding gave him total peace that what came to him was from God. He told them in verse 30, *"He must increase, but I must decrease."* He had total peace about just fulfilling the part that God had given him to do. He had total peace about losing his disciples to Jesus because he understood the sovereignty of God. He even pointed out Jesus to some of his disciples saying, *"Behold the Lamb of God,"* and they followed Him. John was not competitive or jealous, he just knew that he was there to fulfill what God put in his hand. A man can only receive what comes from God.

Denominationalism (or sectarianism) by its very nature is jealous and competitive. Oh, those preachers fight for their turf! If they can make themselves look good enough and everyone else look bad enough, who could go elsewhere? The really bad side-effect is that when their servants leave they just go back to the world, having no hope that there is anything better. However, when some outgrow their system, they go on to something better.

Many times we are concerned as to whether we are in the Will of God. We are in the Will of God more than we think because of the sovereignty of God. We can miss the mark in our actions but be where we need to be in circumstances because God controls our environment. God puts us in the midst of circumstances to crucify us. Jesus was put into circumstances where it appeared that God gave wicked men power over Him.

13

God empowers wicked men for His own purpose. Have you ever been in a situation where God gave power to people over you? This is to humble us and bring us to our cross. When put in that situation, we should submit. God told Paul not to kick against the pricks or painful prods that make us get in line.

(Jn.19:10) Pilate therefore saith unto him, Speakest thou not unto me? Knowest thou not that I have power to release thee, and have power to crucify thee? (11) Jesus answered him, <u>*Thou wouldest have no power against me, except it were given thee from above*</u>; *therefore he that delivered me unto thee hath greater sin.* Jesus had peace in the midst of this situation because He knew He was in the hand of God. The perceived competition between God and the devil always takes away our peace because we never quite know whether we are in the Will of God or in the hand of the devil. Nevertheless, we are in the hand of God. Jesus knew that no one would have any power over Him except it was given from God. It was true about Jesus, and it is true about us. *(Ps.91:11) For* <u>*he will give his angels charge over thee, To keep thee in all thy ways*</u>. *(12) They shall bear thee up in their hands, lest thou dash thy foot against a stone.* This is talking about all who are *"in the secret place of the Most High" (Ps.91:1)*. God's angels are with us. We cannot even have an "accident" against a stone without God's angels being there to deliver us. There is no such thing as an accident anyway. Accidents are for people who believe in luck, not an omnipotent (all-powerful) God. Blaming fate is a "cop-out" because we reap what we sow. *(Gal.6:7) Be not deceived; God is not mocked: for whatsoever a man soweth, that shall he also reap.* This also shows the absolute sovereignty and justice of God.

(Jn.3:27) … A man can receive nothing, except it have been given him from heaven. Everything primarily comes from God. How could God be our Father if He let us have a free will to do anything we want with impunity? How could God be our Father if He gave the devil a free hand with us? We

would never consider doing either of these with our children. There is something else with which this understanding really helps us. If all we ever see is the devil behind everything bad that happens, we never have a reason to repent or change our ways. But, if we look past the devil and see God, we have a reason to repent. This is why it is important that we understand the sovereignty of God. We can always look behind the devil and see God and wonder why God granted the devil to have his way with us.

Job understood more than most people in the New Testament about the sovereignty of God. *(Job 2:10) What? shall we receive good at the <u>hand of God</u>, and <u>shall we not receive evil</u>? In all this did not Job sin with his lips.* God made it very plain that Job was not sinning by saying that good and evil comes our way from God. It was the devil doing the works, but Job was giving no credit to the devil. The devil is just a vessel. We have to look behind the vessel and see the sovereign God. If we can do that, we have a reason to wonder why we are in a bad circumstance or situation. If there is something we need to change, we will be motivated to change it. We will not be motivated to change it if we only see the devil. We will keep on with our sinful ways and think it is the mean old devil. It is convenient for the flesh to say, "The devil is doing this because I am so good," rather than, "God is doing this because I deserve it or need it." No, think again; it is God!

This verse came to my mind when the first space shuttle blew up. *(Lk.13:4) Or those eighteen, upon whom the tower in Siloam fell, and killed them, think ye that they were offenders above all the men that dwell in Jerusalem? (5) I tell you, Nay: but, <u>except ye repent, ye shall all likewise perish</u>.* It may be politically correct to blame national catastrophes on the bad guys, but the truth is we will not repent. We see God's purpose of judging the unrepentant being fulfilled in this verse. God destroyed everything on the earth by the flood in the days of Noah. On the whole earth, only eight people were

15

considered righteous by God and saved in the ark. Is our day any different? *(Mt.24:37) And as [were] the days of Noah, so shall be the coming of the Son of man.* God destroyed Sodom and Gomorrah by fire from heaven. God told Abraham that He would not destroy those evil cities if there were only ten righteous people in them. Is our day any different percentage wise? *(Lk.17:29) But in the day that Lot went out from Sodom* <u>*it rained fire and brimstone from heaven*</u>*, and destroyed them all: (30) after the same manner shall it be in the day that the Son of man is revealed.*

I am not saying that God does not send the devil sometimes so that we can practice overcoming evil. I am saying that God also sends the devil so that He can whip us when we are outside of His Will. We need to look beyond the devil, who is only a vessel of dishonor, and see God's hand in everything. He alone is sovereign. By doing this, we will be constantly motivated to walk and obey Him. I can hear someone offended saying, "God does not send the devil." Just as God works in vessels of honor *"to will and to work, for his good pleasure" (Phil.2:13)*, He also works in vessels of dishonor. *(Rom.9:21) Or hath not the potter a right over the clay, from the same lump to make one part a vessel unto honor, and another unto dishonor?* The devil is the head of God's vessels of dishonor whether he knows it or not. He is a created being. God would not be very smart to make a being that could out do Him, much less beat up on His children without a purpose.

(Mt.28:18) And Jesus came to them and spake unto them, saying, <u>All authority</u> hath been given unto me in heaven and on earth. That does not leave any authority for the devil except what is given him. Jesus said, "All authority," not "All power." Authority is the right to use power. Jesus had the right to use all power because He had <u>all</u> authority. Jesus has authority over the devil's power and, as we shall see in a later chapter, authority to use the devil's power.

16

(1 Cor.11:12 and 2 Cor.5:18) But <u>all things are of God</u>. Wow! That little phrase is used twice in the New Testament. I dare say, if you made this statement among most Christians and they did not know it was in the Scriptures, they would probably rebuke you for it. Have you ever heard people say, "This is of the devil," or "That is of God"? The Bible says, *"All things are of God."* Why does He say that? That does not sound right, does it? The problem is between our ears. We know that some things are through the devil. That is true, they are, but they are primarily of God. God's plan is what is being fulfilled here on earth, not the devil's plan.

(Jn.3:27) … A man can receive nothing, except it have been given him from heaven. That really does not fit with what we have been taught. Most of God's people are absorbed in the teaching that some things are of God, and some things are not. This doctrine has been passed down through the traditions of men. All of the reformers warred against this faith-robbing lie, including those in the Catholic Church like Augustine. We need to see God as being on the throne, always ruling. The circumstances in our lives motivate us to fear, respect, and to have faith in Him.

We learn nothing when we blame the devil or people. For instance, in James 5:16 the Lord says, *"Confess therefore your sins one to another, and pray one for another, that ye may be healed."* It is common to blame the devil instead of seeing sickness as a chastening from God for our sins. Some go their whole lives and die in their sicknesses, never repenting, because they never saw a reason to since they were just being persecuted by a bad devil. *(Gal.6:7) Be not deceived; God is not mocked: for whatsoever a man soweth, that shall he also reap.* In other words, we receive from God according to our actions. On a secondary level we make our own future. Through repentance and faith the sins of our former life are forgiven and washed away, but if we continue in those sins, then we will reap what we have sown. Now that makes us respect and fear God.

17

(1 Cor.8:5) For though there be that are called gods, whether in heaven or on earth; as there are gods many, and lords many; (6) yet to us there is one God, the Father, <u>of whom are all things</u>, and we unto him; and one Lord, Jesus Christ, <u>through whom are all things</u>, and we through him. Everything comes from the Father, through Christ. Everything! Why is this so difficult to understand when, obviously, it is being repeated all through the Scriptures? Conversely, there are no Scriptures to back up what we have been taught in most of the churches.

For almost three decades, as I studied the Scriptures, I would often find a verse that I thought had to do with the sovereignty of God. I would write it in a common place in the margin of my Bible. Then I would go back and study it to see how it fit with other verses. It became very plain to me that God is always in control, which gave me peace and faith in God and rest in circumstances. Later, I started reading the reformer's writings and was shocked to find that they generally agreed with that teaching, which almost nobody around us has taught.

The doctrine of the sovereignty of God is generally called Calvinism. However, much of what John Calvin taught, Martin Luther taught before him and Augustine before that. Most of the reformers taught the sovereignty of God to draw whom He chooses by putting His Will in them. Arminians, on the other hand, taught that those who are bound in sin are able to make good or free choices, which is impossible. The Arminians wrongly accuse Calvin of teaching fatalism. Fatalism is, "What will be, will be. I do not have to worry about it because whatever God decides is what is going to happen anyway. I will just sit back and watch and see what is going to happen." The reformers did not teach that. In fact, they almost all taught that the way God predestines and brings His Will to pass is that He uses your will to do it.

Those who overcome do so because God's grace moves through them to will and to do what He wants. The lost are

18

given a gift of faith to come to God. As a Christian we can receive God's grace to desire what is right by our faith. Fatalistic thinking destroys motivation. The truth always motivates to holiness. If we are going to manifest our sonship, it will be because we desire it. We are going to get there because we were overcomers. Not because we thought, "Well, I am chosen therefore I am going to make it." That kind of thinking prevails in some Calvinistic churches. Calvinists do not necessarily teach what Calvin taught. Calvin's ***Institutes of the Christian Religion*** is a thorough revelation of the sovereignty of God. Those who desire God's holiness will prove that they were chosen.

Chapter 2
God's Sovereignty in Creating the Scriptures

Knowing this first that no prophecy of scripture is of private interpretation. For <u>no prophecy ever came by the will of man</u>: but <u>men spake from God, being moved by the Holy Spirit</u> (2 Pet.1:20,21).

There is no mistaking the fact that the Bible claims God as its author. It seems fantastic that God could give perfect thoughts to imperfect men and make sure that what they write is perfectly inspired. *(2 Tim.3:16) Every scripture inspired of God* (Greek: "is God breathed") *[is] also profitable for teaching, for reproof, for correction, for instruction, which is in righteousness.* He was so perfectly sovereign in this that it was said that He used men's mouths. *(Lk.1:70) As he spake by the mouth of his holy prophets that have been from of old. (Jer.1:9) … The Lord said unto me, Behold, I have put my words in thy mouth.* The prophets themselves also claimed this by prefacing their words with "Thus saith the Lord."

Jesus not only said that <u>His words</u> were from God but that they also would judge us and that <u>they are eternal life</u>. *(Jn.12:48) He that rejecteth me, and receiveth not my sayings, hath one that judgeth him: <u>the word that I spake, the same shall judge</u> him in the last day. (49) For <u>I spake not from myself</u>; but the Father that sent me, <u>he hath given me a commandment, what I should say</u>, and what I should speak. (50) And I know that his <u>commandment is life eternal</u>: the things therefore which I speak, even <u>as the Father hath said</u> unto me, <u>so I speak</u>.* Jesus passed on this inspiration to those whom He sent. *(Mt.10:40) He that receiveth you receiveth me, and he that receiveth me receiveth him that sent me.* New Testament teachers and prophets like Paul claimed this inspiration. *(1 Cor.14:37) If any man thinketh himself to be a prophet, or* *spiritual, let him take knowledge of <u>the things which I write</u> <u>unto you, that they are the commandment of the Lord</u>.*

Can the divine inspiration of Scriptures be proven? In this book, I will relate to you a few miracles that have happened to me, which have no reasonable explanation other than the supernatural power of a living, loving God, Who reacts to our faith in the Scriptures. The most impressive miracle to me is what happened to me when a friend challenged me to read the Scriptures. I was not at all convinced that God wrote them and I was, I thought, fairly happy living in sin. I enjoyed my dope, alcohol, hobbies, and generally pleasing myself with no desire to serve God or to be holy. However I had a curiosity about the supernatural fulfillment of prophecies thousands of years old that were attributed to the Bible. So never having had an interest in reading, I started to read. At the time, I really did not know what was happening to me. This was the first time I really could not put a book down. I found myself neglecting everything I held dear in the world, reading almost every spare moment. Before long, I really wanted to know the One who wrote this book, and I knew Him to be God.

About this time, I noticed that my stash of dope had been sitting in the cabinet untouched and my almost finished Kawasaki Z-1 show chopper got no attention. This was not the old me. My ski boat, racecar, school bus camper, and gun collection all fared the same. I eventually sold or gave them away. I knew that God's hand was upon me to reveal Himself to me. When we put the Word in us, we put God in us. He is the Word (John 1:1). I desired to obey what I was reading. When the Word said to be baptized and filled with the Holy Spirit, I did. Sin was running off me like water off a duck's back. When my new TV got in the way, I got rid of it. I respected the Word more than men or religion for its power to deliver and bless.

<u>Can the divine inspiration of Scripture be proven</u> <u>scientifically</u>? Science is observable and demonstrable. My

testimony is just that to those who knew me and to myself but for further skeptics, I will share another miracle. Ivan Panin was forced to leave Russia during the Bolshevik Revolution and come to the United States. He became a Harvard Scholar, professor, and mathematician, who once tutored Albert Einstein. His training, devotion to Christ and the Scriptures well-equipped him for his future work. Here he found his life's work in scientifically proving the divine inspiration of Scriptures. For fifty years, Dr. Panin devoted twelve to eighteen hours a day to this work. The basis for his revelation, which he called numerics, was the ancient Hebrew Old Testament and Greek New Testament Scriptures. The Hebrews and Greeks used their letters also for their numbers. In other words, the whole Bible was actually written in numbers also. What Dr. Panin discovered is that when he used the numbers, the 66 books of the Bible showed a pattern of numbers and divisibility that no other writing had. He diligently researched other Hebrew and Greek writings and found no pattern. This included the apocryphal books added in the Catholic and other early Protestant Bibles, including the original King James Version before its many revisions.

I have read Dr. Panin's works for many years and am totally impressed. Below is a small sample of his volumes of work from a pamphlet titled *Astounding New Discoveries.* The number seven is by far the most common number used in the surface text of the Bible, used in Revelation alone more than fifty times, but it is also common beneath the surface of the whole Bible.

GENESIS CHAPTER ONE, VERSE ONE
"In the beginning God created the heavens and the earth."

FEATURE ONE
The number of Hebrew words in this verse is exactly *seven*.

FEATURE TWO
The number of letters in the *seven* words is exactly *twenty-eight*, or four *sevens*.

FEATURE THREE
The first three of these *seven* Hebrew words contain the subject and predicate of the sentence. These three words are translated – "In the beginning God created." The number of letters in these first three Hebrew words is exactly *fourteen*, or two *sevens*. The last four of these *seven* words contain the object of the sentence. These four words are translated – "the heavens and the earth." The number of letters in these last four Hebrew words is *fourteen*, or two *sevens*.

FEATURE FOUR
These last four Hebrew words consist of two objects. The first is "the heavens," and the second is "and the earth." The number of letters in the first object is exactly *seven*. The number of letters in the second object is *seven*.

FEATURE FIVE
The three leading words in this verse of *seven* words are **God** – the subject – and **heavens** and **earth**– the objects. The number of letters in these three Hebrew words is exactly *fourteen*, or two *sevens*. The number of letters in the other four words of the verse is *fourteen*, or two *sevens*.

FEATURE SIX
The shortest word is in the middle. The number of letters in this word and the word to its left is exactly *seven*.

FEATURE SEVEN
The number of letters in the middle word and the word to its right is exactly *seven*.

These are only a few examples of the many amazing numeric facts, which have been discovered in the structure of this first verse of only seven Hebrew words. Literally dozens of other phenomenal numeric features strangely underlie the structure of this verse. (Many additional features are given in the complete, 167-page edition of *Astounding New Discoveries* © 1941, by Karl Sabiers, a student of Panin. Some later versions were edited or even plagiarized to prove poor manuscripts.)

Thus, according to the law of chances, for twenty-four features to occur in a passage accidentally, there is only one chance in 191,581,231,380,566,414,401 – only one chance in one hundred ninety-one quintillion, five hundred eighty-one quadrillion, two hundred thirty-one trillion, three hundred eighty billion, five hundred sixty-six million, four hundred fourteen thousand, four hundred one. (The nomenclature herein used is the American, not the British.)

Many brief Bible passages have as many as seventy or one hundred or more amazing numeric features in the very structure of their text. If there is only one chance in quintillions that twenty-four features could occur together accidentally, what would the chance be for seventy features to occur together accidentally?

When there is only one chance in *thousands* for something to happen accidentally, it is already considered highly improbable that it will occur at all. When there is only one chance in *hundreds of thousands*, it is considered practically impossible. But here there is one chance in not only *millions*, but *billions*, and *trillions*, and *quadrillions*, and *quintillions*, that merely twenty-four features could occur together in a passage accidentally.

If that is not enough to convince any sane man, there are patterns of eight, eleven, thirteen, seventeen, nineteen, twenty-three, thirty-seven, forty-three, etc., on top of the sevens throughout the Word. Larger patterns connect book to book, Old Testament to New Testament and show the correct order of the books. What all this proves is that one divine, brilliant mind wrote the Bible rather than thirty-three simple men, with relatively no schooling, who lived in different countries over a span of 1,600 years. If men wrote the Bible, they would

24

have all had to live at the same time and place and all been mathematical geniuses. Then they would have each had to write their book last with the knowledge of the numeric pattern in all the other books. Men have tried to write a simple numeric text with very few features and failed miserably.

The Hebrews had extremely stringent rules for the scribes to follow in copying the ancient manuscripts. God did this through them in order to preserve this pattern of perfection in the Scriptures that we might have the "God-breathed" Word of God. If a Greek or Hebrew letter is added, removed, or changed, the pattern breaks in that text.

The main problem today in publishing Bibles is deciding which manuscript to use. It makes common sense to use only ancient manuscripts, which were close to the original with less likelihood of human mistake. Using a copy of a copy of a copy, etc. makes no sense, and yet, because of prejudices or lack of availability of ancient manuscripts, some have published Bibles from these. Needless to say, the ancient manuscripts proved to be much more numeric. What God has done through numerics is to give us a method by which we can find out which manuscript is right and where each one is right or wrong. Numerics has made searching multiple translations obsolete. It also makes it possible to find out which translation is the most accurate. In comparing the Bibles up through the early 1900's, Dr. Panin rated the ***Revised Version***, which was slightly revised for Americans and called the ***American Standard Version***, as "head and shoulders above its competitors." Before discovering Dr. Panin's work I came to this conclusion from ***Vine's Expository Dictionary of New Testament Words*** and comparing manuscripts. I want to point out in almost any Bible you pick up, you will find the needed knowledge of salvation and holiness. Some may want to start with easy reader versions until they gain a little knowledge, but for the finer points in teaching, accuracy is important. Toward this end, Dr. Panin worked diligently. Two outstanding results of his work are the numerically correct *Numeric English New Testament* and the *Numeric Greek New Testament*. In my own research, I consider them the most accurate available.

There are words or word groups or verses that when added up have values that tend to connect things theologically and sometimes show up in the surface text. Some have called this Bible science "theomatics." This is also the name of the first book on the subject by Jerry Lucas and Del Washburn. Here are a few examples of their calculation discoveries with my notes, which prove God's sovereign design in Scriptures.

EXAMPLE

Add up the numbers in Jesus and you get 888.

This is divisible by 111. Lord God in Gen.3:9 = 111.

Notice the divisible value 111 ties Jesus to God in the Old Testament.

Jesus = 888 or 111 x 8
Lord God = 888 or 111 x 8 – in Rev.15:3
Lord Jesus = 111 x 11 – in Rev. 22:20
Word = 111 x 2
Nazarene = 111 x 2
My beloved Son = 111 x 14

Some hidden values show up in the surface text.

SURFACE TEXT

(Rev.13:16) … the number of the beast … is Six hundred and sixty and six.

HIDDEN IN THE VALUES

(1 Pet.5:8) Adversary = 666
(Jn.1:9) In the world = 666
(Rev.12:12) Great wrath = 666
(Rev.18:3) Merchants of the earth = 666
(Rev.17:15) Where the harlot sits = 666
(Rev.13:6) Blasphemy against God = 666 x 3
(Rev.16:13) Mouth of the dragon = 666 x 3
(Rev.13:3) The whole world wondered after the beast = 666 x 5
(Rev.11:18) And to destroy the ones destroying the earth = 666 x 5

Notice that 666 ties together Satan, the wicked, and the kingdom of the world.

SURFACE TEXT

(Rev.14:1) …behold, the Lamb … and with him <u>a hundred and forty and four thousand</u> ….

HIDDEN IN THE VALUES

(Rom.11:7) The elect = 144
(Rev.14:12) The faith = 144 x 7
(Rev.22:17) The bride = 144 x 7
(Rev.14:3) The 144 thousands = 144 x 7
(Lk.12:37) Blessed are those servants = 144 x 7
(Rom.9:11) Elect of God = 144 x 10
(Rev.14:4) Purchased firstfruits = 144 x 10
(Rev.1:7) Clouds = 144 x 10 ("Behold He cometh with the <u>clouds</u>")
[These are obviously clouds of white-robed saints.]

Notice that 144 ties together God's kingdom of the righteous elect. While the number "666" identifies those who manifest the name (Greek: "character and authority") of the beast in their forehead in Revelation 13:16-18, the number "144" identifies those who have the name (Greek: "character and authority") of Jesus and the Father in Revelation 14:1.

I hope you get the idea. These were some of the shorter phrases. Notice that doctrines of the beast, the harlot, and the world are connected. Doctrines of the righteous, the elect, and the Lord's coming for them are connected. The whole Bible is full of this connection of doctrines by common values like 100, 144, 111, 153, 276, 666, 700, 1000, 1500, etc. Del Washburn continued to research and wrote several more books on theomatics.

Another fantastic mathematical proof of the inspiration of Scriptures has been discovered. It has been popularly called "the Bible code," which is also the name of the first book on the subject by Michael Drosnin. Below is a summary of things gleaned from his book.

John Maynard Keynes, who was provost of Cambridge University, discovered the papers of an earlier provost from 1696, Sir Isaac Newton. Keynes, who wrote Newton's biography, reported that most of Newton's writings were not about math, gravity, or the solar system, but theology. He reported that Newton believed there was a code in the Bible that recorded human history, past and future. Newton had been diligently searching for this for many years before he died. The Genius of Vilna, an 18th century sage said, "The rule is that all that was, is, and will be unto the end of time is included in the Torah, from the first word to the last word. And not merely in a general sense, but as to the details of every species and each one individually, and details of everything that happened to him from the day of his birth until his end."

More than fifty-five years ago, Rabbi Weissmandel of Czechoslovakia discovered that if he picked every fiftieth letter from the beginning of Genesis the word "Torah" was spelled out. He found this skip sequence also in the rest of the books of the Torah, which are the five books given through Moses. Dr. Eliyahu Rips, a renowned Israeli mathematician, eventually unlocked this code by computer, an instrument that his predecessors lacked. His findings have been affirmed by first class mathematicians around the world in scientific journals, at Harvard, Yale, and Hebrew University, where he is Associate Professor of Mathematics. He has termed this code as "equidistant letter sequences" or "ELS."

The sequences can skip one or many thousands of letters and can go from right to left or left to right in the text with the same letter being used more times than we know. This makes layer on top of layer on top of layer, etc. of information beneath the text of the Scriptures. Of course, words with few letters can be found randomly in other writings this way. However, in Scriptures, the words, phrases, or sentences grouped with other related words, phrases, or sentences of different skip sequence in the same text make this happening by chance beyond the realm of reason. Since Michael Drosnin's book, many Bible code software programs have become available. By using this software, volumes of discoveries are being made around the world. I have found discoveries with my own software. A friend found my wife's name and my own with our marriage date. Another friend found his family tree. If relatively unimportant things are found, just think about how much is actually there. It is probable that the Genius of Vilna was correct.

Revelations of the future are harder to come by because a person must have some kind of idea what to ask the software to search for. Drosnin found the assassination of Yitzhak Rabin and the year it was predicted a year before it actually happened. He also warned the Prime Minister, but sadly the prediction was fulfilled on time. Later, the assassin's name was also found. He also found two months in advance the collision of the following: Shoemaker-Levy / will pound Jupiter / 8th AV (July 16).

Another thing that has been found is that the surface text is many times connected to the code beneath it. Drosnin shared an example of this in Daniel 12:4 where "computer" is encoded beginning with the words *"shut up the words, and seal the book, even to the time of the end."* It is clear that the information sealed up in the Bible code could not be revealed until the time of the end when computers became available. Confirming this fact, beginning in Deuteronomy 12:11, "Bible code" is encoded and in Deuteronomy 12:12, "sealed before God" is encoded.

A few of the other codes found in his book are the Holocaust, the moon landing, WWII, Watergate with the impeachment, the Wright brothers with their airplane, Edison with his light bulb, Newton with gravity, both Kennedy assassinations with the assassins, Bill Clinton's election, the Oklahoma City bombing with Murrah Building and Timothy McVeigh, etc. Most of these are given with pertinent information and sometimes dates. Also, there are future warnings of nuclear world wars, comets and asteroids striking the earth, terrible earthquakes, plagues, economic collapse, etc. Most of these are given with pertinent information and many times dates. Some of these are warnings just as Jonah warned Nineveh, which are conditional upon man's actions, and some are prophecies that will surely come to pass.

The above codes have been in the Torah for over 3,000 years. Even more important proof of God's sovereignty in the inspiration of Scriptures are the hundreds of prophecies in the surface text and the thousands of prophecies in the types and shadows of all the Bible that are consistently coming true after 2,000-3,000 years. No psychic, palm reader, crystal-ball reader, prognosticator, etc. can do such a thing, as Daniel also said. King Nebuchadnezzar had a dream in which was hidden the future of the kingdoms of the world until the end. When the devil's false prophets could not reveal the dream or the future therein, Daniel by the Spirit of God did. First he told the king of his error in seeking the future from these people. *(Dan.2:27) ... The secret which the king hath demanded can neither wise men, enchanters, magicians, nor soothsayers, show unto the king; (28) but there is a God in heaven that revealeth secrets, and he hath made known ... <u>what shall be in the latter days</u>.* Only a sovereign God could reveal to the king this future revelation of the history of the world. It is evident that the devil cannot accurately predict the future through his prophets because he has no sovereignty to bring it to pass. He can predict in the short term what he plans to bring to pass that is also ordained of God, but since all of his plans are not ordained, he makes many false prophecies.

Codes have been found recently throughout the Bible by various other researchers, such as Jesus' name found throughout the Old Testament beneath prophecies of the coming Messiah, the World Trade Center attack, the involvement of Osama Bin Laden, the anthrax attack, the soon coming nuclear wars, the

Gulf War, Saddam Hussein's missile attack on Israel, Yasser Arafat and his war on Israel, the Enron catastrophe and its domino effect, the coming one-world currency, Flight 587, Flight 800 hit by a missile, the coming national ID card, the future bombing of the United States by al Qaeda and Bin Laden, the future nuclear attack by terrorists, the terrible government decisions that take away freedoms, abortion bringing the wrath of God, etc.

Numerics, theomatics, and the Bible code are several of the many different types of hidden codes found in Scriptures. I am convinced that a combination of these will uncover the greatest mysteries. To Bible code researchers of the New Testament, I have some advice: use Dr. Panin's numerically correct <u>Numeric Greek New Testament</u> and you will find more and longer codes because only one letter added or subtracted from the original will destroy the numeric pattern in the text.

Only a mind beyond our comprehension could have designed these codes simultaneously beneath an intelligible text. Dear Friends, since God has made His Word so impressively exact, do you think He would ever depart from it? *(Ps.119:89) For ever, O Lord, Thy word is settled in heaven. (Ps.89:34) My covenant will I not break, Nor alter the thing that is gone out of my lips. (Heb.6:18) … It is impossible for God to lie ….* Since this is true and God has spoken, He has bound His actions by His Word. His Word not only sets the conditions for eternal life but also sets the conditions for blessings and curses in our earthly life. There is nothing more important than studying God's Word that we may learn to live in God's kingdom and in so doing avoid the curses and live under the blessings.

Chapter 3
God's Sovereignty in World Order

The <u>king's heart</u> is in the hand of the Lord as the watercourses: He turneth it whithersoever he will (Pr.21:1).

It is amazing to me how many Christians today can be so ignorant of the sovereignty of God when there is so much of it in the Word, though so many, even in the Old Testament, understood this truth. We would get a good argument if we said some of these things in most any church, but we should be able to say anything that the Scripture says and feel good about it. When we quote the Scriptures and we do not feel easy about it, it is because we are wrong in our thinking. In this way, we can know if we have false doctrine and our mind needs to be renewed. There are many verses ignored by the modern church because they are uncomfortable to the carnal mind.

Here is one of those verses. *(Dan.4:17) The sentence is by the decree of the watchers, and the demand by the word of the holy ones; to the intent that the living may know that the <u>Most High ruleth in the kingdom of men</u>, and <u>giveth it to whomsoever he will</u>, and setteth up over it the <u>lowest of men</u>.* Why is it that people do not understand this today? There are so many Christians today that are so politically-minded they think that they have the ability by banding together to put somebody in office that God does not want. Be careful about matching numbers with the wicked. According to the truth of the broad road, there is no moral majority. It is not by might and not by power. Throughout history, God has set up over the kingdoms of men the <u>lowest of men</u>. God has a good reason for doing this. It was the reason that the lowest of men judged Jesus, and it is the same reason that we need the lowest of men to rule over us now. Good people will not nail you to a cross, but without the cross there is no crown.

In Biblical times, when God's people fell into apostasy, He raised up a beast kingdom to crucify them into repentance. Six world-ruling kingdoms – Egypt, Assyria, Babylon, Media-Persia, Greece and Rome – were raised up to bring little Israel to their cross. Is it an accident that world kingdoms thought it important to subject the smallest of kingdoms? History and the Word of God are plain. *(Eccl.1:9) That which hath been is that which shall be; and that which hath been done is that which shall be done: and there is no new thing under the sun.* Now, to bring to repentance a worldwide apostate (fallen away) church, God is raising up a seventh and eighth worldwide beast kingdom, which will incorporate the seed of all the previous kingdoms (Rev.17:11).

We read about Nebuchadnezzar, a man who was so proud of the great kingdom that he thought he had built. *(Dan.4:30) The king spake and said, Is not this great Babylon, which I have built for the royal dwelling-place, by the might of my power and for the glory of my majesty? (31) While the word was in the king's mouth, there fell a voice from heaven, [saying], O king Nebuchadnezzar, to thee it is spoken: The kingdom is departed from thee: (32) and thou shalt be driven from men; and thy dwelling shall be with the <u>beasts of the field</u>; thou shalt be made to eat grass as oxen; and <u>seven times</u> shall pass over thee; until thou know that the <u>Most High ruleth in the kingdom of men, and giveth it to whomsoever he will</u>.* This vessel of clay taking credit for God's work reminds me of the engineer of the Titanic's statement, "We built a boat that God could not sink." *(Eccl.5:2) Be not rash with thy mouth, and let not thy heart be hasty to utter anything before God; for God is in heaven, and thou upon earth: therefore let thy words be few.*

The sovereignty of God instills respect. When King Nebuchadnezzar was walking in his palace bragging about his accomplishments, the Lord turned his mind over to the mind of a beast for seven times. This is a type of the last seven years of tribulation when God will turn the kingdoms of the world over to "Mystery Babylon" with the mind of a beast (Rev.17). For seven seasons, that great boastful king ate the grass of the fields until he came to the revelation that *"the Most High ruleth in the kingdom of men and giveth it to whomsoever He will" (Dan.4:25)*. The first thing we should see here is that God made this arrogant man king and gave the rebellious people of God into his hand. God has repeated this habit throughout history. God through Daniel warned the king of his judgment ahead of time to make him responsible to repent. This is an example to us to fear God and not touch His glory.

(Dan.4:35) And all the inhabitants of the earth are reputed as nothing; (It is not the world that is important in God's plan but those who are born from above.) *and he doeth according to his will in the army of heaven, and among the inhabitants of the earth; and none can stay his hand, or say unto him, What doest thou?* Nobody can push God's hand away and say, "What are you doing?" Nobody can stop Him from doing what He wants to do. This should give us faith, rest, and the fear of God. Since God is doing exactly what He wants, why does He set up these evil men over the world? We thought God wanted to go the other way with the world. He, obviously, does not share the majority's opinion on that. God has no interest in saving the world through world politics; He has never done it before. This is the thinking of ignorant Christians who want to help out God. Their plan is to always put Christians at the head to make favorable laws and judgments for us so that we will never be under persecution, oppression, or the cross. The problem with this is that deeply spiritual men have no desire to rule over men. They only desire to serve the kingdom in fulfilling the Great Commission. *(Mk.10:42) And Jesus …saith unto them, Ye know that they who are accounted to rule over the Gentiles lord it over them; and their great ones exercise authority over them. (43) But it is not so among you: but whosoever would become great among you, shall be your minister* (Greek: "servant").

Political Christians are left with those who desire power among men as their choice. These people and the world they rule over serve the larger plan of bringing sons to maturity. *(2 Sam. 7:14) I will be his father, and he shall be my son: if he commit iniquity, <u>I will chasten him with the rod of men</u>, and with the stripes of the children of men.* Political Christians would love to take away God's rod. If so many Christians did not have a name that lives while they are dead (Rev. 3:1), there would be no need for the rod of men.

When it comes to politics, I am totally neutral because I want to be on God's side not man's side. God does not always want to put in the good man we think He wants to put in. He did not do it with Clinton, did He? Most Christians would agree with me there. God wanted to put a wicked man in office, because a wicked man is the only kind that would bring this wicked country into the chastening it needs. God elected Clinton. *(Rom. 13:1) Let every soul be in subjection to the higher powers: for there is no power but of God; and the powers that be are ordained of God.* God did not put Clinton in because that was His preference as a person but because that was what we needed. No father prefers to chasten his child, but bless him. God put Bush in office because Christians asked Him to. Now, He can prove that Bush cannot save nor keep us from chastening, either.

You may ask, "Is it God's Will to use the Christian vote to put in office someone like Bill Clinton?" No, because if God uses a Christian, He wants to use them as a vessel of honor. Then would He have us not vote? When He desires to put someone like that in office, the answer is yes. When does He want us to vote? The short answer is when He tells us to. *(Rom. 8:14) For as many as are led by the Spirit of God, these are sons of God.* He wants us to vote when He wants to do something very unusual, like put a better man in office. God wants to always use us as vessels of honor. God will use those who refuse to be used as vessels of honor as vessels of dishonor. God will use the wicked to put in a wicked man if He wants the wicked in there.

If you disagree with me on that, at least agree with me on this. *"There is no power but of God; and the powers that be are ordained of God."* This was written in the time of the Herods, Caesars and the Neros, and after that it was true of Hitler and Stalin. Listen, we cannot argue with the Scripture if we want the truth. According to the Word, if wicked men are in a position of power, God put them there. This gives me peace. I do not have to worry. I saw so many Christians worried that Bill Clinton was going to get into office. They were erroneously thinking that it was their responsibility to make sure the right man went in, instead of just obeying God. I did not have to worry about that because my God reigns. I told many before Clinton's first term that God was going to put him into office. I was told that God would not do that. Well, He overruled them. God rules in the kingdom of men, and He rules in the heavens, and He never falls off the throne. Many are deceived into thinking that God's plan is to rule the world by democracy. In such a case, the broad road gang wins. He already rules through theocracy. Romans 9:21 clearly states that He has vessels of honor and vessels of dishonor. God has a good purpose for His vessels of dishonor, as we shall see.

Who was it that killed Jesus? The Jews who were recognized as the people of God were the voters who cried, "Crucify Him! Crucify Him!" Let me show you Who was behind the voters. Do you know what "Barabbas" means? "Barabbas" means "Son of the father." Barabbas was the criminal that represented us. The voters set Barabbas free and demanded that Jesus be crucified. *(Acts 2:22) Ye men of Israel, hear these words: Jesus of Nazareth, a man approved of God unto you by mighty works and wonders and signs which God did by him in the midst of you, even as ye yourselves know; (23) him, being delivered up by the determinate counsel and foreknowledge of God, ye by the hand of lawless men did crucify and slay.*

God delivered up Jesus to lawless men. God could not use men who would not slay the Lamb. God put the people in power that would carry out His *"determinate counsel."* Who was it that delivered up and smote the shepherd? It was not just Judas, Caiaphas, Herod, Pilate, the Romans, and the Jews (voters). We have to look behind all of them. *(Mt.26:31) Then saith Jesus unto them, All ye shall be offended in me this night: for it is written, I will smite the shepherd, and the sheep of the flock shall be scattered abroad.* Even though all these vessels of dishonor are guilty, these are only secondary wills. We have to look behind the secondary wills and see the sovereign Will of God. God said, *"I will smite the shepherd."* Thank God His plan was not to stop there because there is a lot more crucifying necessary. *(Zech.13:7) Awake, O sword, against my shepherd, and against the man that is my fellow, saith the Lord of hosts: smite the shepherd, and the sheep shall be scattered; and I will turn my hand upon the little ones.* God is sovereign, and His plan is to crucify the sheep, the little ones. How else can we account for the persecution of Christians throughout history, throughout the world? Unless we take up our cross and follow Jesus, we cannot be His disciples. Of course, we would like to get rid of evil governments and be accepted by the world so that we could enjoy the good life, but *"all that would live godly in Christ Jesus shall suffer persecution" (2 Tim.3:12)*. If we are disciples of Christ, we will be persecuted.

Jesus said, "I am the way." The way to what? The way to heaven. How do you go? The same way Jesus went. If God were going to turn His hand upon the little ones in the way of crucifixion, would you take away His tools? How is God going to bring His plan to pass without the wicked being in rule? Can you see the earth, the dirt, and the plant? The dirt kills the seed coat, and the plant brings forth fruit. Sometimes God permits childlike thinking. If we understood some of these things without a good foundation, we might be tempted

37

to charge God with doing evil and, of course, God never does evil. For this reason, God permits baby Christians to have this "God is in a war with the devil" concept. But when they mature and study the Scriptures, they should come into the knowledge and understanding that God is sovereign and does not make mistakes. He is creating sons. He created and is using the wicked for the day of evil, and they are necessary to crucify the sons. Prosperity and freedom have caused us to lose sight of this fact. *(Mt.16:24) Then said Jesus unto his disciples, If any man would come after me, let him deny himself, and <u>take up his cross</u>, and follow me. (25) For <u>whosoever would save his life shall lose it: and whosoever shall lose his life for my sake shall find it</u>.*

(Acts 4:27) For of a truth in this city against thy holy Servant Jesus, whom thou didst anoint, both Herod and Pontius Pilate, with the Gentiles and the peoples of Israel, were gathered together, (28) <u>to do whatsoever thy hand and thy counsel foreordained to come to pass</u>. God foreordained these wicked men to crucify Jesus for our salvation and His plan for us to be crucified as well. Not always physically, but absolutely the old man must die that the new man may live.

God uses people around us to bring us to our cross. If you have you ever thought, "I don't need this person in my life," you do need this person in order to bear the fruit of Jesus. Difficult people are used to bring out the worst in us so that we may choose to walk in the light of the Word and be cleansed of this corruption (1 Jn.1:7), or disobey the Word and not bear fruit. This is the whole reason for the most hated command in Scriptures: non-resistance to evil. We are commanded to be as sheep in the midst of wolves (Mt.10:16), to resist not evil and turn the other cheek (Mt.5:39), to love our enemies (Mt.5:44), to bless those who persecute us (Rom.12:14), and to avenge not ourselves (Rom.12:19) to list a few. These are the natural actions of the one who obeys Jesus and forgives from the heart. God will turn all others over to the tormentors or demons. *(Mt.18:34) And his lord was wroth, and delivered him to the tormentors, till he should pay all that was due. (35) So shall also my heavenly Father do unto you, if ye forgive not every one his brother from your hearts.*

When we are faced with the wicked and we obey these commands of non-resistance, we can feel the fiery trial burning up the wood, hay, and stubble of our old life. Every time our flesh rises up on the inside and we deny it, it dies, and we get more of the gold, silver, and precious stones. We are to consider flesh, self or the old man, to be dead (Rom.6:6,11). You can slap, insult, or rob a dead man and he will ignore you. Stop feeding the flesh and see how quickly it dies. We should see the crucifiers as God's gift to us, even if they are being used as vessels of dishonor. All these wicked people are gathered together to do whatsoever God's hand and God's counsel has foreordained to come to pass. In other words, God does not have any trouble out of any of them. They all do exactly what they are supposed to do. All these rebellious people fulfill the Will of God perfectly. Just as God works in us to will and do of His good pleasure, He also does in them. *(Pr.16:9) A man's heart deviseth his way; But the Lord directeth his steps.* Decide what you want to be, but no matter what you are, God will use you. Pity, forgive, and have mercy on those who are being used of God, through the devil, as vessels of dishonor. Some of them will repent through your prayers and faith.

(Ps.75:5) Lift not up your horn on high (your might, power, or voice being heard)*; Speak not with a stiff neck. (6) For neither from the east, nor from the west, Nor yet from the south, cometh lifting up. (7) But <u>God is the judge: He putteth down one, and liftest up another</u>.* Much has been said recently about the hidden powers that are manipulating the duped masses to get their man into office, and there is truth to this, but God is sovereignly behind it all to work His Will. Fleshly power, wisdom, manipulation, or money lifts no one up. The men of means do not rule this world by their own design; it only

appears that way for God's purpose. Just as God sovereignly puts into office, He takes out of office. He also gives us signs of this control along the way. The president in office on every twentieth year died in office until Reagan. 1840: William Henry Harrison (Died in office) 1860: Abraham Lincoln (Assassinated) 1880: James A. Garfield (Assassinated) 1900: William McKinley (Assassinated) 1920: Warren G. Harding (Died in office) 1940: Franklin D. Roosevelt (Died in office) 1960: John F. Kennedy (Assassinated) 1980: Ronald Reagan (Survived assassination attempt) 2000: George W. Bush? Why did this obvious pattern stop with Reagan and is he the last? God knows. I believe God used the faith and prayers of many Christians who knew about this cycle to bring it to an end. The millennial Sabbath or the actual year 6000 A.M. (September 2001 - 2002) may be the beginning of a new dealing with the sins of God's people. Spiritually, according to type, judgment comes on those who do not cease from their works on the Sabbath.

- Two of the most famous of these Presidents who were 100 years apart had obviously God ordained parallels.
- Abraham Lincoln was elected to Congress in 1846. John F. Kennedy was elected to Congress in 1946.
- Abraham Lincoln was elected President in 1860. John F. Kennedy was elected President in 1960.
- Both were concerned with civil rights. Both their wives lost children while living in the White House.
- Both Presidents were shot on a Friday. Both Presidents were shot in the head.
- Lincoln's secretary was named Kennedy. Kennedy's secretary was named Lincoln.
- Both were assassinated by Southerners.
- Both were succeeded by Southerners named Johnson.
- Andrew Johnson, who succeeded Lincoln, was born in 1808. Lyndon Johnson, who succeeded Kennedy, was born in 1908.
- John Wilkes Booth, who assassinated Lincoln, was born in

1839. Lee Harvey Oswald, who assassinated Kennedy, was born in 1939.
- Both assassins were known by their three names.
- Both names are composed of 15 letters.
- Lincoln was shot at the theater named "Ford." Kennedy was shot in a car called "Lincoln" made by Ford.
- Booth ran from the theater and was caught in a warehouse. Oswald ran from a warehouse and was caught in a theater.
- Booth and Oswald were assassinated before their trials.
- A week before Lincoln was shot, he was in Monroe, Maryland. A week before Kennedy was shot, he was with Marilyn Monroe.

Coincidence? It takes less faith to believe in a sovereign God!

(Ps.75:7) But God is the judge: He putteth down one, and liftest up another. You cannot always judge by looking at the circumstances whether one is being lifted up or put down. For instance, look at Job. Job's friends certainly thought that God was putting him down, but God was lifting him up to sanctify him and to double what he had before (Job 42:10). Joseph is another good example of this. He was sold into bondage by his brothers, falsely accused by his master's wife, and thrown into prison, all as a type of Jesus. Through all Joseph's tribulations, God was actually promoting him over all. Pharaoh then promoted him, making him second only to himself. Joseph confirmed that all of the evil his brothers had done against him was for his good. *(Gen.50:20) And as for you, ye meant evil against me; but God meant it for good, to bring to pass, as it is this day, to save much people alive.* When God is through manifesting His sons, they will be promoted, and the usefulness of the vessels of wrath will come to an end. *(Isa.10:24) Therefore thus saith the Lord God of hosts, O my people that dwellest in Zion, be not afraid of the Assyrian, though he smite thee with the rod, and lift up his staff against thee, after the manner of Egypt. (25) For yet a very little while,*

41

and the <u>*indignation [against thee] shall be accomplished, and*</u> <u>*mine anger [shall be directed] to his destruction*</u>. Then God's elect will rule by Him. *(Ps.75:10) All the horns* (power) *of the wicked will I cut off; But the horns of the righteous shall be lifted up.*

Someone recently made the following comment to me: "So raising all these millions of dollars to promote a candidate is not necessary." God is behind that also, even to put the one He wants into office. Those who do not love God need a natural reason for why things happen. Have you ever watched an ant colony behind glass? They carry on through instinct their own purposes, not realizing that they are being watched, and in our case tried. As long as only the natural is seen, God's purpose of a trial environment is established. It is God's purpose that both He and the devil stay hidden until the end. God is looking for those who will overcome walking by sight and will mature to a higher order of living by faith. After the candidate gets into office, it makes no difference. You may think that if you vote for a good conservative, he will be God's servant. He will always make decisions and choices we can trust because he is "God's man." Has not God shown us the fallacy of that? G.W. Bush has taken away more civil rights because of terrorism than Clinton ever did. We know of a Christian, voted into office by Christians, because they believed he would further the Christian cause. He made some of the most ignorant mistakes and foolish decisions, accomplishing near nothing. God teaches us lessons, not by might of the Republican Party, nor by power of the ballot.

The issue is not about God's Will being done, because whoever gets elected, what he does will be God's Will. It will not, however, always be His wish. Let me explain. *(2 Pet.3:9) The Lord is not slack concerning his promise, as some count slackness; but is longsuffering to you-ward, not <u>wishing</u> that any should perish, but that all should come to repentance.* "Wishing" in this verse has been incorrectly translated "willing" in some versions. If God was not willing that any should perish, believe me, none would perish since He *"worketh all things after the counsel of His own will" (Epe.1:11)*. Every good parent does things they do not wish to do, but they will to do, in order to train children. In like manner, these world rulers will do the Will of God but not necessarily His wish. The real issue is who we put our faith and trust in. If we believe that we can blindly follow the good conservative we helped to elect instead of God, we will trip and fall on our misplaced trust. And this, too, is God's Will.

(Pr.21:1) The king's heart is in the hand of the Lord as the watercourses: He turneth it whithersoever he will. Just as a channel turns the water, the Lord turns the king's heart. If He rules the head, He rules the tail. If He rules the king, He rules the people. God does what He wants by turning hearts. Either He turns their hearts as vessels of dishonor for our sake or He turns their hearts to righteousness. He has given us a method by which we can be His vessels to do this. If we forsake His way for the world's ways, the country will crumble. If we think we are going to turn our country around through politics, we are deceived. We cannot politically force evil people to be good. Only the Gospel has the power to change the hearts of the wicked. It is the power of God to save the one that believes it (Rom.1:16). Therefore we should be focused on obeying the Lord and preaching the Gospel to change this nation. Jesus and the apostles are our examples. They focused on the spiritual war and were not deceived into wrestling with flesh and blood. If our country is turned around, it is because people repent; when people repent, God gives them a good government. Since God's people rarely repent without chastening, our nation will hate us. *(Mt.24:9) Ye shall be hated of all the nations for my name's sake.* We must never fear the will or conspiracies of men or governments. They are all working for His Name's sake.

God predestines and does according to His Will. *(Ps.103:19) The Lord hath established his throne in the heavens; And <u>his kingdom ruleth over all</u>. (20) Bless the Lord, ye his angels, That are mighty in strength, that fulfil his word, Hearkening unto the voice of his word, (21) Bless the Lord, all ye his hosts, Ye ministers of his, that do his pleasure. (22) Bless the Lord, <u>all ye his works, In all places</u> of his dominion: Bless the Lord, O my soul.* God is doing everything that is being done. Through many vessels, He is bringing to pass His eternal creation through the last Adam, Jesus Christ.

We need to differentiate between the kingdoms of the world and the kingdom of God. The devil offered Jesus authority over all the kingdoms of the world (even your country!) as a temptation, but He turned the position down (Lk.4:5). Some Christians are not turning the devil down. They are being deceived into working in and for the wrong kingdom. Politics is the world's method for ruling the world. The Gospel is God's only method for building His kingdom. Jesus said, *"My kingdom is not of this world" (Jn.18:36)*. Although God has people everywhere, in order for them to obey the Great Commission, they are forbidden to entangle themselves with the affairs of this life (2 Tim.2:4).

Jesus said, *"… The kingdom of God cometh not with observation: neither shall they say, Lo, here! or, There! for lo, the kingdom of God is within you" (Lk.17:20,21)*. In other words, the kingdom of God is not to be seen or physical. It is within you; it is the spiritual or born again man, the one who submits to Jesus as King. Many Christians are building a physical kingdom thinking it to be God's kingdom. Many are worshipping God and country, thinking their country to be God's kingdom. We are here to seek first the kingdom of God, but many are seeking and serving the world and the flesh, which are passing away. Have you ever noticed how the church usually aligns itself in any dispute according to their patriotic nationalism? For instance, during WWII the church in Germany for the most part aligned itself with Hitler while the church in the United States aligned itself patriotically with this country. Christians went out to kill Christians, members of their own kingdom! *(1 Pet.2:9) But <u>ye are an elect race</u>, a royal priesthood, <u>a holy nation</u>, a people for [God's] own possession, that ye may show forth the excellencies of him who called you out of darkness into his marvellous light.* Our kingdom is one race in the midst of all races and one nation in the midst of all nations. Our brothers and sisters do not have national bounds or ethnic divisions as the world. We are a spiritual race and nation sent to the fleshly races and nations to *"show forth the excellencies of him."*

Shall we show the world how to kill in the name of Christ? The lost, who are killed, will never have another opportunity to have eternal life. The following excerpts from God's Word should answer that question: *"All they that take the sword shall perish with the sword"; "Love your enemies"; "Resist not him that is evil"; "I send you forth as sheep in the midst of wolves"; "Bless them that persecute you; bless, and curse not"; "Render to no man evil for evil"; "Avenge not yourselves"; "If thine enemy hunger, feed him; if he thirst, give him to drink";* and *"Overcome evil with good."* God's people are confused into being members of the wrong kingdom. If we align ourselves with the world, we are God's enemies! *(Jas.4:1) Whence [come] <u>wars</u> and whence [come] <u>fightings</u> among you? [come they] not hence, [even] of your pleasures that war in your members? (2) … <u>ye fight and war</u>; ye have not, because ye ask not. (4) Ye adulteresses, know ye not that <u>the friendship of the world</u> is enmity with God? <u>Whosoever therefore would be a friend of the world maketh himself an enemy of God</u>.* Religion or patriotism is the cause of most wars, sending multitudes to hell. We are forbidden to fight with people, only evil spirits. *(Epe.6:12) For our wrestling is not against flesh and blood, but against the principalities, against the powers, against the world-rulers of*

45

this darkness, against the spiritual [hosts] of wickedness in the heavenly [places].

In the days ahead, God will open our eyes to this adultery with the world. The whole world, including apostate (fallen away) Christianity, will unite against God's people. When this happens it will cause true Christians to unite behind Christ. *(Mt.24:9) Then shall they deliver you up unto tribulation, and shall kill you: and <u>ye shall be hated of all the nations</u> for my name's sake.* The whole world will follow the beast to make war on the saints (Rev.13:7,8). To those same saints, God says, *"If any man [is] for captivity, into captivity he goeth: <u>if any man shall kill with the sword, with the sword must he be killed</u>. Here is the patience and the faith of the saints"* (Rev.13:10).

Many will disagree with me on the grounds of their own reasoning instead of God's Word. I have been asked, "If we do not fight for our country, who will?" Those who are on the broad road, who are not disciples, will and God will use them as well if He wants to save their country that way. We can and should fight for our country God's way. *(2 Cor.10:4) For the weapons of our <u>warfare are not of the flesh</u>, but mighty before God to the casting down of strongholds.* In the pages ahead, we will understand God's power and methods available to us to fight the principalities and powers that are plundering the earth.

Chapter 4
God's Sovereignty Over Evil

I form the light, and <u>create darkness</u>; I make peace, and <u>create evil</u>. I am the Lord, that doeth <u>all</u> these things (Isa.45:7).

What good reason could God possibly have in creating darkness and evil? Be patient and believe the Scriptures ahead to receive a wonderful understanding of this. But first, let us examine how God exercises His Will over evil and to what extent. *(Isa.10:5) Ho <u>Assyrian, the rod of mine anger, the staff in whose hand is mine indignation!</u>* In this verse, God calls the enemy of Israel His rod and staff to correct them. In Psalm 23, the Good Shepherd uses His rod and staff to comfort David. The rod and staff were tools of the shepherd. The Lord, our Shepherd, uses our enemies as tools to correct us and keep us in line. *(Isa.10:6) <u>I will send him against a profane nation</u>* (Israel), *and against the people of my wrath will I give him a charge, to take the spoil, and to take the prey, and to tread them down like the mire of the streets. (7) Howbeit <u>he meaneth not so, neither doth his heart think so</u>; but it is in his heart to destroy, and to cut off nations not a few.* Notice that the Assyrians did not know they were sent by God to fulfill His plan. It was in their heart to take a spoil and a prey. Whenever God uses vessels of dishonor, they are just fulfilling their lusts. God worked in the Assyrians to will and to do of His good pleasure. We will see that God does this with all of His vessels of dishonor. He has purpose for the wicked in the earth, otherwise, He would have removed them long ago. After God fulfills that purpose, He will do away with them.

(Isa.10:12) Wherefore it shall come to pass, that, <u>when the Lord hath performed his whole work upon mount Zion and on Jerusalem, I will punish the fruit of the stout heart of the king of Assyria</u>, and the glory of his high looks. (13) For he hath said, <u>By the strength of my hand I have done it</u>.... Notice that the

king of Assyria thought that he had done this by his own strength. As history and this verse prove, when God is finished using the wicked for His people, He will destroy them. From the beginning, God did not intend to permanently do away with the wicked but to use them to perfect His people. He commanded the angels to let the tares grow together with the wheat until the end (Mt.13:30), and only then will He separate and destroy the wicked (Mt.13:41,42). He explained that if you *"gather up the tares ye root up the wheat with them" (Mt.13:29).* If God took away the tares, the wheat would die for lack of chastening and object lessons.

(Isa.10:13) For he hath said, By the strength of my hand I have done it, and by my wisdom …. The Assyrians believed that this victory was by their wisdom and strength, but God claimed to be using them as a tool. *(Isa.10:15) Shall the axe boast itself against him that heweth therewith? shall the saw magnify itself against him that wieldeth it? as if a rod should wield them that lift it up, or as if a staff should lift up him that is not wood.* That is the way God sees this army, like a dumb tool. God wielded the axe, saw, rod, and staff and lifted it up to work on His creation. How ludicrous for men to take any credit. God is sovereign, and everything else is a tool to be used by Him in the chastening and perfecting of His saints. We should know that God sends these tools to us to carve us into a vessel for His use and that we need to submit for our own sake. These tools will be necessary until the saints are the finished creation of God. Then God will put them away. Meanwhile, we need not fear that the purpose of evil is prospering. *(Isa.54:16) I have created the waster to destroy. (17) No weapon that is formed against thee shall prosper ….* How comforting it is to know that only God's purpose is prospering!

Even Satan is not put in his place until the end when the tempting and crucifying of the saints is over. *(Rev.20:1) And I saw an angel coming down out of heaven, having the key of the abyss and a great chain in his hand.*

(2) And <u>he laid hold on the dragon, the old serpent, which is the devil and Satan, and bound him</u> for a thousand years, (3) and cast him into the abyss, and shut [it], and sealed [it] over him, that he should deceive the nations no more, until the thousand years should be finished: <u>after this he must be loosed for a little time</u>. One angel had no trouble chaining Satan and casting him into the pit. That was so easy that God could have done it a long time ago <u>if He wanted to</u>. According to the theology of most, God would have had to send an army of angels to get that "heavyweight." After all, has he not been resisting God for over 6,000 years? Wrong! Notice that after 1,000 years God looses him again! Does that give you any idea about who loosed him the first time in the Garden of Eden? Does God loose Satan to do His Will, or to thwart His Will?

(Rev.20:7) And <u>when the thousand years are finished, Satan shall be loosed out of his prison, (8) and shall come forth <u>to deceive the nations</u> which are in the four corners of the earth, Gog and Magog, to gather them together to the war: the number of whom is as the sand of the sea. (9) And they went up over the breadth of the earth, and compassed the camp of the saints about, and the beloved city: and <u>fire came down out of heaven, and devoured them</u>. (10) And the devil that deceived them was cast into the lake of fire … (11) And I saw a great white throne ….* God loosed the devil to deceive all the evil nations, to make war on the saints. He did this so that He could rain down fire on the nations to destroy them, just in time for the great white throne judgment of the wicked. God did not even need the angels to destroy the devil and all of his children. He could have done this in the garden and saved us the trial, but it was not His plan!

Who cast the devil and his angels down to the earth to deceive the nations and to make war on the saints during the tribulation period? *(Rev.12:7) And there was war in heaven: <u>Michael and his angels</u> [going forth] to war with the dragon; and the dragon warred and his angels; (8) And they prevailed not, neither was their place found any more in heaven. (9) And* *the great dragon was cast down, the old serpent, <u>he that is called the Devil and Satan, the deceiver of the whole world; he was cast down to the earth, and his angels were cast down with him.</u>* Then the devil in the beast made war with the saints. *(Rev.13:7) And <u>it was given unto him</u>* (the beast) *to make war with the saints, and to overcome them: and <u>there was given to him authority</u> over every tribe and people and tongue and nation.* If God was going to cast the devil and his angels down, why not cast them into the lake of fire? Instead, God restrained them to the earth where we are! God needed the hoards of evil to separate the tares from the wheat and to mature the saints. Notice, *"there was given unto him"* (the beast), both authority over the nations and authority to make war on the saints. You see, Friends, God gave authority to the devil, who dwelt in the beast and gave authority to the beast, to try the saints and to crucify their flesh.

(Isa.10:20) And it shall come to pass in that day, that the remnant of Israel, and they that are escaped of the house of Jacob, <u>shall no more again lean upon him that smote them, but shall lean upon the Lord</u>, the Holy One of Israel, in truth. One of our problems is that we lean on the flesh and the world. We trust in America to defend and make us socially secure. The world has our love, respect, honor, and fear, all of which belongs only to God. God has a remedy for that. God brought the illicit lovers of Israel against her so that she would learn who the true enemies of her soul were. In this case, the Lord is showing us the same thing. One of His remedies for us loving the things, people, and thinking of the world is that He is going to bring all that against us. *(Mt.24:9) "<u>Ye shall be hated of all the nations for my name's sake</u>."* It is necessary that we be hated of all nations so that God's name is manifest in us. It is necessary that the world hate us to turn our heart away from the love of the world. God's people were too comfortable in Egypt so He turned the Egyptians' heart to hate His people (Ps.105:25). Then *"He saved them from the hand of him that*

hated them ... " *(Ps.106:10)*. First, God turned their heart against Israel, then, God delivered Israel out of their hand, and they were so grateful.

(2 Sam.7:14) I will be his father, and <u>he shall be my son: if he commit iniquity, I will chasten him with the rod of men</u>, and with the stripes of the children of men. God's purpose in creating sons is going to be fulfilled by using vessels of dishonor to chasten His sons for their sins. The rod is physical men, armies, and nations. God uses spiritual principalities and powers to motivate these vessels of dishonor. If I were to pick up a stick and hit my neighbor with it, you would accuse me of evil. On the other hand, if I take the same stick and go chasten my child because of willful disobedience, you should think that good (Pr.23:13,14). What is the difference? The same stick was used, but the purpose was opposite. To attribute evil to God for using evil shows a lack of understanding of His purpose or motive. God is going to use evil to do good. God is good and all things that God does are good. We cannot limit God with self-righteous thinking.

God is going to do a good work with evil. In fact, without evil, God cannot do this work. *(1 Tim.1:20) of whom is Hymenaeus and Alexander; whom <u>I delivered unto Satan</u>, that they might be <u>taught</u> not to blaspheme.* The word "blaspheme" here means "to speak evil against." These men were speaking evil against either someone or the truth, and Paul, for God, turned them over to Satan so that they might be taught not to blaspheme. Satan teaches us much. In most cases, it is Satan and his demons that execute the curse on those that sin. The curse was spoken and ordained by God in Deuteronomy 28 to motivate sinners to repent. Satan tempts us with lusts, but when we give in, he legally may administer the curse until we repent. When we get out from under the Blood, Satan is waiting. It is not in Satan's mind to teach us anything or chasten us. That is God's purpose. Satan is full of lust, and hates mankind and wants to do evil against mankind. Satan's does not wish to

51

teach us, mature us, or bring us to an understanding of God but he brings that to pass.

Jesus said, *"If a kingdom be divided against itself, that kingdom cannot stand" (Mk.3:24)*. Satan's kingdom is divided against itself because what he does to the people of God causes them to repent and mature. It is not just Satan, but everything around us that God is going to use to bring us to maturity. Satan, the leader over the vessels of dishonor, is very important to this process. Satan is in command over the wicked spirits and thus, wicked people. God is in command over Satan. The Scripture says, *"All things work together for the good."* According to this, what Satan does to us is for our good. Does Satan understand what he is doing? No, he does not understand. According to the law of sowing and reaping, he has sown deceit, therefore he is deceived. He is out to take man's position of authority by tempting him to sin. Satan is also a created being. God did not create any being that was going to be able to thwart His Will. He created everything for the purpose of bringing His chosen into the image of Jesus Christ. There are several methods that God uses to move the wicked, Satan, and the demons. One is by the power of suggestion. He works in them to will and to do of His good pleasure. He also commands or gives permission to them.

(1 Cor.5:5) to deliver such a one unto Satan for the destruction of the flesh, that the spirit may be saved in the day of the Lord Jesus. Paul is taking authority over the power of the enemy and using that power to chasten rebellious children of God. *(Lk.10:19) Behold, I have given you authority to tread upon serpents and scorpions, and over all the power of the enemy ... (20) Nevertheless in this rejoice not, that the spirits are subject unto you ....* Jesus delegated authority over the power of enemy spirits to disciples. Disciples have a right by the Spirit of God to use their power or to forbid their power. *(Mt.18:18) Verily I say unto you, what things soever ye shall bind* (forbid) *on earth shall be bound* (forbidden) *in heaven;*

and what things soever ye shall loose (permit) *on earth shall be loosed* (permitted) *in heaven.* Disciples have authority to forbid or permit. With the guidance of God's Spirit, mature disciples can permit the devil's power for a good purpose, *"that the spirit may be saved."* Notice the condition that Paul, by the Spirit, laid upon Satan, *"for the destruction of the flesh."* In this way, God exercises His sovereignty through His disciples.

When Jesus sent out His disciples to make disciples, He commanded them to pass on the same authority and commands that He had given them. *(Mt.28:20) Teaching them to observe all things whatsoever I commanded you: and lo, I am with you always, even unto the end of the world.* If we are disciples (Greek: *methetes,* "learners and followers") of Christ, we have the same commands. Jesus said that He would be with them to do this *"even unto the end of the world."* Obviously, the original disciples did not live that long, therefore He is speaking to all disciples.

In our assembly, there was a woman who regularly offended the saints. I loved this sister and had only her best interest at heart. After much correction, I asked the Lord what to do about her. He instructed me to "turn her over to Satan for the destruction of the flesh." I wanted to be careful to not judge on my own. I asked God to confirm this direction with a sign, which He did. In my study I vocally spoke this judgment, turning her over to Satan. I found out that she almost immediately got so sick that she could not get out of her bed. She told me later that when she was lying in her own waste and vomit she cried out to the Lord for answers. He told her that she had offended His people and that she must confess her sin before them and ask forgiveness. She decided to obey. God temporarily delivered her from this affliction so that she could obey. At the next meeting, she asked the assembly's forgiveness which she received. When she went home, the affliction came right back upon her. She cried out to the Lord again asking why it had come back since she had obeyed. She got an answer and called me on the phone. She related to me what happened and then said, "David, the Lord said that I have been turned over to the devil." I told her, "It is true, I did this at God's direction, but you have repented, and I see no reason not to release you. You are free in Jesus' name." The Lord healed her and because of this instance gave her a new respect for ministerial authority.

Modern day ministry goes from one extreme to the other. Either God's ministers are totally powerless in the face of rebellion or they exercise carnal dominion like the Pharisees. Just as a father and mother have authority in a family to chasten their children physically, the leadership in the Church has authority, because of the love of Jesus, over His children. This authority is not for the purpose of personal animosity, anger, or vengeance. It is because we do not want to see God's people come to the end of their lives having never repented of their sins and fall off into the pit. God's purpose has to be continually working in a person's life to bring them to maturity, to get them ready to face Him. Paul turned this man over to Satan in obedience to the Spirit, out of love. Some worry about the possibility of abuse here, but *"the curse that is causeless alighteth not" (Pr.26:2)*.

(1 Cor.5:5) To deliver such a one unto Satan for the destruction of the flesh, <u>that the spirit may be saved</u> in the day of the Lord Jesus. This man had his father's wife, probably what we would call a stepmother. Paul spoke to the elders in Corinth and determined to agree with them to turn this man over to Satan. Do you think that Satan is thinking about destroying people's fleshly nature to save their spirit? The flesh is Satan's ally and a manifestation of his very nature. *(Rom.8:7) Because the mind of the flesh is enmity against God; for it is not subject to the law of God, neither indeed can it be.* No, it is God's plan for Satan to administer chastening. It is Satan's lust to do what he is permitted, to destroy man. Satan has been given power over the flesh. Do you remember the serpent in the garden? He

was cursed to crawl on his belly and to eat the dust of the earth. What is the dust of the earth? It is what our flesh was made from. Satan has been given authority to come against flesh. I am speaking not only of this body but also of the carnal desires and appetites that gratify self. Satan's job is to devour the old man, and he is very good at it. The benefit is the saving of the spiritual man.

God commonly turns us over to Satan for chastening when we walk in willful disobedience. In Matthew 18, we have a case of unforgiveness. *(Mt.18:34) And his lord was wroth, and __delivered him to the tormentors__* (demons), *till he should pay all that was due. (35) __So shall also my heavenly Father do unto you__, if ye forgive not every one his brother from your hearts.* This is a common thing. When we see ourselves delivered over to the curse, we should examine our conscience to see if there is cause to repent. I say "if," because sometimes Satan is permitted to come against us to build our faith and to prove our authority over him. God uses a very bad devil to do a very good work in more ways than one.

(2 Pet.2:9) The Lord knoweth how to deliver the godly out of temptation, and to __keep the unrighteous under punishment unto the day of judgment; (10) but chiefly them that walk after the flesh__ in the lust of defilement, and despise dominion. God takes credit for keeping the rebellious under judgment. Some live under judgment all their life because they *"walk after the flesh."* If we do not understand the sovereignty of God, many times we are going to go through a lot more judgment. We need to recognize God's purpose in everything. He is using Satan, one of his demons, or the wicked people around us to chasten and bring us to repentance or to build our faith through trials. Many only see the vessel; they do not see God behind the vessel whose purpose is being fulfilled. They only see it as a work of Satan and not the work of God. Satan would have us believe that the reason he comes against us is because we are good children of God. However, God would have us

believe that when Satan comes against us it is because He loves us and chastens our corrupt nature and acts, or to give our faith a spiritual workout. If you only see Satan coming against you and not God, you do not have any motivation to change. But, if you see God sending Satan against you, you are motivated to change. *(Jn.3:27) … A man can receive nothing, except it have been given him from heaven.*

(Heb.2:2) … Every <u>transgression</u> and disobedience received a just <u>recompense</u> of reward. All you have to do is look at the recompense, and you can tell when something is a transgression. Some people have asked me if I thought it was wrong to do this or that. Look at the recompense and you will see if it is wrong. Is it wrong to recreationally indulge in hard liquor? Look at the recompense, deterioration of the body and spirit. Is it wrong to smoke? Look at the recompense, chronic obstructive pulmonary disease (COPD), cancer, and other physical complications. People who are bitter, angry, and unforgiving are delivered over to cancer, arthritis, and other immune deficiencies. Many with cancer or arthritis have kept up anger and bitterness in their lives. Anxiety and worry gives way to ulcers. You do not have to ask if it is sin; look at what it does to people. Even if you do not know a verse that tells you it is a sin, look at the fruit of it. Look at what comes against you because of it. God has ordained the entire curse system to come against those who transgress. Whether God is using the devil, his demons, wicked people around you, sickness, or any other part of the curse, He is doing it to bring us to repentance and fruit.

God will use evil spirits to humble us and bring about good fruit in us. Paul is a good example. He was caught up to the third heaven and received wonderful revelations that tempted him to be proud. *(2 Cor.12:7) And by reason of the exceeding greatness of the revelations, <u>that I should not be exalted overmuch there was given to me a thorn in the flesh, a messenger</u>* (Greek: *angelos,* "angel") *of Satan to buffet me, that I should not be exalted overmuch.* Paul says the thorn was an angel of Satan to buffet him. The word "buffet" means "to hit over and over." You can see that this evil spirit was given to Paul to fulfill God's purpose of humbling him. *(2 Cor.12:8) Concerning this thing I besought the Lord thrice that it might depart from me. (9) And he hath said unto me, My grace is sufficient for thee: for my power is made perfect in weakness.* This angel of Satan was bringing about a humbling in Paul's life that God called grace. When Paul was in a position of personal weakness or inability to save himself, he got to see God's power to save. It should be the same with us. The Scriptures are full of instances where God purposely brought people such as Moses, Abraham, Jehoshaphat, Gideon, and Lazarus to a position of human weakness so that He could perform a miracle to save them and no one would get the credit but Him. Paul understood this. *(2 Cor.12:10) Wherefore I take pleasure in weaknesses* (K.J.V.: infirmities)*, in injuries* (insults)*, in necessities, in persecutions, in distresses, for Christ's sake: for when I am weak, then am I strong.* "Thorn in the flesh" is mentioned four other times in the Scriptures, and not once is it an infirmity. This word "weaknesses" is from the Greek word *astheneia* meaning "want of strength." The King James Version translated this word "infirmities," but the same Greek word in many other places, including this text, is translated "weak" or "weakness" (1 Cor.1:25; 2 Cor.11:29; 2 Cor.12:9,10; 2 Cor.13:4). The same Greek word *astheneia* in the following two verses shows us that "infirmity" is a bad translation. *(1 Cor.1:25) ... The weakness of God is stronger than men.* Now we know that God is not infirm or sick so this word has to be "weakness." *(2 Cor.13:4) For he was crucified through weakness, yet he liveth through the power of God. For we also are weak in him, but we shall live with him through the power of God toward you.* We know that Jesus Christ was not crucified through infirmity, but weakness. He would

57

not defend Himself when He was brought before Pilate and the Jewish leaders. Likewise, we are crucified when we are weak to save ourselves while we trust in God. Earlier in the text, Paul lists what he calls weaknesses. He lists things such as shipwrecks, prisons, persecutions from enemies, and stripes. Not once does Paul mention sickness in the list. The point is that God uses evil angels to come against our lusts, to humble us, to chasten us, and to cause us to repent. *(2 Cor.12:8) Concerning this thing I besought the Lord thrice, that it* (the angel of Satan or demon) *might depart from me. (9) And he hath said unto me, My grace is sufficient for thee.* God was saying that He would deliver Paul from the individual buffetings, but not from the angel of Satan. Paul said as much to Timothy. *(2 Tim.3:11) Persecutions, sufferings. What things befell me at Antioch, at Iconium, at Lystra; what persecutions I endured. And* <u>*out of them all the Lord delivered me*</u>. *(2 Tim.4:18) The Lord will deliver me from every evil work.* In this, we see the sovereignty of God in both bringing the chastening and supplying the deliverance. The demon was as a dumb animal to be used for God's purpose.

(2 Thes.1:4) So that we ourselves glory in you in the churches of God for your patience and faith in all your <u>*persecutions*</u> *and in the* <u>*afflictions*</u> *which ye endure.* When Paul was going through persecutions and afflictions, who was it that was bringing them? It was an angel of Satan. In each case, Paul was chastened and sanctified, and his faith delivered him. God never does anything just for one purpose. *(2 Thes.1:5) Which is a manifest token of the* <u>*righteous judgment of God*</u>; *to the end that ye* <u>*may be counted worthy*</u> *of the kingdom of God, for which ye also suffer.* Sometimes God's method is to use an angel of Satan to bring us into persecution and affliction, which Paul said was a token of the judgment of God to get us ready for His kingdom. Most often, the demons are administering the curse to do that. All things, curses and blessings, are working together for our good.

We have a covenant right to deliverance from the curse. *(Gal. 3:13)* <u>*Christ redeemed us from the curse*</u> *of the law,* <u>*having become a curse for us*</u> ....

(Ps.78:43) How he set <u>*his signs*</u> *in Egypt, And his wonders in the field of Zoan, (44) And* <u>*turned*</u> *their rivers into blood, And their streams, so that they could not drink. (45)* <u>*He sent*</u> *among them swarms of flies, which devoured them; and frogs, which destroyed them. (46)* <u>*He gave*</u> *also their increase unto the caterpillar, And their labor unto the locust. (47)* <u>*He destroyed*</u> *their vines with hail, And their sycomore-trees with frost. (48)* <u>*He gave*</u> *over their cattle also to the hail, And their flocks to hot thunderbolts. (49)* <u>*He cast upon them*</u> *the fierceness of his* <u>*anger, wrath, and indignation, and trouble, A band of angels of evil*</u>*. (50) He made a path for his anger; He spared not their soul from death, But gave their life over to the pestilence (51) And smote all the first-born in Egypt.* Here we have God sending judgments, which He called *"a band of angels of evil,"* to chasten His people and destroy their enemies. When God sent all these judgments through *"angels of evil,"* they came against both the Egyptians and the Israelites in the beginning until His people were willing to come out of Egypt. Then God made a separation between Goshen and Egypt. The judgments then fell only on the Egyptians so that God's people would be set free. When we repent of living in Egypt, we do not have to live under the judgments.

(Ex.12:23) For the <u>*Lord will pass through to smite*</u> *the Egyptians; and when he seeth the blood upon the lintel, and on the two side-posts, the* <u>*Lord will pass over the door*</u>*, and will* <u>*not suffer the destroyer*</u> *to come in unto your houses to smite you.* Notice that the Lord passed over the Israelites' door with the destroyer and smote the Egyptians. The king angel of the abyss in Revelation 9:11 was Apollyon (in the Greek) or Abaddon (in the Hebrew), and both of these names mean "destroyer." These are probably just two of the many names for the devil. He was the king demon over death, but God had authority over

him. The destroyer came through at midnight, exactly when God said he would. God's purpose was for him to destroy God's enemies and anyone who did not partake of the lamb. God told them to eat the lamb, and the destroyer would not smite them. That is how we come out from under the curse of sin and death. We must eat the lamb, Jesus Christ, the Word. Physically we are what we eat. Spiritually we are what we spiritually eat. By consuming and digesting the Word of God, we are delivered from the curse and manifest our sonship.

Sennacherib, king of the Assyrian Empire, had sent his vast army against Judah, but God promised them victory through Isaiah. *(Isa.37:7)* ***Behold, I will put a spirit in him, and he shall hear tidings***, *and shall return unto his own land; and I will cause him to fall by the sword in his own land.* God put a demon spirit in Sennacherib, who, hearing voices, was then afraid of being away from home. Many demon-possessed people hear voices. The demons want to destroy God's people. Sometimes they have no choice in what they do. God used this demon to take the king home where he fell by the sword of two of his sons (Isa.37:38).

Mary and I were praying for a friend to come to the Lord. I was dumbfounded at the way the Lord did this. The friend received a spirit of fear, and for some time he was very fearful that he was going to lose his soul and go to hell. This is a man that had no interest in Jesus. His thoughts and fears were unreasonable to him, so in seeking answers he went to a priest, because that was his background. The priest gave him no satisfaction. Ultimately, he came to us, and we showed him from the Word the way of salvation, and he was saved. Your objection may be that God has not given us a spirit of fear. That verse was written to believers who know and serve God. But in this case, my friend did not know the Lord. God gave him a spirit of fear to cause him to fear eternal damnation, so he went looking for salvation, and found it. *(Ps.111:10) The fear of the Lord is the beginning of wisdom ….*

Some ministers who have not lived righteous lives and yet retain authority over God's people have been demon-possessed. King Saul was just such a man. God called him and anointed him, but he rebelled. *(1 Sam.16:14) Now the Spirit of the Lord departed from Saul, and <u>an evil spirit from the Lord</u> troubled him.* I am sure that if most did not know this was in the Word, they would accuse me of heresy. We see here an evil spirit from the Lord troubling Saul because he would not obey. *(15) And Saul's servants said unto him, Behold now, <u>an evil spirit from God troubleth thee</u>. (16) Let our lord now command thy servants that are before thee, to seek out a man who is a skillful player on the harp: and it shall come to pass, when <u>the evil spirit from God</u> is upon thee, that he shall play with his hand, and thou shalt be well.* Of course, they found David with his harp to comfort the king. Isn't that something? God sent an evil spirit to trouble Saul and then sent David with his harp to give him some relief from the torment. He works on us from both sides.

I ministered in an assembly once where I discerned that the pastor had demons. He was having problems with women, money, and honesty. He told me three times that God had spoken to him that he was Saul and I was David. I shared with him truths that would help him to overcome, but he was self-willed. I asked the Lord what to do about him because he was causing believers to stumble. God said, "Let the Philistines take him out." The Philistines were the enemies of God's people who took Saul out. The enemies of God's people did take this man out, too. I ended up taking over the ministering there for a short time. It was Saul and David all over again. God worked on this man from both sides. In Deuteronomy 28, God says over and over that He would send the curse to the rebellious, and now we know that He sent Jesus to deliver from that curse.

God refused to give Balaam permission to curse the children of Israel in Numbers 22. After being offered a bribe, Balaam went back to God hoping His mind had changed. Seeing the proud, covetous heart of Balaam, God gave him permission. When Balaam went, the angel of the Lord was standing in the way with sword drawn to kill him. Balaam did not see the angel of the Lord, but his ass did and tried to warn him. *(2 Pet.2:16) But he was rebuked for his own transgression: a dumb ass spake with man's voice and stayed the madness of the prophet.* God through the angel was waiting to kill Balaam if he continued, and God through the donkey was reasoning with him to stop him. God is doing that with all of us. We are constantly faced with a choice. God has put us here for our soul to make a decision between our flesh and our spirit. We are the highest creation of God and the lowest creation of God. We are between heaven and hell, between demons and the angels, between God and the devil. Every way we turn, there is a decision to be made. God planned it that way. He is saying to rebellious people, "The curse is in front of you; do not go. But if you do, it is your own fault, and you will pay a penalty." At the same time He offers grace to make the right decision.

God raised up Gideon to conquer Israel's enemies. After this, Gideon would not accept a position of authority over Israel. In fact, he would not let his sons take a position of authority over Israel while he was alive (Jdg.8:23). Gideon had seventy-one sons, one of these by a concubine in Shechem. This son lusted after authority and wanted to be the next king over Israel. So he conspired with the men of Shechem to kill Gideon's seventy sons. All but Jotham were murdered. Jotham prophesied the following to the men of Shechem after they had executed the dastardly deed: *(Jdg.9:20) ... Let fire come out from Abimelech, and devour the men of Shechem, and the house of Millo; and let fire come out from the men of Shechem, and from the house of Millo, and devour Abimelech.* God was pronouncing through Jotham a curse of division upon the guilty parties. *(Jdg.9:22) And Abimelech was prince over Israel three years. (23) And <u>God sent an evil spirit between Abimelech and the men of Shechem</u>; and the men of Shechem dealt treacherously with Abimelech: (24) that the violence done to the threescore and ten sons of Jerubbaal might come, and that their blood might be laid upon Abimelech their brother, who slew them, and upon the men of Shechem, who strengthened his hands to slay his brethren.* God wanted to judge and destroy this evil alliance so He sent an evil spirit between them to divide and conquer. Both Abimelech and the men of Shechem were destroyed because of this one evil spirit. God used evil to judge the guilty and to deliver His people from their hand.

Once I was ministering in an assembly along with two other ministers. These two ministers were grieving me because they were continually patting each other on the back, even while they were agreeing to disagree with God's Word. When I went home one evening after witnessing them confirm one another's errors in front of the congregation, I felt that the Lord put in my heart to pray that He would send an evil spirit between these two ministers to break up this evil alliance. I was shocked. The next day, I found out that on the very evening of my prayer, those two had fallen out with one another to the degree that they had separated. God used that to separate this evil alliance between these two people.

God uses this method all through the Scriptures. Let me share another example. *(Rev.16:14) For they are <u>spirits of demons</u>, working signs; <u>which go forth</u> unto the kings of the whole world, to gather them together unto the war of the great day of God, the Almighty.* Here demons gather the whole world to fight the battle of Armageddon. The same account in Zechariah says that <u>God</u> gathered the whole world to that battle. *(Zech.14:2) For <u>I will gather all nations</u> against Jerusalem to battle ... (3) Then shall <u>the Lord go forth</u>, and fight against those nations, as when he fought in the day of battle.* So now we see that God will use the demons to gather the enemy army against His people just so that He can destroy them and save His people. Friend, can you see that *"if God is for us who is against us?" (Rom.8:31)* On the other hand, if God is against us then who can be for us?

After gathering the nations to the battle, the Lord said that He would *"fight against those nations, as <u>when He fought in the day of battle</u>."* In 2 Chronicles 20:17, the Lord told Jehoshaphat, *"Ye shall not need to fight in this [battle]: set yourselves, stand ye still, and see the salvation of the Lord."* He was going to fight this battle. His method of warfare is described in the following verses: *(2 Chr.20:22) And when they began to sing and to praise, <u>the Lord set liars-in-wait</u> against the children of Ammon, Moab, and mount Seir, that were come against Judah; and they were smitten. (23) For the children of Ammon and Moab stood up against the inhabitants of mount Seir, utterly to slay and destroy them: and when they had made an end of the inhabitants of Seir, <u>every one helped to destroy another</u>.* I used to think that they waited in ambush for one another. But as I looked at the Scripture more carefully, I discovered that God set liars-in-wait for the whole army so that they fell out with one another. The demon spirits who brought them there were waiting to assemble them so that they could ambush them with suspicion, greed, anger, fear, etc., and cause them to destroy one another. He divided three armies that came as one into three, and they killed off one another. Since God is paralleling this to the battle of Armageddon, He will cause a civil war in the midst of the end time beast kingdom, and they will divide into kings of the north, kings of the south (Dan.11:40), and kings of the East (Rev.16:12) to destroy one another and save God's people. God is in control of demons, therefore, He is also in control of their obedient servants, men. All this is for the purpose of bringing us to repentance and glorifying Himself in our eyes and the world's. This should be a word of encouragement to anyone.

Though God uses evil spirits to divide, He also uses us to forbid them when appropriate. God wants us to resist the devil, to not permit his lies or his accusing of the brethren. God expects us to be vigilant and to test the spirits at all times. The ability to test with discernment comes from the practice of seeking to be a vessel of honor and having our spiritual senses exercised by the Word to discern good and evil (Heb.5:13,14). It is a pity more of God's people do not hear from the Lord today.

Many falsely believe that the division of an assembly of Christians could not possibly be the Will of God. The assembly at Jerusalem was scattered by persecution in order to spread the Gospel. Israel rebelled from under the house of David leaving only Judah and Benjamin. King Rehoboam gathered his army to bring the rebels back into the fold, but the Lord through the prophet spoke to them. *(1 Ki.12:24) Thus saith the Lord, Ye shall not go up, nor fight against your brethren the children of Israel: return every man to his house; for this thing is of me.* Other reasons for division could be because the assembly is too large to meet the needs of the individual or because the assembly is apostate and ruled by men, in which case, the people would not grow up in Christ. God divided Babel because their unity was for the purpose of evil. Notice it was the tongue that divided them just as the denominations are divided now. God's purpose in division is always good but man's purpose is generally evil. Denominationalism is the tendency to divide into sects and is a work of the flesh according to the Word (Gal.5:20; 1 Cor.1:10-13; 1 Cor.3:1-8; 1 Cor.11:17-19; Acts 20:29,30; Jude 16,19). Jesus prayed that His disciples would be one even as He and the Father were one (Jn.17:21,22). This can only happen when in the tribulation the righteous give up their sects to be one flock with one Shepherd (Jn.10:16).

(2 Sam.24:1) And again the anger of the Lord was kindled against Israel, and he moved David against them, saying, Go,

number Israel and Judah. If Israel and David had been pleasing God, God would not have done this. The Lord was angry at Israel and moved David to do something that would bring them into judgment. Even though God moved David, he listened to what was against the principles of God and was guilty. *(10) And David's heart smote him after that he had numbered the people. And David said unto the Lord, I have sinned greatly in that which I have done* …. God sent a judgment and 70,000 men lost their lives to a plague. David made a sacrifice in the threshing floor of Araunah, which stayed the angel (in this case a good angel) that was bringing this judgment against God's people. What was wrong with numbering Israel? God never wanted His people to count on their own strength. He wanted them to count on His strength. *(Jer.17:5) Thus saith the Lord: Cursed is the man that trusteth in man, and maketh flesh his arm, and whose heart departeth from the Lord*. God does not want us to tally up what we can do against the enemy. He wants us to go in His might, trusting in His Word.

How did God move David to number Israel?

(1 Chr.21:1) And Satan stood up against Israel, and moved David to number Israel. First, check to see if this is the same instance as in 2 Samuel 24:1 which was previously quoted. In both places, David repented and sacrificed on the threshing floor after 70,000 men were killed by the pestilence, so it is the same instance. In 2 Samuel 24, God moved David against Israel. In this account, it was Satan who stood up against Israel, and moved David to number his people. Both verses are right, so it is obvious that God used Satan to put it in the heart of David to number Israel, because God wanted to bring a chastening upon Israel. Satan was *"against Israel."* His purpose was evil, but God's was good. It does not matter who speaks convincing us to rebel against the Word of God; if we rebel, we are wrong. It could be our pastor, a prophet, a denomination, a government, or close Christian friends that speak, but we are responsible to the Word.

(Rom.9:17) For the scripture saith unto Pharaoh, For this very purpose did I raise thee up, that I might show in thee my power, and that my name might be published abroad in all the earth. (18) So then <u>he hath mercy on whom he will, and whom he will he hardeneth</u>. Here it is hard to escape the fact that God made Pharaoh stubborn in order to make Himself famous and powerful in the eyes of men. God knows that we need to perceive a great God and Savior. Those who ignorantly think they are defending God's reputation usually say that Pharaoh hardened his own heart first. *(Ex.4:21) And the Lord said unto Moses, When thou goest back into Egypt, see that thou do before Pharaoh all the wonders which I have put in thy hand: but <u>I will harden his heart and he will not let the people go</u>. (Ex.7:3) <u>And I will harden Pharaoh's heart, and multiply my signs and my wonders in the land of Egypt</u>*. Five times in Exodus, God says that He hardened Pharaoh's heart before we are told that *"Pharaoh hardened his heart" (Ex.8:15)*. God sent Moses to tell Pharaoh to set His people free. He then hardened Pharaoh's heart to refuse to set them free. To Israel this made their freedom naturally impossible. God's power is made perfect in our weakness (2 Cor.12:9). God gave to them what they perceived as hopeless in order to glorify Himself in their eyes. They needed to know that He could save them from anything in their coming wilderness trial. God and you are a majority in any situation. If that was not enough, God hardened Pharaoh's heart again to cause him to follow the Israelites into the Red Sea to the Egyptians' destruction. *(Ex.14:4) And <u>I will harden Pharaoh's heart</u>, and he shall follow after them; <u>and I will get me honor</u> upon Pharaoh, and upon all his host.* Unlike the movies, this is the only Pharaoh that they have found that died of drowning. All this was just to impress Israel with God's power to set free. They were going to need this in the trials to come.

Have you ever had some hardened heart in a position of power over you? Go to God, not Pharaoh. All Moses ever got from him was insolence. Have you considered your flesh? Does it seem more powerful than your ability to obey God? That was God's plan. He wants to show us His power to save from sin. *(2 Cor.4:7) But <u>we have this treasure in earthen vessels, that the exceeding greatness of the power may be of God, and not from ourselves</u>.* God wants no competition from our own ability. He wants to prove the power of His grace through our faith in Him.

(Pr.26:2) As the sparrow in her wandering, as the swallow in her flying, So <u>the curse that is causeless alighteth not</u>. No curse can alight upon us unless there is a cause. Sin and corruption is the most likely cause. Whose purpose is fulfilled in a curse? God's! *(Num.23:8) <u>How shall I curse, whom God hath not cursed? And how shall I defy, whom the Lord hath not defied?</u>* We are really wise if we are looking for the cause, and not looking at the curse, or looking at the devil. If we deal with the cause, we do not have to live with the curse. The problem is people will not deal with the cause. They just live with the curse and try by man's methods to be delivered from it. If man, by his own methods, could deliver us from the curse that God sent to cause us to repent, man would be detrimental. What if we examine our conscience and do not see the cause? Then it is very possible that the cause is so that we renew our mind with the Word and fight the good fight of faith. Sometimes the Lord sends Satan against us so that we can whip him. Yes, God does that to prove to us that His Word is true and that we have authority over all the power of the enemy. <u>God's ultimate purpose is to manifest His sovereignty through us, as we shall see</u>. God wants us to learn to fight a spiritual warfare. God gives us practice sometimes. When Satan comes against us through demons, wicked people, or circumstances, we should examine our conscience. If we do not find guilt because of willful disobedience (Heb.10:26), then we should exercise the authority that Jesus gave us against Satan, because we are going to win. In coming against Satan, we are also crucifying

our old man because our old man is created in the image of Satan. When we fight with Satan, we fight with self. When we win against Satan, we win against self. That is another part of God's plan that is so perfect and so beautiful.

(Lam.3:37) **Who is he that saith, and it cometh to pass, when the Lord commandeth it not?** Can evil command something and it come to pass if the Lord has not commanded it? No! God is sovereign. Jesus said His words were not His but the Father's (Jn.14:24). We know this was true because they came to pass. By the grace of God, I have commanded healings, miracles, provisions and deliverances that have come to pass. Religious people have told me that my faith was presumptuous because we cannot know the Will of God. I have thought, "How ludicrous! Do I have power to do these things? God did them. I merely agreed with His Word." The proof that I was in agreement with God is that they came to pass. If the devil commands something and it comes to pass, is it because he is more powerful than God? Not according to this verse. It is because God commanded it whether the devil knew it or not. *(Lam.3:38)* **Out of the mouth of the Most High cometh there not evil and good?**

Where does evil and good come from? God says that it comes out of the mouth of the Most High. Does that mean God is evil? No, it means we deserve or need the ministry of evil. *(Lam.3:39) Wherefore doth a living man complain, a man for the punishment of his sins?* We have been brainwashed to believe that man is basically good and deserving of good, so we are shocked when bad things happen to "good" people. *(Mk.10:18) And Jesus said unto him … None is good save one, [even] God.* From God's mouth comes blessing and curse, good and evil. The evil here represents the hard things that happen to "good" people in order to turn them towards good and to stop them from continuing in sin. Any evil that comes against the life of those *"who are called according to His purpose"* is for good. We blame Satan for coming against us because we are children of God but we should examine our conscience and the Word to find out if God is sending Satan against us because of the sin in us or the actions of sin that we do.

Arminianism is the erroneous belief that everyone has a free will. God is the only one who has a free will. We have a limited free will, limited by our ability, thinking, nature, body, and circumstances. If you have a free will, stick a feather in both ears and let us see if you can get off the ground, or better yet, let us see if you can stop sinning. We cannot do just anything we would like to do. The only one the Bible credits with the ability to do everything He wishes is God. *(Epe.1:11) In whom also we were made a heritage, having been foreordained* (predestined) *according to the purpose of him who worketh all things after the counsel of his will*. Like this verse, Calvinism teaches the sovereignty of God over election, predestination, evil, and everything. The only way that we can do what we want to do is to get God's Will in us. *(Phl.2:13) For it is God who worketh in you both to will and to work, for his good pleasure.* Then we can do what we want to do because we want what He wants, and what He wants He gets.

That is how the Son sets us free, by giving us a will to do His Will. While we have our own will, we will be at war with ourselves. *(Gal.5:17) For the flesh lusteth against the Spirit, and the Spirit against the flesh; for these are contrary the one to the other; that ye may not do the things that ye would*. We have God's Will in us, and we have our will in us. They are tugging away at each other. That is not freedom or a free will. This means that *"ye may not do the things that ye would."* We did not even have the freedom of will to come to God. *(Jn.6:44) No man can come to me, except the Father that sent me draw him: and I will raise him up in the last day*. That is not a free will. We choose not to come to God, unless He draws us. You may choose to sin, most do, but God will choose the time, place, and extent. *(Pr.16:9) A man's heart deviseth his way; But the Lord directeth*

70

his steps. God directs the steps of His vessels of honor or dishonor. The only reason we make the choice in God's direction is because of grace. *(Jn.15:16) Ye did not choose me, but I chose you, and appointed you, that ye should go and bear fruit* .... Jesus first chose us and gave us the will to choose Him because of His unmerited favor. We bear fruit because of a gift of His Will in us.

The Lord brings spirits against us to chasten us and to cause us to repent, then after we overcome, He has total ability to make our enemies to be at peace with us. *(Pr.16:7) When a man's ways please the Lord, He maketh even his enemies to be at peace with him*. We see here that God has total control over our enemies and He can put peace in their heart toward us when we overcome. We should remember this when we are tempted to take care of our enemies ourselves. So we see, God uses our enemies when our ways do not please the Lord. God created our enemies just for that purpose. *(Pr.16:4) The Lord hath made everything for its own end* (Some manuscripts say: *for His own purpose*.): *Yea, even the wicked for the day of evil*. Need I say that we should not argue with God? We see God's hand as sovereign in all of this. God can send the wicked to us, for a day of evil, because our ways do not please the Lord. When we overcome, God can give us total peace in the midst of our enemies. Whether they are wicked men or demon spirits, it does not make any difference.

Should we reason with our puny understanding that God would be wrong to make the wicked? He has an answer. *(Rom.9:21) Or hath not the potter a right over the clay, from the same lump to make one part a vessel unto honor, and another unto dishonor? (22) What if God, willing to show his wrath, and to make his power known, endured with much longsuffering vessels of wrath fitted* (Greek: "to complete thoroughly") *unto destruction*. Notice that they are vessels of dishonor and wrath, made to be destroyed. *(2 Pet.2:12) But these, as creatures without reason, born*

71

mere animals to be taken and destroyed. In instances like this, we must repent and conform our reasoning to God's if we want truth. We, obviously, value these wicked beasts more than God does. In God's opinion, and His is the only one that counts, the wicked are animals, made to be destroyed when they have served their purpose. *(Pr.21:18) The wicked is a ransom for the righteous; And the treacherous [cometh] in the stead of the upright*. A ransom is a price that must be paid for someone's freedom. The wicked are a price that God pays to create sons who are free from the bondage of corruption, so let us not waste their sacrifice.

When Joseph was revealed unto his brethren who came out of Canaan's land into Egypt, they were repenting to him because of the way that they had treated him. Joseph understood the cause for all the tribulation he had been through. *(Gen.50:20) And as for you, ye meant evil against me; but God meant it for good, to bring to pass, as it is this day, to save much people alive*. Joseph credited God for using evil to bring him into Egypt *"to save much people alive."* The Israelites who came out of Canaan's land were starving to death. When they came to Egypt, Joseph, who was sent on ahead because of his Judas brothers, fed them. God used them to crucify Joseph and prepare him as a vessel of honor.

Because Abraham feared the people of the land, he asked Sarah to tell everyone that she was his sister. She was beautiful and he thought they would kill him for her. Abimelech, the king, thinking Sarah was only Abraham's sister, took Sarah to be his wife. God threatened Abimelech telling him that if he did not give Abraham back his wife, he was a dead man. Abimelech protested to the Lord. *(Gen.20:4) Now Abimelech had not come near her: and he said, Lord, wilt thou slay even a righteous nation? (5) Said he not himself unto me, She is my sister? And she, even she herself said, He is my brother: in the integrity of my heart and the innocency of my hands have I done this*. Abimelech took full credit for his integrity of heart.

(6) And God said unto him in the dream, Yea, <u>I know that in the integrity of thy heart thou hast done this, and I also withheld thee from sinning against me: therefore suffered I thee not to touch her</u>. God admitted his integrity but claimed credit for it. Sometimes we take credit because we do not understand God's favor. God puts it in us to do right. God is able to put integrity into the heart of a heathen king to keep him from sinning against God's people.

Recently, I bought a used car from a heathen. We had agreed on a price and were to close the deal the next day. I had asked God for a better price. The next day, when I went to close the deal, he said he would sell it for the better price that I had only spoken about to the Lord. Only God could put in the heart of a lost used car salesman to suggest selling for a cheaper price after we had already agreed. I realized that God had put this in his heart even though it did not come naturally to him. God works in us to will and to do of His good pleasure, so also them.

The Lord said to Peter, *(Lk.22:31)* "*Simon, Simon, behold, <u>Satan asked to have you, that he might sift you as wheat: (32) but I made supplication for thee, that thy faith fail not</u>; and do thou, when once thou hast turned again, establish thy brethren.*" Satan asked to sift Peter, but why would God give any heed to what he asks unless it is for our good? If Peter had been like most people, he would ask, "Lord, why did you give Satan permission to have me? Just say, 'No, Satan, you cannot have him.'" But Jesus knew that was not God's Will.

God's purpose is for Satan to get what belongs to him in our lives. The purpose of sifting is to separate and remove what you want. He keeps what is his. The Lord said, "*The evil one cometh but he hath nothing in me.*" Jesus was pure; there was nothing in Him that belonged to Satan. Satan is sifting to get what belongs to him. God only wants what is left. God could have destroyed him back at the beginning of the world but God ordained Satan for God's good purpose .

In the same way, God used the Assyrians to chasten Israel. *(Isa.10:12) Wherefore it shall come to pass, that, when the Lord hath performed his whole work upon mount Zion and on Jerusalem, I will punish the fruit of the stout heart of the king of Assyria, and the glory of his high looks.* When God is through doing His whole work upon the people of God, guess what He is going to do with Satan, the demons, the wicked, the false prophet and the beast, too? That is right, the lake of fire.

Jesus set the sheep on His right hand and the goats on His left (Mt.25:31). That is exactly how God uses the righteous and the wicked, as His right hand and His left. His right hand is the vessels of honor, and His left hand is the vessels of dishonor. Satan is, in effect, one of God's hands to create sons. A close spiritual brother shared a dream with me. *He saw a line of the saints coming before Jesus in heaven. At Jesus' left hand was Satan with an old style cannon in front of him pointed at the first person in line. Satan with a lighter in his hand eagerly wanted to light the fuse on the cannon and blow them away. Jesus' left hand was in front of him stopping him.* From that dream, you can see that when the Lord moves His left hand, Satan moves.

Here is a clear case of that. *(Job 1:8) And the <u>Lord said unto Satan, Hast thou considered my servant Job</u> for there is none like him in the earth, a perfect and upright man, one that feareth God, and turneth away from evil.* God brought Job to Satan's attention and bragged about him. That is just like waving a red flag in a bull's face. Satan did not want to hear that. In fact, Satan is trying to prove just the opposite to God. He is the accuser of the brethren. God inflicted Satan on Job by the power of suggestion. *(9) Then Satan answered the Lord, and said, Doth Job fear God for naught? (10) <u>Hast not thou made a hedge about him, and about his house, and about all that he hath, on every side?</u> thou hast blessed the work of his hands, and his substance is increased in the land.* Satan is admitting he did not have the power to get at Job because of God's hedge. The same is true of us. *(11) But <u>put forth thy hand</u> now, and* *touch all that he hath, and he will renounce thee to thy face. (12) And the Lord said unto Satan, Behold, all that he hath is in thy power; only upon himself put not forth thy hand. So Satan went forth from the presence of the Lord.* Satan suggests to God that He drop the hedge and put forth *"His hand"* against Job to try him. So why drop the hedge? It was not keeping God's hand out unless you see that the left hand of the Lord was Satan! God confirms this by using the terms *"in thy power,"* and *"thy hand."*

Satan was the one who brought the Sabeans, the fire of God, the Chaldeans and the great wind from the wilderness against Job and his family to try him. Look at what Job said about it. *(Job 1:21) And he said, Naked came I out of my mother's womb, and naked shall I return thither: the Lord gave, and the Lord hath taken away; blessed be the name of the Lord. (22) In all this Job sinned not, nor charged God foolishly.* God says plainly here that Job was not sinning by attributing all this to Him. The Lord gave on the right hand, and the Lord took away on the left. Some people would say that the Sabeans, Chaldeans, and the fire took everything away from Job. Some would look behind those and say that Satan did it. Then some would look a little further back and say that God did it. That is what Job did. That is what we have to do if we are to have the purpose of God fulfilled in our lives. We have to look all the way back and see God's purpose in our lives. Job did not stumble because he understood that. Anyone who sees only the vessel will stumble. If we see only an evil vessel, we will end up fighting and wrestling with flesh and blood. Even though Job was hurting, in his spirit he had rest because he saw God's purpose.

(Job 2:3) And the Lord said unto Satan, Hast thou considered my servant Job? for there is none like him in the earth, a perfect and an upright man, one that feareth God. And turneth away from evil: and he still holdeth fast his integrity (God was rubbing Satan's nose in it.) *although thou movedst me against*

him, to destroy him without cause. God appears to be using reverse psychology on Satan, letting him believe that he was moving God when it was the other way around. God was moved against Job, but Satan was the instrument. It was God who pointed Job out to Satan in the first place in order to fulfill His own purpose. *(4) And Satan answered the Lord, and said, Skin for skin, yea, all that a man hath will he give for his life. (5) But put forth thy hand now, and touch his bone and his flesh, and he will renounce thee to thy face. (6) And the Lord said unto Satan, Behold, he is in thy hand; only spare his life*. God always laid down the conditions of Satan's involvement even as he does today. *(9) Then said his wife unto him, Dost thou still hold fast thine integrity? Renounce God, and die. (10) But he said unto her, Thou speakest as one of the foolish women speaketh. What? shall we receive good at the hand of God, and shall we not receive evil? In all this did not Job sin with his lips*. God wanted to make it plain to us, using two witnesses, that what Job was saying was correct. Shall we receive good at the hand of God and not evil? Job never gave credit to Satan. He never even gave credit to the Sabeans, Chaldeans, or the wind from the wilderness. He did not even look at all the secondary vessels that God used. Job only looked at the primary purpose of God.

Jesus, in teaching us to cooperate with God's purpose of crucifixion in our lives, said, *"Resist not him that is evil,"* speaking of men. However, we are commanded to, *"Resist the devil,"* speaking of evil spirits. We should never get caught up and wrestle with flesh and blood. Jesus would not. *(Isa.53:7) He was oppressed, yet when he was afflicted he opened not his mouth; as a lamb that is led to the slaughter, and as a sheep that before its shearers is dumb, so he opened not his mouth*. We are to wrestle with principalities and powers. God wants us to see evil people as victims of Satan and the curse, vessels to be pitied. *(Lk.23:34) And Jesus said, Father, forgive them; for they know not what they do*. God wants us to see through those vessels of evil and see Him. Jesus had peace because He believed in the sovereignty of our Father. Jesus knew where all power comes from. *(Jn.19:10) Pilate therefore saith unto him, Speakest thou not unto me? Knowest thou not that <u>I have power</u> to release thee, and have power to crucify thee? (11) Jesus answered him, <u>Thou wouldest have no power against me, except it were given thee from above</u> ....*

Eli rebuked his sons for their apostasy.

(1 Sam.2:24) Nay, my sons; for it is no good report that I hear: ye make the Lord's people to transgress. (25) ... Notwithstanding, <u>they hearkened not unto the voice of their father, because the Lord was minded to slay them</u>. The purpose of the Lord is ultimate. Many will not repent because it is in the mind of the Lord to slay them for their evil. We could justly receive the same treatment, but God gave us grace. *(Epe.2:8) For by grace have ye been saved through faith; and that not of yourselves, [it is] the gift of God.* Only God gives the gift of faith to believe and repent. We have to go to God; He grants faith and repentance. True understanding of salvation by unmerited grace causes us to fear God. Some do not value the gift of God only to have it taken away and given to ones who do value it. The Jews lost out to the Gentiles. *(Rev.3:11) Let no man take your crown.* The self-righteous flirt with catastrophe. *(1 Cor.4:7) For who maketh thee to differ? and <u>what hast thou that thou didst not receive</u>? but if thou didst receive it, <u>why dost thou glory as if thou hadst not received it?</u>* If we have anything more than our neighbor, it is a gift of God, not cause for pride.

Chapter 5
God's Sovereignty Over Time and Election

I have <u>declared the former things from old</u>; yea, they went forth out of my mouth, and <u>I showed them</u>: suddenly <u>I did them</u>, and they came to pass (Isa.48:3).

Predict means to tell the future in advance. What the world calls predictions rarely come to pass. It seems they have a warped idea of what a prediction is. When God predicts the future, He declares it and then does it. Not only does God's Word show the future but also it brings it to pass. The *"worlds* (Greek: "ages") *have been framed by the word of God" (Heb.11:3)*. The word "framed" in this verse means "to make complete." The history (or His-story) of all ages was completed before the beginning. *(Isa.48:4) Because I knew that thou art obstinate, and thy neck is an iron sinew, and thy brow brass; (5) therefore <u>I have declared it to thee from of old; before it came to pass I showed it thee</u>; lest thou shouldest say, Mine idol hath done them, and my graven image, and my molten image, hath commanded them.* He is a *"jealous God" (Ex.20:5)*. He will not share His glory with the idol of self or an idol of man's creation (Isa.42:8). God receives glory from telling of His works hundreds or thousands of years beforehand. His *"works were finished from the foundation of the world" (Heb.4:3)*. Because His works were finished from the foundation of the world, no one can say, "My might, my power, my god has done this."

It is important to God that we know He is sovereign. Our God has done something that no other "god" has done; He accurately tells the future long before it comes to pass. It is hard to live the Christian life without knowing that God is sovereign. Without this knowledge, we will not have the peace, rest, and the fear of God that we need in the midst of trials. We will always be wrestling with people and circumstances and trusting in our own strength, instead of seeing God's hand and trusting in His strength. *(Hos.4:6) My people are destroyed for lack of knowledge. (Isa.46:8) Remember this, and show yourselves men; bring it again to mind, O ye transgressors. (9) Remember the former things of old: for I am God, and there is none else; I am God, and there is none like me; (10) <u>declaring the end from the beginning</u>, and from ancient times things that are not yet done; saying, <u>My counsel shall stand</u>, and <u>I will do all my pleasure</u>.* God does all of His pleasure so that only His counsel comes to pass. The proof, that God is the only God, is that He declares the end from the beginning. All the prognosticators, psychics, seers, and stargazers of the devil have only come up with slightly better than random accuracy on the future because their lord is not sovereign. The devil does have an edge. He knows the prophetic Word better than we do, and he predicts what he plans to do, but God is sovereign and often overrules him.

(Isa.46:11) … I have spoken, I will also bring it to pass; I have purposed, I will also do it. God is very self-willed. He has a right to be. His self is not corrupt, but ours is. He brings to pass what He desires because it is right. In the text, God is speaking of Cyrus, the pagan king of the Media-Persian Empire. God raised up Cyrus to destroy Babylon in order to set His people free from bondage. At that time, Cyrus had no idea that the Lord had put the desire in him to do exactly what He wanted. *(Isa.44:28) That saith of Cyrus, [He is] <u>my shepherd, and shall perform all my pleasure</u>, even saying of Jerusalem, She shall be built; and of the temple, Thy foundation shall be laid.* How can God be so sure that a man who has been a pagan all his life will do everything that will please Him? We see here that nothing or no one can resist God's good purpose for His people. God is sovereign over the future of the great empires of the world in order to deliver and prepare His people.

(Isa.45:1) <u>Thus saith the Lord to his anointed, to Cyrus, whose right hand I have holden, to subdue nations before him</u>, and I will loose the loins of kings; to open the doors before him,

and the gates shall not be shut: (2) I will go before thee, and make the rough places smooth; I will break in pieces the doors of brass, and cut in sunder the bars of iron; (3) and I will give thee the treasures of darkness, and hidden riches of secret places, that thou mayest know that it is I, the Lord, who call thee by thy name, even the God of Israel. (4) <u>For Jacob my servant's sake, and Israel my chosen</u>, I have called thee by thy name: I have surnamed thee, <u>though thou hast not known me</u>. The Euphrates River passed through the city of Babylon. One of the gates spoken of here crossed in the Euphrates River to keep the enemy out. Cyrus by the help of God performed a monumental feat in diverting the Euphrates so that his army could enter the city beneath this gate. After they had entered the city, they discovered that the gates on either bank leading into the city had been left unlocked (by God, verses 1 and 2), which was strange, considering that the Babylonians were at war. After Cyrus conquered Babylon, the high priest showed him these prophecies and more that were written about him hundreds of years before he was born. The Jews say Cyrus was very impressed to see his name and works written in prophecy before the fact and became a believer in the God of Israel. God stated clearly that He was going to open those gates for Cyrus to do His Will. After hearing these revelations, Cyrus knew that God had empowered, planned, and made his way.

Christian leaders have turned God into a mere prophet, claiming God sees into the future and then reveals it. Every type and shadow in the Old Testament is fulfilled in the New Testament to prove that God sits on the throne and One Mind rules over time and the future. One loose canon, would change everything. According to the law of geometric progression, one change at the beginning makes an immense change at the end. Chance or more than one in control could not possibly bring to pass what we see. The Arminian thinkers teach that God predestines and predicts by seeing into the future then tells us how the dice rolled. "Predestine" means "to determine destiny before it happens." "Foreordain," which is the same Greek word, means "to ordain an event before it takes place." *(Epe.1:4) Even as <u>he chose us in him before the foundation of the world</u>, that we should be holy and without blemish before him in love: (5) having <u>foreordained us unto adoption as sons through Jesus Christ</u> unto himself, <u>according to the good pleasure of his will</u>.* You who are manifesting sonship by bearing fruit have been chosen and are being drawn by God.

(Rom.8:29) For whom he <u>foreknew</u>, he also foreordained (predestined) *[to be] conformed to the image of his Son, that he might be the firstborn among many brethren.* God foreknew and decreed all who come to the likeness of Jesus, but not the apostate. "Foreknew" here does not mean He looked into the future and saw what would be. "Foreknew" here means, "to know before" and is not connected with actions or events, but persons. God knew these people before the foundation of the world because He does not dwell in time. God knows what He creates before He speaks it into existence just as we conceive and design something first in our mind before we make it. "Knew" speaks of intimate knowledge, for instance, Adam knew Eve. Jesus will say to those who called Him Lord but do not do the Will of the Father, *(Mt.7:23) "And then will I profess unto them, I never <u>knew</u> you* (from the foundation of the world)*: depart from me, ye that work iniquity."* To the foolish virgins without the oil of the Spirit, Jesus said, *"I <u>know</u> you not."* The ones that God intimately knew He *"foreordained"* before the creation to be conformed to the image of Jesus. God creates us through His gift of faith and the Word in us; His people who are on the narrow road. This is grace.

(Rom.8:30) And <u>whom he foreordained</u>, them he also called: and whom he called, them he also justified: and whom he justified, them <u>he also glorified</u>. This says all who are foreordained will be called, justified, and glorified. They will not fall away but will bear the fruit of Christ. Are there others who are called but not foreordained?

(2 Tim.1:9) Who <u>saved us, and called us</u> with a holy calling. Notice that only the saved are called. Called is from the Greek word *kaleo*, which means, "to invite." Called is an invitation given only to God's people (more proof: Heb.3:1; Hos.11:1; 1 Tim.6:11,12; Mt.25:14; Rom.1:6,7) to partake of his heavenly benefits in Christ in order to bear fruit. Those who bear fruit 30, 60, or 100-fold will be proven to be the chosen or picked. If at harvest time you have no fruit, rotten fruit, or unripe fruit, you will not be picked. The called are the vineyard of God (Isa.5:7). The chosen are the smaller percentage who bear fruit (Isa.5:10). *(Mt.22:14) For many are called, but few chosen* (Greek: *eklektos*, "elect").

The called can fall, but the elect or chosen will not. *(Hos.11:1) When Israel was a child, then I loved him, and <u>called</u> my son out of Egypt. (2) The more [the prophets] <u>called</u> them, the more they went from them ....* The Lord saved those that ate the lamb and were baptized in the Red Sea. He then tried them in the wilderness to see who would be a believer in the midst of trials, and only those entered the Promised Land. Jude warned the called of this very thing. *(Jude 1) Jude, a servant of Jesus Christ, and brother of James, to them that are <u>called</u> ... (5) Now I desire to put you in remembrance, though ye know all things once for all, that the Lord, having <u>saved</u> a people out of the land of Egypt, afterward <u>destroyed them that believed not</u>*. Notice that the called were saved, but some did not continue in faith and were destroyed. Friends, God is not looking for what we loosely call "Christians," but believers or disciples, as they were called.

Jesus gave us very clear examples of His servants who are called but do not come and partake in order to bear fruit. Jesus shared a parable in which a king made a marriage feast for His son. *(Mt.22:3) And sent forth his servants to <u>call</u> them that were <u>bidden</u>* (Greek: "called") *to the marriage feast: and <u>they would not come</u>*. They were full of excuses (a farm, merchandise, etc.). *(Mt.22:8) Then saith he to his servants, The wedding is* *ready, but they that were bidden were not worthy.* Even one who appeared to come did not have on a wedding garment which implies putting on Christ (Rom.13:14) or putting on righteousness (Rev.19:8). *(Mt.22:13) Then the king said to the servants, Bind him hand and foot, and cast him out into the outer darkness; there shall be the weeping and the gnashing of teeth. (14) For many are called, but few chosen.* A few of the called are chosen or elect because they bear fruit.

(Mt.25:14) For [it is] as [when] a man, going into another country, called his own servants (Greek: "bondservants"), *and delivered unto them his goods. (15) And unto one he gave five talents, to another two, to another one; to each according to his several ability; and he went on his journey.* Obviously, the man who went away was the Lord, and His bondservants are His people. Two of these example servants brought forth fruit of the talent given them (Mt.25:20-22), but one buried his in the earth (used his talent for the earthly, Mt.25:24,25). When our Lord returns, He will say, *"And cast ye out the unprofitable servant into the outer darkness: there shall be the weeping and the gnashing of teeth" (Mt.25:30)*.

The apostle Paul, who said of himself that he was called in Galatians 1:6, also said, *"But I buffet my body, and bring it into bondage: lest by any means, after that I have preached to others, I myself should be rejected"* (Greek: "reprobated") *(1 Cor.9:27).* There is much more proof that the saved and the called can fall (2 Pet.1:9-11; 1 Tim.6:11,12; Heb.3:1,6,12,14; Rom.11:1-7,19-23).

Friend, you probably know if you are called, but are you chosen? You must be diligent in your walk of faith to prove this. *(2 Pet.1:10) Wherefore, brethren, give the more diligence to make your calling and election* (choosing) *sure: for if ye do these things* (the attributes of Christ, verses 5-7), *ye shall never stumble: (11) for thus shall be richly supplied unto you the entrance into the eternal kingdom of our Lord and Savior Jesus Christ.* God at the cross has already given us everything that we need to bear fruit through faith. *(2 Pet.1:3) seeing that his divine power hath granted unto us <u>all things</u> that pertain unto life and godliness, through the knowledge of him that called us by his own glory and virtue.* Faith in the promises in the midst of trials will give us the fruit. *(2 Pet.1:4) Whereby he hath granted unto us his precious and exceeding great <u>promises; that through these ye may become partakers of the divine nature</u>, having escaped from the corruption that is in the world by lust.* The called have the power and the opportunity. The called and the chosen, or foreordained, use the power by faith and take the opportunity. The only ones who will ultimately be with the Lord are identified in this verse. *(Rev.17:14) These shall war against the Lamb, and the Lamb shall overcome them, for he is Lord of lords and King of kings; and they [also shall overcome] that are with him, <u>called</u> and <u>chosen</u> and <u>faithful</u>.* Notice that the called that are chosen will be faithful. I did not make these verses up; they are the Word of God. Those who have eyes and ears will see and understand, but the rest will justify their religion and ignore the Scriptures. Before time and the future, God sovereignly spoke the end from the beginning, bringing these things into existence in time.

Some would argue, "How could God make a promise to all of His called and then not keep it for those who do not bear fruit?" Every promise in the Bible is useless until someone walks by faith in it. Our part of the covenant is faith; God's part is power and salvation. We can break the covenant through unbelief. *(Num.14:11) And the Lord said unto Moses, How long will <u>this people</u> despise me? and how long will they <u>not believe in me</u>, for all the signs which I have wrought among them? (12) I will smite them with the pestilence, and <u>disinherit them</u>, and will make of thee a nation greater and mightier than they.* Notice that God is saying to <u>His own</u> people who did not believe that He would <u>disinherit</u> them.

Lest any believe that God cannot make a promise and then take it back when they do not walk in faith, pay attention to this: *(Num.14:23) Surely <u>they shall not see the land which I sware unto their fathers</u>, neither shall any of them that despised me see it. (30) surely <u>ye shall not come into the land, concerning which I sware that I would make you dwell therein</u>, save Caleb the son of Jephunneh, and Joshua the son of Nun. (34) and ye shall know <u>my alienation</u>* (Hebrew: "<u>revoking of my promise</u>"). Unless we mix faith with God's promises, they are void. *(Heb.4:2) For indeed <u>we</u> have had good tidings preached unto us, even as also <u>they</u>* (God's people)*: but the word of hearing did not profit them, because it was not united by faith with them that heard.* The Israelites who walked in sin were disinherited and blotted out of God's book. *(Ex.32:33) And the Lord said unto Moses, Whosoever hath sinned against me, him will I <u>blot out of my book</u>.*

The same is true of the Christians who do not overcome sin. Notice what the Lord said to the Church. *(Rev.3:5) He that overcometh shall thus be arrayed in white garments; and I will in no wise <u>blot his name out of the book of life</u> ....* Those who do not overcome will be rejected from the body of Christ. *(Rev.3:16) So because thou art lukewarm, and neither hot nor cold, I will <u>spew thee out of my mouth</u>.* God's people Israel were broken off because of unbelief, and Christians who were grafted in but do not walk by faith will be, too. *(Rom.11:20) Well; by their <u>unbelief they were broken off</u>, and thou standest by thy faith. Be not highminded, but fear: (21) for if God spared not the natural branches, <u>neither will he spare thee</u>. (22) Behold then the goodness and severity of God: toward them that fell, severity; but toward thee, God's goodness, if thou continue in his goodness: otherwise <u>thou also shalt be cut off</u>.* Those who are still grafted in at the end are called *"all Israel." (Rom.11:26) and so <u>all Israel shall be saved</u>.* Those who are still in the book of life, still grafted in, are the elect (Greek: "chosen"). *(Rom.11:2) <u>God did not cast off his people</u>,* *which he foreknew* (5) *Even so then at this present time also there is a remnant according to the election* (chosen) *of grace.* A remnant is those who are left. Notice they are foreknown and chosen. Sovereign God will have those who are truly His.

Abiding in Christ is where salvation is. Some say God gave us the gift of eternal life so He cannot take it back. In Galatians 3:16, we are told, *"To Abraham were the promises spoken, and to his seed. He saith not, And to seeds, as of many, but as of one, And to thy seed, which is Christ."* So the promises were given to Christ, not to us individually. The only way the promises are ours is if we abide in Christ. Abiding in Christ is bearing fruit (Jn.15:1-6), walking as He walked (1 Jn.2:3-6), believing the same teachings given by Jesus and the apostles (1 Jn.2:24; Jude 3; Mt.28:20), not adding to or subtracting from the Word (Rev.22:18,19), not walking in sin (1 Jn.3:5,6), and keeping His commandments (1 Jn.3:24). In Christ is the only place we can claim the gift of eternal life. *(1 Jn.5:11) … God gave unto us eternal life, and this life is in his Son.* God does not have to take His gift back; His people walk out of it. *(1 Cor.6:18) … Every sin that a man doeth is without the body ….* When you walk in willful sin, you are not abiding in His body for *"… in him is no sin. Whosoever abideth in him sinneth not" (1 Jn.3:5,6).* For instance, fornication, spiritual or physical, takes away the members of Christ and makes them members of a harlot (1 Cor.6:15,18). Only Christ and those abiding in Him are chosen.

(Epe. 1:4) Even as he chose us in him before the foundation of the world …. Only Christ and those abiding in Him are going to heaven. *(Jn.3:13) And no one hath ascended into heaven, but he that descended out of heaven ….* The manna from heaven, the Word Jesus Christ, who takes up residence in those who love Him, is the fruit that God is coming to choose.

By this time, I am sure some are thinking that they do not measure up. We must first abide in Christ by faith accepting the Gospel report that *"I have been crucified with Christ; and* *it is <u>no longer I that live</u>, but <u>Christ living in me</u>: and that [life] which I now live in the flesh <u>I live in faith</u>, [the faith] which is in the Son of God, who loved me, and gave himself up for me" (Gal.2:20).* Those who walk by faith that they are dead to sin and Christ now lives in them are <u>accounted as righteous</u> until God uses that faith to manifest righteousness in them. *(Gal. 3:6) Even as Abraham believed God, and it was <u>reckoned unto him for righteousness</u>.* We will discuss this good news and its fruit more fully in later chapters.

God does not dwell in time, but eternity. He sees the beginning and the end at the same time, therefore, He can answer a prayer before we pray. We do not have to worry that we have waited too late to pray because He can have the answer coming long before we ask. *(Isa.65:24) And it shall come to pass that, <u>before they call, I will answer</u>; and while they are yet speaking, I will hear.*

I had a friend, who went to the local trade school, offer to take my broken washer for the students to work on. It was only going to cost me for parts. By faith, I told him to go ahead. He called back in a couple of days to say that he would be bringing it back and the cost was $90. My wife and I accounted that we only had $40. In a moment of inspiration, I pointed my finger at the mailbox and said, "$50 is coming in that box today." In the mail that day was a letter from a brother in Maryland. (I had absolutely no foreknowledge of this incident.) He wrote, "It is after midnight, and I just cannot get to sleep until I obey God and write this check for $50." I looked at the post date on the letter and discovered it had been lost in the mail for a whole month! Obviously, God had it found at just the right moment. He had it coming a month before I spoke those words of faith. He merely used me to bring to pass what He had already planned.

I asked God to do something that I believe He may have changed time to accomplish. Many years ago, this very young girl made a mistake and tested pregnant. As I prayed about her situation, a thought came into my head and right out of my mouth. I asked the Lord to make this girl as though she were never pregnant. I believe that this did not come from my mind, but God's Spirit. Because of the way this prayer came, I received it as a confirmation from the Lord that it was the Will of God. Later, tests proved that she was not pregnant. I do not know what God did with the baby, but I am sure He is taking better care of it than that girl would have. Nothing is beyond God's ability to help us, unless it is beyond our faith.

How can God change His mind when He knows and speaks the end in the beginning? Then changing your mind makes you a liar. *(Isa.46:10)* <u>*Declaring the end from the beginning,*</u> *and from ancient times things that are not yet done; saying, My counsel shall stand, and I will do all my pleasure.* If He sees all from the beginning, why would He ever need to change His mind? God will not change what is written in His Word. *(Ps.119:89) Forever, oh Lord, thy word is settled in heaven.* His Word is likened unto a rock, immovable and unchangeable. However, God can change or delay what He speaks to you personally as a warning through prophets, dreams, visions, or His Spirit. When the Word ultimately comes to pass, it will be fulfilled as the Bible says it will.

God gave us an example of this in the book of Jonah. Jonah *"Cried and said, yet <u>forty days, and Nineveh shall be overthrown</u>" (Jnh.3:4).* God told Jonah to *"preach unto it the preaching that I bid thee" (Jnh.3:2)*, so he did. He was not a false prophet. God spared Nineveh, the capital of Assyria, because they repented. This angered Jonah because Assyria was the mortal enemy of Israel and the prophets had already been prophesying that Assyria would conquer rebellious Israel. He wanted them to be destroyed for what he perceived was Israel's sake. Jonah knew that if he preached to Nineveh and they repented, God would not destroy them, so he fled. *(Jnh.4:1) But it displeased Jonah exceedingly, and he was angry. (2) And he prayed unto the Lord, and said, I pray thee, O Lord, was not this my saying,* *when I was yet in my country? Therefore I hasted to flee unto Tarshish; for I knew that thou art a gracious God, and merciful, slow to anger, and abundant in lovingkindness, and <u>repentest thee of the evil.</u>*

God spared Nineveh around 752 B.C. so that Assyria could conquer the northern ten tribes of Israel around 720 B.C. and then Judah around 701 B.C. Nineveh ultimately did fall around 612 B.C. God knew before He threatened Nineveh that He was going to spare them for the purpose of using them to chasten Israel. From Nineveh's perspective, they changed God's mind by repenting, but from God's perspective, He changed Nineveh's mind and fulfilled His plan from the beginning for them, which was to chasten Israel! Jonah's Hebrew word for *"repentest"* here is *nacham*, meaning "to sigh" and by implication "to be sorry." In itself, *nacham* does not admit evil doing, or even a change of mind, only sorrow. As Father, God must do many things that He sorrows over. When the Scriptures speak of God repenting, it is for our perspective because it appears to us that He changed His mind and did not do what He threatened. As a parent five times over, I have done this many times. The difference between God and us is, He plans and sees the delays and repentances from the beginning. *(Num.23:19) <u>God is not a man, that he should lie, Neither the son of man, <u>that he should repent</u>. (1 Sam.15:29) And also the Strength of Israel <u>will not lie nor repent</u>; for he is not a man that he should repent.</u>*

Here is another thing that proves the sovereignty of God in time and the future and that God plans delays or "repentances" beforehand. Israel and the United States share a unique identity. Each was entrusted with the Gospel in their respective time. From 887 B.C., Israel was at war every seventeen years for a period of fifteen cycles until 631 B.C. The United States also has been in a war every seventeen years for a period of fifteen cycles from the forming of the thirteen original states to Grenada in 1983-1984. For both nations, in the sixth and tenth cycle there was no war. The only possible exceptions to the parallel are that Israel appears to have had a devastating famine in the forth cycle instead of a war and there seems to be no record for a war in their thirteenth cycle. The cycles could be more exact than our knowledge, but no sane person could think that this is chance. The repetitions of history clearly show that one mind is in control of past and future.

Chapter 6
God's Sovereignty Over the Fall and Salvation

No man can come to me, except the Father that sent me draw him: and I will raise him up in the last day (Jn.6:44).

Some parents feel very guilty that, though they did the best they could, their children seem to be going the wrong way. The following teaching is not against those who have faithfully served the Lord from their youth but rather for those who feel that the Lord has passed them or their children by.

Walk by faith for those wayward children, not sight. Believe in your prayers, expect miracles, but be patient. God has a plan that starts for them long before their salvation. Give some deep thought to this. It will free you from worry, strife, condemnation and self-effort to bring about God's will in them. They will have to be saved after tribulation and failure of their worldly expectations, as we were. Children who are raised knowing about the Lord are sometimes very self-righteous. They think they deserve what they have and do not understand grace. They will also have to see themselves as sinners in order to be the dirt that can receive the Word and bear the fruit of Jesus. God only saves sinners. We have all been one. This is a necessary revelation in order to appreciate the great value of salvation and to be saved by unmerited favor. I remember my oldest daughter when she was three years old going around our lost friends and relatives saying, "God does not like that." She was quickly deflecting what we had taught her. We thought, "You little Pharisee."

Our heavenly Father has had many prodigal sons just as Jesus' parable shows, but that does not make Him a bad Father (Lk.15:11-32). In this parable, the "good" son who never left home was self-righteous, judgmental, and merciless. On the other hand, the younger son, who spent his inheritance on riotous living, realized his low estate and came to his father very humbly saying, *"Father, I have sinned against heaven, and in thy sight: I am no more worthy to be called thy son." (Lk.15:21)*. The once rebellious son now understood mercy and grace and was a much better man for it. Prophetically, the firstborn son who never left the Father was the righteous among Israel, but they did not understand grace. The younger, second son of the Father who fell away through the dark ages for 2,000 years is the Church who is returning in these days to understand the grace of God. The Father said to these, *"Bring forth quickly the best robe* (the robe of righteousness [Isa.61:10]), *and put it on him; and put a ring on his hand* (symbol of authority and of the Bride), *and shoes on his feet* (the walk of separation from the world)*" (Lk.15:22)*. The prodigal son will have more of everything than the first son.

Those who have been sinners know their need of God, but many times, those who are raised as God's people do not. *(Mt.21:28) But what think ye? A man had two sons; and he came to the first, and said, Son, go work today in the vineyard. (29) And he answered and said, <u>I will not: but afterward he repented himself, and went</u>. (30) And he came to the second, and said likewise. And he answered and said, <u>I [go], sir: and went not</u>. (31) Which of the two did the will of his father? They say, The first. Jesus saith unto them, Verily I say unto you, that <u>the publicans and the harlots go into the kingdom of God before you</u>. (32) For John came unto you in the way of righteousness, and ye believed him not; but the <u>publicans and the harlots believed him</u>: and ye, when ye saw it, did not even repent yourselves afterward, that ye might believe him.* Many times, it is not the son who says he will go to work in the Father's vineyard who actually goes, but the son whose first inclination is to rebel. This rebel who comes to see himself as a sinner goes while the other son who feigns righteousness does not. Many career Christians are bored with the work of God and are distracted by the allure of the world. The publicans and harlots are so appreciative of a place in the kingdom that they throw their whole heart into it, willing to be servants rather than be served. They understand the great value of the gift of grace that is given them and their own unworthiness.

In the last days of the Gentiles, it will be the same as it was in the last days of the Jews. There are many self-righteous "Christians" today who are not the creation that the Father desires. Those who have been raised in the church should humble themselves to the Word of God and not religion so that no man takes their crown (Rev.3:11). It appears Jesus had this in mind when He shared this parable. *(Lk.18:9) And he spake also this parable unto certain who <u>trusted in themselves that they were righteous, and set all others at nought</u>: (10) Two men went up into the temple to pray; the one a Pharisee, and the other a publican. (11) The Pharisee stood and prayed thus <u>with himself</u>, God, <u>I thank thee, that I am not as the rest of men</u>, extortioners, unjust, adulterers, or even as this publican. (12) I fast twice in the week; I give tithes of all that I get. (13) But the publican, standing afar off, would not lift up so much as his eyes unto heaven, but smote his breast, saying, <u>God, be thou merciful to me a sinner</u>. (14) I say unto you, This man went down to his house justified* (Greek: "accounted righteous") *rather than the other: for every one that exalteth himself shall be humbled; but he that humbleth himself shall be exalted*. The self-righteous child who kept all the religious traditions was not accounted righteous while the poor sinner who was repenting of his unworthiness was.

Jesus told the Pharisees that He had not come to call the righteous but the sinners. He was after those who knew they had been sinners to be His children. Look at the following verse carefully. *(Rom.11:32) For God hath shut up all unto disobedience, that he might have mercy upon all.* God has designed that forgiven sinners become His sons. Those who have been disobedient have a great appreciation for mercy and grace and do not offend God quickly. God has subjected us to this fallen creation for the purpose of a higher creation.

(Rom.8:20) For the creation was subjected to vanity (the fall and corruption), *not of its own will, but by reason of him* (God) *who subjected it, in hope* (Greek: "firm expectation") *(21) that the <u>creation itself also shall be delivered from the bondage of corruption into the liberty of the glory of the children of God</u>.* The children of God can only be created from the fallen creation, and God is the one who subjected them to it to humble them. The Scriptures show us our unfaithfulness and unworthiness so that we might have a reason to truly repent. *(Gal.3:22) But the <u>scriptures shut up all things under sin</u>, that the promise by faith in Jesus Christ might be given to them that believe.* God chose us to be saved in Christ before Adam even fell. *(Epe.1:4) Even as <u>he chose us in him before the foundation of the world</u>, that we should be holy and without blemish before him in love.* He knew we would need a savior before the world was made and Adam fell. He knew the fall would happen, and He went ahead with the creation anyway. From this you can see that the fall was in His plan. Children who are raised with Christ many times take Him for granted and do not really understand grace. God has a plan for them that may involve the temporary lifting of His grace that has been taken for granted. Do not fear this, or walk by sight, but continue to believe God for them.

Peter was Jesus' little one whom He raised up to be a disciple. He self-confidently declared to the Lord that he would never be offended and deny Him but would go with Him to death (Mt.26:33-35). God hates self-confidence but loves God-confidence. So how does God deal with this sin? *(1 Cor.10:12) Wherefore let him that thinketh he standeth take heed lest he fall.* Failure is the best treatment for self-confidence. *(Lk.22:31) Simon, Simon, behold, Satan <u>asked</u> to have you, that he might sift you as wheat: (32) but I made supplication for thee, that thy faith fail not; and do thou, when once thou hast turned again, establish thy brethren. (33) And he said unto him, <u>Lord, with thee I am ready to go</u> both to prison and to death. (34) And* *he said, I tell thee, Peter, the cock shall not crow this day, until thou shalt thrice deny that thou knowest me.* Jesus prophesied failure for this proud man. Jesus, who had authority over Satan, did not forbid him from sifting Peter. Satan sifts to get what belongs to him. In this case, it was Peter's pride, self-righteousness, and self-confidence. What fell through the sieve was what God wanted, the humbled Peter. The sifted Peter who had *"turned again"* or been converted, could now *"establish the brethren."* Before this failure, he would have been a good Pharisee.

(Lk.7:40) *And Jesus answering said unto him, Simon* (the Pharisee, not Peter), *I have somewhat to say unto thee. And he saith, Teacher, say on. (41) A certain lender had two debtors: the one owed five hundred shillings, and the other fifty. (42) When they had not [wherewith] to pay, he forgave them both.* <u>*Which of them therefore will love him most?*</u> *(43) Simon answered and said,* <u>*He, I suppose, to whom he forgave the most.*</u> *And he said unto him, Thou hast rightly judged. (44) And turning to the woman, he said unto Simon, Seest thou this woman? I entered into thy house, thou gavest me no water for my feet: but she hath wetted my feet with her tears, and wiped them with her hair. (45) Thou gavest me no kiss: but she, since the time I came in, hath not ceased to kiss my feet. (46) My head with oil thou didst not anoint: but she hath anointed my feet with ointment. (47) Wherefore I say unto thee,* <u>*Her sins, which are many, are forgiven; for she loved much:*</u> *but to whom* <u>*little is forgiven, [the same] loveth little*</u>. Big sinners make big saints, for they know the value of grace.

According to the previous verses, God wants people who are forgiven of their many sins and saved by grace so that they love and appreciate Him much. This is the creation that He wants, not Adam before the fall. The creation that springs from the last Adam Jesus Christ is the ones who have fallen and then are saved by grace through faith. We need not worry about our children or loved ones becoming sinners, just *"hold fast the confession of your hope that it waver not, for he is faithful that promised."* We must gracefully sow seeds of truth, as we can, without frustrating them. They cannot be convinced without grace. *"God works all things after the counsel of His own will"* and *"a man can receive nothing except it have been given him from heaven,"* and *"no one comes unto the Son except the Father draw him."* God will do it when the time is right, and He will use our faith because *"faith is the substance of the thing hoped for."* We can see why sometimes God does not save people until they are a little older and have tried the world and found it wanting. However, if you have faithfully served the Lord from your youth, you have a great reward.

God can save anyone anytime He desires. It is important that we not try of our own works to save the lost but first honor God's sovereignty with our faith for Him to do it. *(Jn.6:37)* <u>*All that which the Father giveth me shall come unto me*</u> *... (44)* <u>*No man can come to me, except the Father that sent me draw him*</u> *....* Father will draw everyone that He chooses to Christ. God chooses us and gives us a desire to come to Him and only then do we choose Him. *(Ps.65:4) Blessed is the man whom thou choosest, and* <u>*causest to approach [unto thee]*</u>*, that he may dwell in thy courts.* God sometimes chooses the worst in our estimation. If God can save Paul or Mary Magdalene, who had seven demons, he can save those we believe for. Do you remember the conversion of Saul who persecuted the saints with a vengeance? *(Acts 9:3-5) And suddenly there shone round about him a light out of heaven: and he fell upon the earth, and heard a voice saying unto him, Saul, Saul, why persecutest thou me? And he said, Who art thou, Lord? And he [said], I am Jesus whom thou persecutest.* A monkey would get saved with such an experience, which was totally at the discretion of God. This same omnipotent God says, <u>*"All things, whatsoever ye shall ask in prayer, believing, ye shall receive"*</u> *(Mt.21:22)*. God uses His gift of faith in us to manifest the salvation of those He has chosen from the foundation of the world. Pray and thank God for those salvations.

I can hear someone say, "Goody, we will believe God to save the devil; that will solve a lot of problems." I do not think such faith would endure to the end since faith is a gift from God (Epe.2:8), to give or to take, and there is no precedent in Scriptures for such a request. Besides that, the devil is needed in his job for which he would be totally unfit if he got saved. There is precedent for household salvation though (Acts 11:14; 18:8). Paul and Silas offered this to the jailer. *(Acts 16:31) And they said, <u>Believe on the Lord Jesus, and thou shalt be saved, thou and thy house</u>.* They believed and were saved. *(34) … with all his house, having believed in God.* Peter preached this, too. *(Acts 2:39) For <u>to you is the promise, and to your children</u>, and to all that are afar off, [even] as many as the Lord our God shall call unto him.*

In Exodus 12:3, the lamb was slain for a household. Unbelieving family members are sanctified by our faith. *(1 Cor.7:14) For the unbelieving husband is sanctified in the wife, and the unbelieving wife is sanctified in the brother: else were your children unclean; but now are they holy.*

Some object that God would be unrighteous to choose some and not others. We are too late; He has done just that. *(Ps.147:19) He showeth his word unto Jacob, His statutes and his ordinances unto Israel. (20) <u>He hath not dealt so with any nation</u>; And as for his ordinances, they have not known them. Praise ye the Lord.* God did not attempt to share His first covenant with any of the world but Israel. The New Testament He shares only with spiritual Israel. *(Dt.7:6) For thou art a holy people unto the Lord thy God: The Lord thy <u>God hath chosen thee</u> to be a people for his own possession, <u>above all peoples</u> that are upon the face of the earth. (7) The Lord did not set his love upon you, nor choose you, because ye were more in number than any people; for ye were the <u>fewest of all peoples</u>.* God is not worried about multitudes, for He has chosen the least. He still only chooses little spiritual Israel on the narrow road.

Abraham is the father of spiritual Israel, the Church: those who walk in the same gift of faith that Abraham walked in. *(Gal.3:7) Know therefore that they that are of faith, the same are sons of Abraham.* Paul told the Gentile church at Rome that the people of all nations who believe the promise were Abraham's children. *(Rom.4:16) For this cause [it is] of faith, that [it may be] according to grace; to the end that the promise may be sure to all the seed; not to that only which is of the <u>law</u>,* (natural Israel) *but to that also which is <u>of the faith of Abraham</u>, who is the <u>father of us all</u> (17) (as it is written, A <u>father of many nations</u>* [Gentiles] *have I made thee).* True, spiritual Israel believes the promises even now. *(Rom.9:6-9) … For <u>they are not all Israel, that are of Israel</u>: (7) neither, because they are Abraham's seed* (naturally or physically), *are they all children: but, In Isaac shall thy seed be called. (8) That is, it <u>is not the children of the flesh</u>* (natural Israel) *that are children of God; <u>but the children of the promise are reckoned for a seed</u>.* Those who believe the promises are born again children of the promises. These are Abraham's seed.

A New Testament spiritual Jew is circumcised in heart, not flesh. *(Rom.2:28) For <u>he is not a Jew who is one outwardly</u>* (physical)*; neither is that circumcision which is outward in the flesh: (29) but <u>he is a Jew who is one inwardly</u>* (spiritual)*; and circumcision is that of the heart, <u>in the spirit not in the letter</u>.* Notice that a Jew now is not a physical Jew. A Jew now has the flesh cut off from his heart through the new birth. *(Gal.6:15) For neither is circumcision* (in the flesh) *anything, nor uncircumcision, but a <u>new creature</u>. (16) And as many as shall <u>walk by this rule</u>, peace [be] upon them, and mercy, and upon <u>the Israel of God</u>.* The Israel of God are they who walk as new creatures. The unregenerate physical Jews who worship in synagogues are not Jews until they are born again through the New Testament. *(Rev.2:9) I know thy tribulation, and thy poverty (but* *thou art rich), and the blasphemy of them that <u>say they are</u> <u>Jews, and they art not, but are a synagogue of Satan</u>* (the same in Rev.3:9). We were not Jews but now are in Spirit. *(Rom.9:25) As he saith also in Hosea, <u>I will call that my people,</u> <u>which was not my people; And her beloved, that was not beloved.</u> (26) And it shall be, [that] in the place where it was said unto them, Ye are not my people, There shall they be called sons of the living God.* We were not His people but are now beloved sons of God.

   (Rom.9:27) And Isaiah crieth concerning Israel (natural or physical), *If the number of the children of Israel be as the sand of the sea, it is the <u>remnant that shall be saved</u>.* A remnant of natural Israel will be born again mostly after the elect Gentiles have been saved. *(Rom.11:25) … A hardening <u>in part</u> hath befallen Israel, until the fullness of the Gentiles be come in."* "In part" here means that the line between Gentiles and Jews is not a sharp demarcation. Neither was it in the book of Acts. Jews are even now being saved more than ever. This is a sign that we are nearing the end of the times of the Gentiles. Most of the physical Jews will come in after the Gentiles.

   We who sought not after God were given the gift of faith to be spiritual New Testament Israel when natural Israel turned her back on God. *(Rom.10:20) And Isaiah is very bold, and saith, <u>I was found of them that sought me not; I became manifest unto</u> <u>them that asked not of me.</u>* God revealed himself to the Church who on their own neither knew nor sought Him. *(21) But as to Israel he saith, All the day long did I spread out my hands unto a disobedient and gainsaying people. (Rom.11:7) … <u>that</u> <u>which Israel</u>* (physical) *<u>seeketh for, that he obtained not; but the</u> <u>election</u>* (chosen) *<u>obtained it, and the rest were hardened:</u>* (We see here that only the few chosen among the many called of Israel accepted Christ and the New Testament. The rest were reprobated.) *(8) according as it is written, God gave them a spirit of stupor, eyes that they should not see, and ears that they should not hear, unto this very day.* In that day and in this,

99

those who walk by faith are chosen from among the called to be the eternal people of the living God.

Paul said *"all Israel"* is the physical Jews and Gentiles who are part of the olive tree by faith, not those who are broken off by unbelief (Rom.11:19-25). All have sinned and deserve destruction. Is God wrong for giving some mercy and grace and others justice? All deserve justice instead of unmerited favor.

Chapter 7
God's Sovereignty Over Deception

And even if our Gospel is veiled, it is veiled in them that perish: in whom the <u>god of this world hath blinded the minds of the unbelieving</u>, that the light of the Gospel of the glory of Christ, who is the image of God, should not dawn upon them (2 Cor.4:3,4).

The god of this world is Satan, but he does not run this world. He is called the god of this world because this world worships and serves him whether they know it or not. Anyone who serves the lusts of their flesh worships and serves Satan as their god. He is the father of the flesh, which is also called the old man. God never gives Satan credit in the Scriptures for being sovereign. Jesus said, *"All authority in heaven and on earth has been given unto me."* Satan blinds the minds of the unbelievers so that they do not understand and see the light of the Gospel. We can see from other Scriptures that Satan received his authority from the Lord to blind the unbelievers. *(1 Pet.5:8) Be sober, be watchful: your adversary the devil, as a roaring lion, walketh about, <u>seeking whom he may devour:</u> (9) whom withstand steadfast in your faith ....* We have the ability to withstand Satan when we walk by faith, but the word "may" here implies that he has permission to devour those who do not. With Christians or non-Christians, unbelief gives permission to Satan. The faith that resists and binds Satan is a gift from God (Epe.2:8). Satan has permission to devour those who do not have that gift.

(Jn.12:35) Jesus therefore said unto them, Yet a little while is the light among you. <u>Walk while ye have the light, that darkness overtake you not:</u> (Notice that word "overtake." This indicates that darkness is chasing all of us. The Lord is saying that for a little while we are going to receive the light but do something with that light while we have it, so that the darkness does not

overtake us.) *and he that walketh in the darkness knoweth not whither he goeth. (36) <u>While ye have the light, believe</u>* (trust in and act on) *<u>on the light, that ye may become sons of the light</u>.* (If we do not act on the light now, the impression will leave us and the darkness will again close in. When we pass by the moment, we have been tried and failed if we have not done something with the light.) *These things spake Jesus, and he departed and <u>hid himself from them</u>* (Jesus hides Himself from those who do not value the light enough to act upon it.) *(38) that the word of Isaiah the prophet might be fulfilled, which he spake, Lord, who hath believed our report? And to whom hath the arm of the Lord been revealed? (39) <u>For this cause they could not believe, for that Isaiah said again,</u> (40) <u>He hath blinded their eyes, and he hardened their heart</u>; Lest they should see with their eyes, and perceive with their heart, And should turn, And I should heal them.* It is clear from the text of Isaiah 6:9,10 quoted below that the "He" who blinded their eyes and hardened their hearts is the Lord. Israel had the light for a long time, and they did not bear fruit of it. Many Christians have the light, but do not act on it. They start out in a blaze of glory, but soon the cares of the world, the deceitfulness of riches, trials, and persecutions hardens their hearts and allows the darkness to overcome them (Mt.13:19-23). We must believe and walk in the light while we have it so that Jesus does not withdraw and hide himself.

(Isa.6:8) And I heard the voice of the <u>Lord, saying</u>, Whom shall I send, and who will go for us? Then I said, Here am I; send me. (9) Then he said, Go, and tell this people, Hear ye indeed, yet understand not; and see ye indeed, but perceive not. (10) Make the heart of this people fat, and make their ears heavy, and shut their eyes; lest they see with their eyes, and hear with their ears, and understand with their heart, and turn again, and be healed. God is blinding eyes and hearts through the devil. God makes us responsible when we see His Word to walk in the light of its truth. *(1 Jn.1:7) But if we walk in the light, as he is in the light, we*

have fellowship one with another, and <u>the blood of Jesus his Son cleanseth us from all sin</u>. Walking in the light sanctifies us.

God has a method for weeding the Church which most do not understand. *(2 Thes.2:3) Let no man beguile you in any wise: for [it will not be,] except the falling away come first ... (8) And then shall be revealed the lawless one, whom the Lord Jesus shall slay with the breath of his mouth, and bring to naught by the manifestation of his coming; (9) even <u>he, whose coming is according to the working of Satan</u> with all power and signs and lying wonders, (10) and with all deceit of unrighteousness for them that perish; <u>because they received not the love of the truth</u>, that they might be saved. (11) And for this cause <u>God sendeth them a working of error</u>, that they should believe a lie: (12) that they all might be judged who believed not the truth, but had pleasure in unrighteousness.* We see here that falling away comes through the deception of Satan. However, God is sending this working of error to those who do not love the truth so that they might be judged. By the way, this letter is addressed to the Church. Only Christians, using the term loosely, can fall away. There is a great falling away today, but an even greater deception is coming. Before God sends judgment, He sends *"a working of error"* to weed out the Church. Who will believe a lie? It is the evil and wicked who will believe a lie. *(Pr.17:4) An evildoer giveth heed to wicked lips; And a liar giveth ear to a mischievous tongue. (11) An evil man seeketh only rebellion; Therefore a cruel messenger shall be sent against him.* The evildoer will be weeded out by deception. They are going to be seen clearly for who they are because they are going to buy the lie and fall away. The righteous love God's Word and the truth, and will not be deceived.

(1 Cor.11:19) For there must be also <u>factions</u> (Greek: "heresies") *<u>among you, that they that are approved may be made manifest among you</u>.* It is necessary for heresies to be among us, so that they that are approved by God may be known. God is doing two things with deception and evil: He

is revealing the wicked, and revealing the true. This is God's method throughout history for separating His people from the tares. Birds of a feather flock together. God will gather the tares into bundles to burn them.

Deception is one of God's methods for proving who will be counted worthy of the kingdom of heaven. Remember this working of Satan will come through power, signs, and lying wonders. These are placebos to pacify the Church with replacements for the genuine to confirm the lies being taught. The genuine are listed as gifts of the Holy Spirit in 1 Corinthians 12:4-11. The gifts of the Holy Spirit are the word of wisdom, word of knowledge, faith, healings, workings of miracles, prophecy, discernings of spirits, kinds of tongues, and interpretation of tongues. For our own safety, we should obey Paul who said, ***"Learn not to go beyond the things that are written."*** How so many can believe that some of these things we have been seeing are Scriptural manifestations of the Holy Spirit is beyond me. When we look at the value of these silly signs as far as salvation, healing, deliverance, or provision, there is no comparison.

(Dt.13:1) If there arise in the midst of thee a prophet, or a dreamer of dreams, and <u>he give thee a sign or a wonder,</u> <u>(2) and the sign or the wonder come to pass</u>, whereof he spake unto thee, saying, <u>Let us go after other gods</u> (Elohim), *which thou hast not known, and let us serve them.* Here we have a false prophet speaking a sign that comes to pass. No false prophet can command something and have it come to pass unless God says so. *(Lam.3:37) Who is he who saith, and it cometh to pass, when the Lord commandeth not?* This is clear that God is trying His people with error. This prophet is saying, *"Let us go after other gods."* This is not as uncommon as we may think. Actually, the Hebrew word for "gods" here is the same word used everywhere else in the Old Testament for our God "Elohim." In this case, he is talking about a false elohim. There are many false elohim, because anyone who has a Jesus

of their own making and not the Jesus of the Bible has a false elohim. *(Dt.13:3) Thou shalt not hearken unto the words of that prophet, or unto that dreamer of dreams: for the Lord your <u>God proveth you</u>, to know whether ye love the Lord your God with all your heart and with all your soul.* False prophets prove us for God by deception. God is saying it is necessary for us to be proven by deception to see if we love Him. Those who love Him will not buy the lie. *(Dt.8:2) And thou shalt remember all the way which the Lord thy God hath led thee these forty years in the wilderness, that he might humble thee, <u>to prove thee, to know what was in thy heart, whether thou wouldest keep his commandments, or not</u>.* This is the whole point. A prophet, a dream, a vision, a teaching, or anything that comes to us that is not according to the commandments is a trial from God, to see if we are going to be counted worthy of the kingdom.

(Eze.14:1) Then came certain of the <u>elders of Israel</u> unto me, and sat before me. (2) And the word of the Lord came unto me, saying, (3) Son of man, <u>these men have taken their idols into their heart, and put the stumbling block of their iniquity before their face: should I be inquired of at all by them</u>? An idol is anything that demands more of our love, time, or money than God; self-will being the most evil idol. Should we ask the Lord's direction if all we want is what we want? It is dangerous to inquire of the Lord with self-willed motives before our face. We may satisfy our flesh but lose a blessing. *(Eze.14:4) Therefore speak unto them, and say unto them, Thus saith the Lord: <u>Every man of the house of Israel that taketh his idols into his heart</u>, and putteth the stumbling block of his iniquity before his face, and cometh to the prophet; <u>I the Lord will answer him therein according to the multitude of his idols</u>.*

God is not our God, and we are not His servants when our will is more important than His Will. Before we ask God, we should ask ourselves if we would be as willing to go in the opposite direction should He give that answer. If we would not, then we have an idol. We should deal with our idol first.

(Epe.5:5) For this you know of a surety that no ... covetousness man, who is an idolater, hath any inheritance in the kingdom of Christ and God. The Greek word for "covetous" only means "to desire more." A person who desires more than is necessary is an idolater. The word "idolater" comes from two words, *eidolo*, meaning "that which is seen" and *latres* meaning "a servant to." Those who constantly desire more are servants to that which is seen (physical things), not the Lord. These things can be anything – possessions, a job, a religion, or people to name a few. People can be serving themselves. They can be their own idol, like the son of perdition who sits in the temple of God making himself god. Judas, whom Jesus called the son of perdition, sat among the disciples who were the temple of God. He was his own idol because he only wanted to please himself. There are many Judas' today. *(Ex.20:3) Thou shalt have no other gods before me.* Whatever is more important to us than the Lord is going to deceive us if we do not renounce it.

(Eze.14:7) For every one of the house of Israel, or of the strangers that sojourn in Israel, that separateth himself from me, and taketh his idols into his heart, and putteth the stumblingblock of his iniquity before his face, and cometh to the prophet to inquire for himself of me; I the Lord will answer him by myself: (8) and I will set my face against that man, and will make him an astonishment, for a sign and a proverb, and I will cut him off from the midst of my people; and ye shall know that I am the Lord. Those who are separated from God through their idols will be answered according to the lusts of their own heart. God is going to give them an answer that is not a true answer because He will be answering their lusts. Remember God said, *"I the Lord will answer him by myself."* The Lord's answer may come through an apostate prophet, a religion, a thought, a dream, a word or a doctrine, but it will come to deceive. This could bring chastening or even reprobation as we see in verse eight.

(Eze.14:9) And if the prophet be deceived and speak a word, <u>I, the Lord, have deceived that prophet</u> and I will stretch out my hand upon him, and will destroy him from the midst of my people Israel. A true prophet who has idols or a false prophet can be deceived by a false word from God, as we shall see. *(2 Thes.2:10) … <u>God sendeth them a working of error, that they should believe a lie</u>.* The Lord sends the word because people do not love Him, but the world. *(1 Jn.2:15) … If any man love the world, the love of the Father is not in him.* We are here to prove who it is that loves God.

God is going to cleanse His Church in these days because there are many idols. Religion can be an idol. When the Word of God says one thing, and we believe our religion, which says another, our religion is our Babylonish idol. God will send deception. We can see how it can be an increasingly degenerative road to travel. The more we believe religion, instead of God, the more deception comes in. Nothing but the Word of God should move us. *(Rom.3:4) God forbid: yea, <u>let God be found true, but every man a liar</u>; as it is written, That thou mightest be justified* (accounted righteous) *in thy words, And <u>mightest prevail when thou comest into judgment</u>.* When we agree with God in the midst of judgment, we will prevail. These are the people whom God accounts as righteous. When we receive a prophecy, vision, dream, revelation, or a word that agrees with the Word of God, praise the Lord because the Word does not give many specifics. It does not tell us where God wants us to live or work or whom He wants us to marry. It gives us principles to find out the true will of the Lord in all areas. We can desire something so much, we hear "the Word of the Lord." We can become convinced that this is what the Lord wanted us to do, only to find out later that we missed God. We need to be careful, because if our desires are not for the will of the Lord, <u>first</u>, we can be deceived.

Let us look at Balaam's situation again from another angle. The children of Israel were in the plains of Moab. Balak, the

King of Moab, was very fearful of the Israelites. He gathered together the elders of Midian and Moab. They decided they would <u>hire</u> Balaam to curse these people. Balak said to Balaam, *"I know that he whom thou blessest is blessed, and he whom thou cursest is cursed" (Num.22:6).* He did not realize it was not Balaam but God who counted in this situation because *"the curse that is causeless alighteth not" (Pr.26:2).* If Balaam spoke the Word of the Lord, it was going to come to pass. The "profit" Balaam went to the Lord with the promise of rewards in his heart and a request to curse Israel on his lips. *(Num.22:12) And God said unto Balaam, <u>Thou shalt not go with them; thou shalt not curse the people; for they are blessed</u>. (13) And Balaam rose up in the morning, and said unto the princes of Balak, Get you into your land; for the Lord refuseth to give me leave to go with you.*

Balak did not give up. He sent more honorable princes who offered to bestow upon Balaam a very high honor and give him anything he asked. Balaam decided to ask the Lord again since this sounded like a pretty good offer. *(Num.22:19) Now therefore, I pray you, tarry ye also here this night that I may know what the Lord will speak unto me more. (20) And <u>God came unto Balaam at night, and said unto him, If the men are come to call thee, rise up, go with them</u>; but only the word which I speak unto thee, that shalt thou do.* Balaam did not like God's "no," so God, wanting to put to death his covetous self-will, gave him a "yes." *(21) And Balaam rose up in the morning, and saddled his ass, and went with the princes of Moab. (22) <u>And God's anger was kindled because he went; and the angel of the Lord placed himself in the way for an adversary against him</u>.* Notice that God was angry that He went contrary to the first word spoken to him. The ass carrying Balaam to his reward saw the angel with his sword in the way and stopped, saving his life. Balaam, still ignorant of the angel, was furious and beat the ass. Then God opened the ass's mouth to reason with Balaam, who was so blinded by the prospect of reward that he did not realize that an ass was reasoning with him and making more sense than he was. *(Num.22:32) And the angel of the Lord said unto him, Wherefore hast thou smitten thine ass these three times? Behold, <u>I am come forth for an adversary, because thy way is perverse before me</u>.* The Hebrew word translated "perverse" here means "headlong" or "self-willed." Because of this self-will, the Lord gave Balaam what he wanted to hear and told Balaam to go and speak what he was told to speak, but when Balaam went, the angel of the Lord was waiting to kill him.

Balaam got the following revelation through this: *(Num.23:19) <u>God is not a man, that he should lie, Neither the son of man, that he should repent: Hath he said, and will he not do it? Or hath he spoken, and will he not make it good?</u>* God does not have to change His mind; He is God and does not make mistakes. From our perspective, God changes His mind because He warns or makes promises that are conditional upon our reactions. Balaam really wanted God to change His Word. Have we ever been there? It is a dangerous place to be in if we want a straight answer from God. God can send deception that will lead to crucifixion of the flesh or in more stubborn cases reprobation, like a sword in our way. *(Jer.4:10) Then said I, Ah, Lord God! surely <u>thou hast greatly deceived this people</u> and Jerusalem, saying, Ye shall have peace; whereas the <u>sword reacheth unto the life</u>. (Jude 11) <u>Woe unto them! for they went in the way of Cain, and ran riotously in the error of Balaam for hire</u>, and perished in the gainsaying of Korah.* We can be <u>hired</u> by our own selfish desires. Balaam wanted God to tell him "yes" and refused to hear God's "no," so God told him "yes." Be careful how much you want something from God. God wants us to submit our will to His, to desire what He wants, and to take Him at His Word. Do not let your flesh be pampered by voices that speak contrary to what the Word has already spoken, or God will send deception. *(2 Thes.2:11) And for this cause <u>God sendeth them a working</u>*

of error, that they should believe a lie: (12) that they all might be judged who believed not the truth, but had pleasure in unrighteousness. Many have adopted deceptive doctrines that appease their selfish desires such as doctrines of materialistic prosperity rather than sacrifice, unconditional eternal security so that they may live after the flesh without fear of God's warnings, rapture without purification through trial, eternal life without discipleship and holiness, etc. God's people have justified just about anything to appease their flesh such as unscriptural divorces, abortion, drunkenness, drugs, lying, stealing, etc. Peace for the flesh is deception. Satan and his ministers are anxious to tell us what our flesh wants to hear. *(2 Cor.11:14) And no marvel; for even Satan fashioneth himself into an angel of light. (15) It is no great thing therefore if his ministers also fashion themselves as ministers of righteousness ....*

Balaam learned a lesson temporarily. *(Num.22:18) And Balaam answered and said unto the servants of Balak, If Balak would give me his house full of silver and gold, I cannot go beyond the word of the Lord my God, to do less or more.* These were words of truth that came from a deceitful heart. Balaam still was covetous and eventually gave in to bribery again. He ended up teaching Balak how to cast a stumbling block in front of the children of Israel, in teaching them how to eat food sacrificed to idols and to commit fornication (Rev.2:14). Balaam could not curse the children of Israel, because of their position with God. Therefore, Balaam taught Balak to tempt Israel into a place where God would curse them. And that is exactly what happened. God knew what Balaam was doing. Israel was tried and flunked the test.

After David sinned with Bathsheba, his own son Absalom usurped the kingdom, and David had to flee for his life. Absalom inherited two counselors from David. *(2 Sam.16:23) And the counsel of Ahithophel, which he gave in those days, was as if a man inquired at the oracle of God: so was all the council of Ahithophel both with David and with Absalom.* So the counsel that Ahithophel was giving to Absalom was good, just as if it was coming from God. *(2 Sam.17:1) Moreover Ahithophel said unto Absalom, Let me now choose out twelve thousand men, and I will arise and pursue after David this night: (2) and I will come upon him while he is weary and weak-handed, and will make him afraid; and all the people that are with him shall flee; and I will smite the king only.* He wanted to catch David with a small quick force before David reached the depths of the wilderness.

After they received this counsel from Ahithophel, Absalom called for Hushai the Archite, the other counselor. Hushai was secretly loyal to David. He advised the king to gather all Israel together, and catch David and the people with him, and smite every one of them. Hushai knew that it would take a while to gather all the people of Israel. Meanwhile, he sent word to David to quickly flee into the wilderness where he would be safe. *(2 Sam.17:14) And Absalom and <u>all the men of Israel</u> said, The counsel of Hushai the Archite is better than the counsel of Ahithophel. <u>For the Lord had ordained to defeat the good counsel of Ahithophel, to the intent that the Lord might bring evil upon Absalom</u>.* With God's help, all the men of Israel agreed with the bad advice, which helped David escape and cost Absalom his life.

Never follow the multitudes of those who profess religion. They follow a leadership that has usurped authority. When the Lord wants to judge someone, He can give a multitude of bad advice and lead him to take it. In these days, many will listen to the bad advice of their apostate leaders so that they will be judged. <u>Ten of the twelve tribes of Israel</u> worshiped the image of the beast, the golden calf, at the advice of their leadership (1 Ki.12:25-32). So it is today among those professing to be God's people because history always repeats itself (Eccl.1:9). Most of what is only called Christianity will take the mark of the beast, but the true disciples will not be deceived for they love truth.

Ahab, the evil king of the apostate northern ten tribes of Israel, was trying to convince Jehoshaphat, the good king of Judah, to align with him and go to war against the Syrians at Ramoth-gilead. This story applies to making alliances with evil and deception today. *(1 Ki.22:5) Then Jehoshaphat said unto the king of Israel, Inquire first, I pray thee, for the word of the Lord. (6) Then the king of Israel gathered the prophets together, about four hundred men, and said unto them, Shall I go against Ramoth-gilead to battle, or shall I forbear?*

Remember these four hundred men were not the prophets of Baal. They were killed in 1 Kings 18 by Elijah. Then, the prophets of the Lord took over. We shall see, these prophets of the Lord belonged to Ahab. So he gathered up these four hundred "yes-men" and inquired of them about going to battle with the Syrians. *(1 Ki.22:6) And they said, Go up; for the Lord will deliver it into the hand of the king.* (Jehoshaphat still felt uneasy because the Lord put this in his heart to warn him.) *(7) But Jehoshaphat said, is there not here a prophet of the Lord besides that we may inquire of him? (8) And the king of Israel said unto Jehoshaphat, There is yet one man by whom we may inquire of the Lord, Micaiah the son of Imlah: but I hate him; for he doth not prophesy good concerning me, but evil. And Jehoshaphat said, Let not the king say so. (9) Then the king of Israel called an officer, and said, Fetch quickly Micaiah the son of Imlah … (11) And Zedekiah the son of Chenaanah made him horns of iron, and said, Thus saith the Lord, With these shalt thou push the Syrians, until they be consumed. (12) And all the prophets prophesied so, saying, Go up to Ramoth-gilead, and prosper; for the Lord will deliver it into the hand of the king. (13) And the messenger that went to call Micaiah spake unto him, saying, Behold now, the words of the prophets declare good unto the king with one mouth: let thy word, I pray thee, be like the word of one of them, and speak thou good.* (It is tempting to agree with consensus.)*(14) And Micaiah said, As the Lord liveth, what the Lord saith unto me, that will I speak. (15) And*

112

when he was come to the king, the king said unto him, Micaiah, shall we go to Ramoth-gilead to battle, or shall we forbear? And he answered him, <u>Go up and prosper; and the Lord will deliver it into the hand of the king</u>.

Realize that Micaiah's words *"Go up and prosper"* were from the Lord. Micaiah made a vow that what the Lord said, he would say. God through Micaiah was telling the king to go up and prosper because that was the answer King Ahab wanted. Like Balaam, he got the answer he wanted. God is sovereign over deception but no one is guiltless when they are deceived. *(16) And the king said unto him, How many times shall I adjure thee that thou speak unto me nothing but the truth in the name of the Lord. (17) And he* (Micaiah) *said, I saw all Israel scattered upon the mountains, as sheep that have no shepherd: and the Lord said, These have no master; let them return every man to his house in peace.* (One truthful prophet who was not motivated by gain prophesied the death of Ahab and the loss of the battle.) *(18) And the king of Israel said to Jehoshaphat, Did I not tell thee that he would not prophesy good concerning me, but evil? (19) And Micaiah said, Therefore hear thou the word of the Lord: I saw the Lord sitting on his throne, and <u>all the host of heaven</u> standing by him on his <u>right hand and on his left</u>.*

In Job 1:6, the sons of God were gathered together before the Lord, and Satan was there among them. What was he doing there? It says here, *"<u>All the hosts</u> of heaven ... on His right hand and on His left.*" Whom did the Lord gather on His left? It was the goats and the wicked (Mt.25:33). *(1 Ki.22:20) And <u>the Lord said, Who shall entice Ahab that he may go up and fall at Ramoth-gilead?</u>* (The Lord was asking for a spirit to deceive Ahab.) *And one said on this manner; and another said on that manner. (21) And <u>there came forth a spirit, and stood before the Lord, and said, I will entice him. (22) And the Lord said unto him, Wherewith? And he said, I will go forth, and will be a lying spirit in the mouth of all his prophets</u>.* (Notice that the spirit said, "his" prophets, not "your" prophets.) *And* *he* (God) *said, Thou shalt entice him, and shalt prevail also: go forth, and do so. (23) Now therefore, behold, <u>the Lord hath put a lying spirit in the mouth of all these thy prophets</u>.* Notice "thy prophets." These prophets did not belong as much to the Lord as they did to Ahab.

The apostate leadership of the northern 10 tribes was deceived by God to lead them into a battle they could not win. Here are four hundred prophets of the Lord prophesying by a lying spirit. They were probably fed from Ahab's table and desired his favor. It was four hundred false prophets to one true prophet. That is the same case we have today. They loved the hire of wrongdoing. What motivates a Christian to agree with their religion or preacher when they disagree with the Word of God? This is the idolatry that deceives their heart.

We must be true to the Lord and not be influenced by respect of men. I was a guest speaker in an assembly once where the pastor was to speak before me. As he walked around sharing some things, he walked by me and said, "Isn't that right, David?" I softly said, "No" and shook my head. The pastor did a double-take but walked away and went right on speaking. Later, he walked by me again and the same thing happened. Finally, the man behind me could not stand it any longer and asked, "Did you say, 'No'?" I answered, "Yes, and if he didn't want my truthful opinion, he shouldn't ask." After the service, the pastor came and asked me what was wrong. I told him that his statements were wrong and the truth was such and such according to the Word. I also asked him not to ask me any more questions in the assembly. Well, he did not throw me out, and I ended up doing a lot of the teaching there for a while.

Ahab did not trust his four hundred prophets and he feared that one prophet. *(1 Ki.22:30) And the king of Israel said unto Jehoshaphat, <u>I will disguise myself</u>, and go into the battle; but put thou on thy robes. And the king of Israel disguised himself, and went into the battle ... (34) And a <u>certain man drew his bow</u> at* *a venture* (Hebrew: "in his simplicity") *and smote the king of Israel between the joints of the armor.* It appears that this Syrian was shooting in the general direction of the enemy, and smote Ahab right in the joints of his armor. We cannot fool God. I do not know who was simpler, the man who drew the bow or Ahab who thought he could hide from the wrath of God by changing his clothes. There are several good morals to this story. Firstly, you cannot go by the majority. Here was a case of four hundred to one, and the majority was wrong. Throughout history, the majority of what is called God's people have been wrong. Secondly, you have to look carefully at your motives when you inquire of the Lord. If your motives are impure, you will get an answer that your flesh wants. In this case, Ahab got the answer he wanted and was killed. Jehoshaphat was chastened and almost lost his life for making an alliance with an evil king. He did not learn his lesson and later aligned with Ahab's evil successor, losing his life and his works (2 Chr.20:35 - 21:1). We can be deceived by wanting our desires or following the majority. It does not have to be a prophet that speaks to us. The Lord can give us a dream, vision, doctrine, or man we respect who can lead us astray. God can answer us according to our idols before our face.

When Jeroboam was the king of the northern ten tribes, he was afraid that his people would go and worship in the ordained temple at Jerusalem and, in so doing, stay and serve the king of Judah. He decided that he would erect altars for the people in Bethel and Dan. Jeroboam then made two golden calves and called them in Hebrew *Elohim* (1 Kings 12:28). He put the name of our God on his own creation. Aaron did the same thing when Israel came out of Egypt. He built a golden calf and called it in Hebrew *YHWH* and *Elohim*. The apostate religions teach a Jesus of their own creation, not the Jesus of the Bible. Paul called him *"another Jesus" (2 Cor.11:4)*. Jeroboam and his people were serving another Jesus. The golden calf was the Egyptian god Apis who

115

was called the creator. In other words, they were worshiping the god they knew in the world before they ate the Lamb and came out of Egypt. Many "Christians" are worshiping a Jesus that is acceptable to the world and the flesh. He is not the true God but an impostor. Jeroboam and his apostates were also making priests (ministers) who were not Levites (1 Ki.12:31). This tells me that in ten of the twelve tribes, the ministers were not ordained of God but apostates. That is exactly what has happened in the church today. Of the twelve spies, ten brought an evil report and died in the wilderness because they made the congregation to speak against the Lord (Num.14:36-38).

God sent a young prophet to prophesy against the altar in Bethel. In Hebrew, "Bethel" means "house of God." Of course, they called it the "house of God," but it was a false house of God because the true house was in Jerusalem. At that time, the king was standing at the altar offering incense before the people. When the prophet prophesied against the altar, the king stretched out his arm and pointed his hand at the prophet and told his men to seize him. At that point, the king's hand dried up and he could not draw it back. The altar rent and ashes poured out, which the prophet prophesied would happen. This, obviously, symbolized that God did not accept their sacrifices in this place of apostasy. The king asked the prophet to restore his hand, so the prophet prayed, and the Lord restored the king's hand. As a result, the king wanted to take the prophet home and reward him. The prophet declined for he was commanded by the Lord to <u>neither eat bread nor drink water in that place</u> (1 Ki.13:8,9). What place was that? It was the place where God's people were in apostasy and where their leaders were not ordained of God. It was an apostate religious system.

We must not eat their bread! This represents partaking of a false Jesus since He was the bread of life (Jn.6:48). Jesus is also the Word (Jn.1:1). Jesus said to beware of the leaven of

116

the Pharisees. Leaven changes the bread (the Word) to make it more acceptable to the flesh. Neither should we drink their water, which represents the false spirit formed by a false word. Jesus commanded us to come unto Him and drink of the living water of the Spirit through the Scriptures. *(Jn. 7:37) … Jesus stood and cried, saying, If any man thirst, let him come unto me and drink. (38) He that believeth on me, <u>as the scripture hath said</u>, from within him shall flow rivers of <u>living water</u>. (39) But this spake he of the <u>Spirit</u>, which they that believed on him were to receive.* Without this, any Jesus we might know is another Jesus.

The prophet was being obedient and was leaving those backslidden people. In this city of Bethel, there was an older prophet who had heard what the young prophet did. He saddled his ass and caught up with him. *(1 Ki. 13:15) Then he said unto him, Come home with me, and eat bread. (16) And he said, I may not return with thee, nor go in with thee; neither will I eat bread nor drink water with thee in this place: (17) for it is said to me by the word of the Lord, Thou shalt eat no bread nor drink water there, nor turn again to go by the way that thou camest. (18) And he said unto him, I also am a prophet as thou art; and <u>an angel spake unto me by the word of the Lord, saying, Bring him back with thee into thy house, that he may eat bread and drink water. But he lied unto him</u>. (19) So he went back with him, and <u>did eat bread in his house, and drank water</u>.* The young prophet falsely believed that God had changed His Word that was originally given and so ate and drank of the apostate word. We are told in Jude 1:3 to contend earnestly for the <u>faith which was once delivered</u> unto the saints. Today many without scriptural foundation tell us that after the apostles God changed what He called an *"eternal covenant."* This lie has robbed the Church of its power by replacing Jesus with a golden calf. Daniel and his three friends would not defile themselves with Babylon's food (Dan. 1:5-16). After refusing Babylon's food, they were said to have ten times the wisdom and understanding of those who did eat (Dan.1:17-21). They also were the only ones to not bow down to the image of the beast (Dan.3:12,18), Babylon's version of the golden calf.

The young prophet was deceived into a modern gospel. *(1 Ki.13:20) And it came to pass, as they sat at the table, that the word of the Lord came unto the prophet that brought him back; (21) and he cried unto the man of God that came from Judah, saying, Thus saith the Lord, Forasmuch as <u>thou hast been disobedient</u> unto the mouth of the Lord, and <u>hast not kept the commandment</u> which the Lord thy God commanded thee, (22) but camest back, and <u>hast eaten bread and drunk water in the place of which he said to thee, Eat no bread, and drink no water; thy body shall not come unto the sepulchre of thy fathers</u>.* The Lord tried the young prophet; but he was said to have *"not kept the commandment"* of the Lord, which was synonymous with partaking of apostate spiritual food. He lost his life in that place as many do today. The old prophet of God spoke a lie for personal gain. That place had leavened him, and he was now a false "profit."

We must respect the Word of God so much that nothing can turn us away from it to another Jesus. We have to remain on guard, for even vessels of honor can be used as vessels of dishonor to try us. When the young prophet left a <u>lion</u> met him in the way and slew him. *(1 Ki.13:26) … <u>Lord hath delivered him unto the lion</u>, which hath torn him, and slain him, according to the word of the Lord ….* The lion was given permission from God to kill the one who ate the apostate spiritual food. *(1 Pet.4:8) … <u>the devil</u>, as a roaring <u>lion</u>, walketh about, seeking whom he <u>may</u> devour.* "May" is used here because the devil must have permission to devour. He is ordained to devour apostates. The penalty for the young prophet's apostasy was that he would *"not come unto the sepulchre of thy fathers,"* spiritually meaning he was not joined with his fathers in death,

118

therefore, he would not be among the righteous resurrection. One who partakes of a false word from the false Jesus will lose his life by the devil and will not be among the righteous in resurrection. *(Rev.22:18) I testify unto every man that heareth the words of the prophecy of this book, if any man shall add unto them, <u>God shall add unto him the plagues</u> which are written in this book: (19) and if any man shall take away from the words of the book of this prophecy, <u>God shall take away his part</u> from the tree of life ... (Gal.1:8) But though we, or an angel from heaven, should preach unto you any gospel other than that which we preached unto you, let him be anathema* (Greek: "cursed; devoted to destruction").

The Lord tested the apostle Paul by His Spirit. *(Acts 19:21) Now after these things were ended, Paul purposed in <u>the spirit</u>, when he had passed through Macedonia and Achaia, to go to Jerusalem, saying, After I have been there, I must also see Rome.* Neither "spirit" here nor "Holy Spirit" in the following verses is capitalized in the Greek because the Greek language has no capitalization. This means we must determine from the text if "spirit" is "Holy Spirit." Since "the" and not "his" is used before spirit, we know that God is speaking of the Holy Spirit. Therefore "spirit" in this and the following verse should be capitalized in English. That was a translator's mistake. Paul determined in the Spirit, that he was going to Jerusalem and then to Rome. He could have only gotten that revelation from God because it was in the future. *(Acts 20:22) And now, behold, I go bound in <u>the spirit</u> unto Jerusalem, not knowing the things that shall befall me there: (23) save that <u>the Holy Spirit</u> testifieth unto me in every city, saying that bonds and afflictions abide me.* It was the Holy Spirit telling Paul to go to Jerusalem where he could expect bonds and afflictions.

(Acts 21:4) And having found the disciples, we tarried there seven days: and these said to Paul through <u>the Spirit</u>, that <u>he should not set foot in Jerusalem</u>. Notice that this was just the opposite of what the Holy Spirit had told Paul he was

119

going to do three times before. I suggest to you that Paul was being proven by *"the Spirit"* as to whom he would listen. Other disciples were offering a <u>new word</u>. He was being given an opportunity to obey his flesh and avoid the spiritual cross just as in the cases of Balaam and the young prophet. *(Acts 21:10) And as we tarried there some days, there came down from Judea a certain prophet, named Agabus. (11) and coming to us, and taking Paul's girdle, he bound his own feet and hands, and said, <u>Thus saith the Holy Spirit, So shall the Jews at Jerusalem bind the man that owneth this girdle</u>, and shall deliver him into the hands of the Gentiles.* Having been told by the Spirit again that he would go to Jerusalem and be persecuted, he was now going to be tried by human sentiment. *(12) And when we heard these things, both we and <u>they of that place besought him not to go up to Jerusalem</u>. (13) Then Paul answered, What do ye, weeping and breaking my heart? for I am ready not to be bound only, but also to die at Jerusalem for the name of the Lord Jesus. (14) And when he would not be persuaded, we ceased, saying, <u>The will of the Lord be done</u>.* Paul was tried by human sentiment and prophecy, and overcame. He obeyed what the Lord told him, which is the important thing.

The Lord will try us by His Spirit to see if we will believe what He has told us. To Abraham was born the long-promised seed Isaac. God promised to make His covenant with Isaac and <u>his seed after him</u> (Gen.17:19), a seed which God said would be as the stars for multitudes (Gen.15:5). *(Gen.15:6) And he believed in the Lord; and He reckoned it to him for righteousness.* This was not enough for God; Abraham's faith had to be tried. After many years of waiting in faith, Isaac was born. Then an even greater trial came. *(Gen.22:1)…<u>God did prove Abraham</u>, and said unto him, Abraham. And he said, Here am I. (2) And he said, Take now thy son, thine only son, whom thou lovest, even Isaac, and get thee into the land of Moriah. And offer him there for a bu rnt-offering upon one of the mountains which I will tell thee of.*

(Heb.11:17) By faith Abraham, <u>being tried</u>, offered up Isaac. (18) even he to whom it was said, In Isaac shall thy seed be called: (19) accounting that God [is] able to raise up, even from the dead; from whence he did also in a figure receive him back. Abraham believed God's original promise to him to the extent that even if he sacrificed Isaac, God would have to raise him up to fulfill the promise. We need to believe the original promises above all that we see and hear. God will prove or try us through religion, ministers, spoken word, or well-meaning friends. We are tried by external circumstances, but we are tempted by our own lusts, not God (Jas.1:13,14). External trials and internal temptations are necessary to prove who loves God (Jas.1:12). God waited until the last seconds, when Abraham was about to plunge the knife into Isaac, stopped him and said unto him, *"Now I know that thou fearest God."* There is no proof that we believe God's promises until we are tried. The Lord then provided a ram caught in a thicket for a sacrifice in the place of Isaac, the seed of Abraham. This, of course, typified Jesus who died in the place of all the seed of Abraham, including we who believe.

I once asked God to give me a new car, which He did six months later. After a year or so, He told me to sell it. I was a little grieved and preferred to sell my other car because it was smaller and I had five children. I obeyed the Lord and offered the car in the papers for a fair market price. After advertising it for a couple of months, I asked the Lord why, if He wanted me to sell it, were there no buyers. He said to me, "I wanted you to sacrifice it as Abraham sacrificed Isaac." I said, "But, Lord, Abraham did not sacrifice Isaac." Then I saw that the Lord was trying me in the same way as Abraham, to see if I would sacrifice what was important to me. God told me to sell my other smaller car, which I did not need at the time. I was relieved.

God will tell our spirit what He wants us to do. Dreams, visions, revelations, or spoken words will agree with our spirit, but not our flesh. When God sends us to a cross, we are going to be tried to not go. We can also be tried to go beyond the Lord. A brother had a vision he believed was from God. I felt it was a trial. In the vision, the Lord told him to sell everything, and go out on the mission field. Many come back from the mission field wounded because they were sent by religion, not God. We considered whether this was a true word from God or a trial. I asked him a few questions. He was afraid to go, but he didn't want to miss God and lacked faith. I knew this brother was there to be fed and prepared to minister, but I knew he was not ready. I advised him to pray, but if God did not speak it in his spirit, to ignore it. Thank God he did. We should do nothing when we are uncertain of God's direction. We should not be led by prophecy or by dreams and visions when they disagree with our own spirit. These are wonderful confirmations and direction for what we feel in our spirit. We are to be led by the Spirit of God.

If God puts something Scriptural in our spirit, we should let no one talk us out of it. Peter was used to try Jesus in this way. Jesus told the disciples that He was to die at Jerusalem, and Peter rebuked Him. *(Mt.16:22) And Peter took him, and began to rebuke him, saying, Be it far from thee, Lord: this shall never be unto thee. (23) But he turned, and said unto Peter, <u>Get thee behind me, Satan:</u> thou art a stumbling-block unto me: for <u>thou mindest not the things of God, but the things of men</u>.* Jesus knew that He was being tempted by Satan through Peter to do his own fleshly will.

122

Chapter 8
God's Sovereignty Over Sickness, Death, and the Curse

See now that I, even I, am he, And there is no god with me: I kill, and I make alive; I wound, and I heal; And there is none that can deliver out of my hand (Dt.32:39).

Our God wounds and kills! Does that make you uncomfortable? For many people, it is very uncomfortable. Most feel that only Satan or men wound and kill. But they are only vessels; only God has all authority in heaven and earth (Mt.28:18). God does all these things because He is the righteous judge. God is truly working on us from both directions. He sent the curse to turn us from sin, and He sent our Savior to deliver those that do. He says, *"I kill, and I make alive; I wound, and I heal."* This motivates us to please, fear, and obey Him.

When God sends the curse to bring repentance, can man deliver from it without repentance? That is what the sinner wants, blessing without repentance. Man has sought out many inventions to try to circumvent repentance, but they have all come back to curse him. Are we stronger than God? God said, *"There is none that can deliver out of my hand."* This is contrary to the deception of the world, but it is God's purpose for the world to be deceived in this. We cannot get anyone out from under a curse except through the Gospel. Sometimes God is merciful, but we cannot guarantee God's deliverance to those who do not walk under the blood. Those ministers who are in agreement with God will administer His gifts of healing, deliverance, and provision to the ones who are in line for God's blessings through repentance, faith, and justification.

God, through Paul, delivered a man to Satan to bring him to repentance. *(1 Cor.5:5)* ***To <u>deliver such a one unto Satan for the destruction of the flesh, that the spirit may be saved</u> in the day of the Lord Jesus.*** Whether we understand it or not, the purpose God turns some over to Satan or demons is good. They chasten and cause some to count the high cost of sin. It is important that we understand that it is God who ultimately is in charge. Otherwise, we had better start fearing the devil. If the devil ever has authority to do what he wants to do, we have reason to fear him, but Jesus forbids that. *(Lk.12:4) **And I say unto you my friends, <u>Be not afraid of them that kill the body</u>*** (Satan and demons through men), ***and after that have no more that they can do. (5) But I will warn you whom ye shall fear: <u>Fear him, who after he hath killed</u>, hath power*** *(Greek: "authority")* ***to cast into hell.*** We are not to be afraid of the vessels that God uses. Only God has authority to cast into hell, after He has killed. Have we ever heard it said, "God does not cast anyone into hell"? There is a shred of truth to that. The demons may cast in, but the Lord has the authority. He alone are we commanded to fear. The reason that God can tell those who follow Him to *"be anxious for nothing"* is because He is always in control.

God is never wrong. People blame God for the death of a loved one or some other tragedy, but He is always right in what He does. We must realize that God has bound Himself with His Word. *(Ps.119:89)* ***<u>For ever</u>, O Lord, <u>Thy word is settled</u> in heaven.*** Once He says something, He must stand by it, or He is a liar and breaks His word. If He makes a condition in the Word for His benefits, we must meet that condition. *(Rom.1:16)* ***The Gospel is the power of God unto salvation <u>to every one that believeth</u>.*** Can we expect God's provisions without believing His Word? Many unbelieving "Christians" endure much hardship because they have not met the condition. Then they say, "It must not have been God's will to deliver, heal, or bless me." Jesus never said that God's will was the reason His people did not receive these things. He said, *"Because of your unbelief"*; *"As thou hast believed, [so] be it done unto thee"*; *"Thy faith hath made thee whole"*; and *"According to your faith be it done unto you."* In His own home town, Jesus could not do many mighty works because of their unbelief (Mt.13:58; Mk.6:5).

If we have a problem, we should blame ourselves. *(Gal.6:7) Be not deceived; God is not mocked: for <u>whatsoever a man soweth, that shall he also reap</u>. (Mt.7:2) For with what judgment ye judge, ye shall be judged: and <u>with what measure ye mete</u>* (give out), *<u>it shall be measured unto you</u>*. If we were living in unforgiveness and yet praying for God to heal our body, would not God have to break His Word in order to heal us? *(Mt.6:15) But <u>if ye forgive not men their trespasses, neither will your Father forgive your trespasses</u>. (Jas.5:16) <u>Confess therefore your sins</u> one to another, and pray one for another, <u>that ye may be healed</u>*. Can we expect God to give to us when we will not first give? *(Lk.6:38) <u>Give and it shall be given unto you</u>*. What God does is right and righteous. Those who start out believing in the sovereignty and good purpose of God do not question God. They believe God is in control and trust Him. If we deal with the cause, we will not have to deal with the curse.

Why is it that we see the devil mentioned so seldom in the Scriptures, but yet so often he is on the lips of Christians? They are constantly saying that the devil did this, and devil did that. He is only an angel (Greek: "messenger"), but the world and the worldly church have made him a god, the *"god of this world."* He is a created being used to bring to pass God's purposes. Jesus through His sacrifice took away the devil's *"power of death"* *(Heb.2:14)* for those who believe. He never had the <u>authority</u> of death. Authority is the right to use power. *(1 Sam.2:6) <u>The Lord killeth, and maketh alive: He bringeth down to Sheol, and bringeth up</u>*. Death and life are in the hand of the Lord, not any other. But again, that does not negate our responsibility.

(Pr.18:21) Death and life are in the power of the tongue. We need to be careful to agree with God's Word that we fall not under the curse (Rev.22:18,19). *(Num.14:28) ... As ye have spoken in mine ears, so will I do to you. (Mt.12:37) For by thy words thou shalt be justified, and by thy words thou shalt be condemned.* God reacts to the way we react to His Word. Everything is subject to the Word God has spoken, even His own will. *(Ps.138:2) ... thou hast magnified thy word above all thy name.* God puts the Word first, as a standard to trust even above His own name, which in Hebrew means "character and authority." God wants us to know that He puts His Word above any desire or purpose that we might think He has. But His Word is His desire and purpose.

(1 Sam.2:7) <u>*The Lord maketh poor, and maketh rich: He bringeth low, he also lifteth up*</u>. Many Christians think that it is by their own wisdom or by hard work alone that they prosper. We are all taught from an early age that to have a prosperous life you must seek out all the worldly means to be "successful." However, God says, *"Seek ye first his kingdom, and his righteousness; and all these things shall be added unto you (Mt.6:33).* If we seek first the world, we will do without the kingdom, but if we seek first the kingdom, we will have our needs met. *(Phl.4:19) And my God shall supply every <u>need</u> of yours according to his riches in glory in Christ Jesus.* God will supply our every need to further His Will and kingdom in our life. He will also do this for us while we promote His kingdom in the lives of others.

By the grace of God, I was doing this when God told me, "You are never going to work for man again." The Lord showed me that I was to promote His kingdom in Pensacola, Florida. Since I had no way to buy a house and car and I had stayed away from debt for many years, I asked the Lord to freely give these to me there. Within six months, He had given me what I had asked, however, He did have me give the house and car that I had away. He has been providing for us ever since. So you see, I believe God will supply our every need. Who fed and cared for the wives and children of the disciples as they followed Jesus for 3-1/2 years and afterwards? Paul said that they had wives in 1 Corinthians 9:5, and where there were wives there were children in those days.

Kingdom prosperity is not the world's prosperity. *(Pr.13:7) There is that <u>maketh himself rich</u>, yet hath nothing.* We have not been put here to make ourselves rich or to make the old man prosperous. We have been put here to make the spiritual man prosperous. Jesus and the disciples are our examples. They had no love for the things of the world (1 Jn.2:15). As much as the prosperity folks would like to make Jesus rich because of His seamless garment or to jam that camel through the eye of the needle, it cannot be done in honesty. The Lord gives authority to the devil to tempt us with riches. *(Mt.4:1) Then was <u>Jesus led up of the Spirit</u> into the wilderness <u>to be tempted of the devil</u>. (8) Again, the devil taketh him unto an exceeding high mountain, and showeth him <u>all the kingdoms of the world</u>, and the glory of them; (9) and he said unto him, <u>All these things will I give thee</u>, if thou wilt fall down and worship me.*

The devil offered Jesus all the things of the world if He would serve him. *(Mt.6:24) No man can serve two masters; for either he will hate the one, and love the other; or else he will hold to one, and despise the other. Ye cannot serve God and mammon.* This is God's way of finding out who loves Him and weeding out His flock. Those who use faith to be rich are asking to be deceived. In 1 Timothy 6:5-11, the believer is commanded to be content with food and covering and to flee the love of money which leads astray from the faith with the temptations of many foolish and hurtful lusts. The rich hoard up someone else's food and supplies for vanity. According to God, there is just enough supply on earth to feed everyone. *(Eccl.5:11) <u>When goods increase, they are increased that eat them</u>; and what advantage is there to the owner thereof, save* *the beholding [of them] with his eyes?* Starving people will point their fingers on judgment day.

God sent the curses to motivate men to repent and obey Him. Here is the portion of the curse that indicates who sent it. *(Dt.28:15) But it shall come to pass, if thou wilt not hearken unto the voice of the Lord thy God, to observe to do all his commandments and his statutes which I command thee this day, that <u>all these curses shall come upon thee</u>, and overtake thee. (20) <u>The Lord will send</u> upon thee cursing, discomfiture, and rebuke, in all that thou puttest thy hand unto to do, until thou be destroyed, and until thou perish quickly; because of the evil of thy doings, whereby thou hast forsaken me. (21) <u>The Lord will make</u> the pestilence cleave unto thee, until he have consumed thee from off the land, whither thou goest in to possess it. (22) <u>The Lord will smite</u> thee with consumption, and with fever, and with inflammation, and with fiery heat, and with the sword, and with blasting, and with mildew; and they shall pursue thee until thou perish. (24) <u>The Lord will make</u> the rain of thy land powder and dust: from heaven shall it come down upon thee, until thou be destroyed. (25) <u>The Lord will cause</u> thee to be smitten before thine enemies; thou shalt go out one way against them, and shalt flee seven ways before them: and thou shalt be tossed to and fro among all the kingdoms of the earth. (27) <u>The Lord will smite</u> thee with the boil of Egypt, and with the emerods, and with the scurvy, and with the itch, whereof thou canst not be healed. (28) <u>The Lord will smite</u> thee with madness, and with blindness, and with astonishment of heart; (35) <u>The Lord will smite</u> thee in the knees, and in the legs, with a sore boil, whereof thou canst not be healed, from the sole of thy foot unto the crown of thy head. (36) <u>The Lord will bring</u> thee, and thy king whom thou shalt set over thee, unto a nation that thou hast not known, thou nor thy fathers; and there shalt thou serve others gods, wood and stone.*

Notice that the Lord will send the curse. Why is it that the worldly church says that God does not do these things? Why and how does God do this? *(47) Because thou <u>servedst not the Lord</u> thy God with joyfulness, and with gladness of heart, by reason of the abundance of all things; (48) therefore shalt <u>thou serve thine enemies that the Lord shall send against thee</u>.* God uses enemies to administer the curse on the rebellious. It is black or white. If we are not serving the Lord, we are serving our enemies that the Lord sends. The Lord sends the curse and the enemy for chastening. That is the part the devil, demons, and the wicked play. It is the Lord taking credit, so we know we have to fear the Lord, and serve Him with joyfulness and a glad heart, by reason of abundance of all things.

Some might think their particular curse is not listed in Deuteronomy 28 and is, therefore, not under the Lord's dominion. *(Dt.28:61) Also every sickness, and every plague, <u>which is not written</u> in the book of this law, them will <u>the Lord bring upon thee</u>, until thou be destroyed.* OOPS! *(Pr.3:7) … Fear the Lord, and depart from evil.* Those who fear and repent have every right to claim the sacrifice of Jesus for deliverance from the curse. *(Gal.3:13) <u>Christ redeemed us from the curse</u> of the law, <u>having become a curse for us</u>; for it is written, Cursed is every one that hangeth on a tree: (14) <u>that upon the Gentiles might come the blessing of Abraham in Christ Jesus</u>.* What was the blessing of Abraham? *(Gen.24:1) … And the Lord had blessed Abraham in <u>all things</u>.* Glory to God! The entire curse that was due us was put on Jesus. All we have to do is repent and believe. We have been blessed in all things.

(Num.14:11) And the Lord said unto Moses, How long will this people despise me? and <u>how long will they not believe</u> in me, for all the signs which I have wrought among them? (12) <u>I will smite them with the pestilence</u>, and <u>disinherit them</u>, and will make of thee a nation greater and mightier than they. It is not as though we do not have an example of God doing this. In Noah's day, God did just that and repopulated His earth with Noah's sons. Our text is speaking about the time when the twelve spies entered into Canaan's land. God had

promised Canaan's land to His people. It was "The Promised Land." The ten spies brought back the evil report that they were not able to go up and take the land from the Canaanites. This angered God because He had told them that He had given them this land.

Canaan's land is a "type" of our body. Both that land and our body are made from dirt. *(1 Cor.3:9) For we are God's fellow-workers: ye are God's husbandry* (Greek: "tilled land"), *God's building.* God wants the fruit of Christ, the spiritual man, to grow up in His land. God warns those who have partaken of His Spirit and Word to not fall away as land that does not bear fruit. *(Heb.6:7) For the land which hath drunk the rain* (Spirit and Word) *that cometh oft upon it, and bringeth forth herbs meet for them for whose sake it is also tilled, receiveth blessing from God: (8) but if it beareth thorns and thistles, it is rejected and nigh unto a curse; whose end is to be burned.* God curses the land that does not bear fruit. For those who have been born again, God has given us this land (body) to be totally controlled by the spiritual man. God sent the Israelite, the spiritual, born again man, to take the Promised Land from the Canaanites, who represented the lusts of the flesh, the old man. The names of the tribes of Canaan in Hebrew describe the lusts of the flesh (Gen.10:15-18). Their kings represent the principalities and powers that rule over the flesh.

Today, ten out of twelve ministers bring the evil report that we are not able to take this land. They teach that we should be satisfied to be forgiven but that we cannot expect to be sanctified of the lusts of the flesh in order to rule this land for God. In this type, God is clearly telling us to take up the sword of the Spirit, which is the Word (Heb.4:12), put to death the old man that lives in our land, take over his house, and raise our own crops (fruit of the Spirit). *(2 Cor.7:1) Having therefore these promises* (sword of the Word), *beloved, let us cleanse ourselves from all defilement of flesh and spirit, perfecting holiness in the fear of God.* God would not tell us to do something that we cannot do by faith in Him. *(Gal.2:20) I have been crucified with Christ; and it is no longer I* (the old man or Canaanite) *that live, but Christ* (the new man or Israelite) *living in me.* To those who do not believe the good report, God *"will smite them with the pestilence, and disinherit them."*

Joshua and Caleb believed that the Promised Land was theirs and that they could take it from the Canaanite. *(Num.14:9) Only rebel not against the Lord, neither fear ye the people of the land; for they are bread for us: their defense is removed from over them, and the Lord is with us: fear them not.* The old man is bread for the new man. The spiritual man grows as he devours the old man. Since they occupy the same territory, the old man has got to die so that the spiritual man can live and grow. For those who believe, the Lord has removed the defense of the old man.

(Josh.1:3) Every place that the sole of your foot shall tread upon, to you have I given it, as I spake unto Moses. The Word of God is also a type of the land of promise. Every promise that we stand on, God is going to give it to us. I am not a denominational person, but I have shared in these churches. It is clear to me that each sect believes a portion of the Word, which yields the promised benefit. Members of these sects are being delivered to believe increasingly more of the Word and consequently to receive increasingly more of the benefits. Today much of what we hear in the churches is the evil report. Their thinking is that we cannot act in faith that God will heal, provide, sanctify, or deliver from the curse because we do not know His Will. To them I say, "Get in the Word and find out His Will so that you do not do without." God in His sovereignty says, *"To you have I given it."*

(Gen.7:4) For yet seven days, and I will cause it to rain upon the earth forty days and forty nights; and every living thing that I have made will I destroy from off the face of the ground. Why would God destroy the whole earth? *(Gen.6:12) And God saw*

the earth, and, behold, it was corrupt; for <u>all flesh had corrupted their way upon the earth</u>. So it is in our day. *(Mt.24:37) And as [were] the days of Noah, so shall be the coming of the Son of man.* Today if we say that God is the one that is causing the destruction that is coming, people would be offended. Until our mind is renewed with the Word, we think that man is basically good and not deserving of such treatment. God is about to prove the fallacy of this thinking.

God sees man as a beast. Man, obviously, is capable of things that even beasts do not do. Contrary to the apostate theologians, man has no preeminence above the beasts. *(Eccl.3:18) I said in my heart, It is because of the sons of men, that God may prove them, and <u>that they may see</u> that <u>they themselves are but as beasts</u>. (19) … yea, they have all one breath* (Hebrew: "spirit")*; and <u>man hath no preeminence above the beasts</u>.* Notice that unregenerate man is one spirit with the beasts. Some say that beasts do not have spirits, which is also false. *(Eccl.3:21) Who knoweth the spirit of man, whether it goeth upward, and the <u>spirit of the beast</u>, whether it goeth downward to the earth?* As you can see, all beasts do not go down and all men do not go up. "Breath" in these verses is the Hebrew word for the spirit of beasts (Gen.7:22; Ps.104:29,30). They say that man is a higher creation because he has a soul and the beasts do not. False! *(Gen.1:30) And to every <u>beast</u> of the earth, and to every bird of the heavens, and to everything that creepeth upon the earth, wherein there is <u>life</u>* (Hebrew: "soul" [see also: Job 12:10; Lev.17:11]).

God says that unregenerate man is no higher than an animal. *(Epe.2:3) Among whom we also all once lived in the lust of our flesh, doing the desires of the flesh and of the mind, and <u>were by nature children of wrath, even as the rest</u>.* Before we knew God, the only good thing about us is that we made good dirt for God to throw His seed into. Our dirt is no better than the next man's dirt. *(Rom.9:21) Or hath not the potter a right over the clay, from the <u>same lump</u> to make one part a vessel unto honor, and* *another unto dishonor?* Individually, we ask, "God, why would you choose me?" It is purely election. We think, "There has got to be something different about me." Well, maybe a few things. *(1 Cor.1:27-28) But God chose the foolish ... the weak ... the base ... and the ... despised, did God choose ... (29) that no flesh should glory before God.* Our old man is no better than the pagan's old man, who will never know God and will reject Him all of his life. God chose our old man to be a surrogate mother for His spiritual man that He sows in us by the Word from above. That is the old fleshly man's primary value to God. God does not want the fleshly old man but the fruit that is born in him. *(1 Cor.15:50) ... Flesh and blood can not inherit the kingdom of God. (Jn.3:3) Jesus answered and said unto him, Verily, verily, I say unto thee, Except one be born anew* (Greek: "from above"), *he cannot see the kingdom of God.*

The Lord destroyed all mankind except Noah and seven others! *(Gen.6:8) Noah found <u>grace</u> in the eyes of the Lord.* That means he did not earn or merit God's salvation. It is only those who have found grace through faith and are bringing forth the fruit that are building the ark of Jesus. The judgments on Egypt were a type of the tribulation judgments coming on the world. In the Exodus, only those who ate <u>all</u> of the <u>Passover</u> Lamb, which was a type of Christ, were passed over in judgment (Ex.12:9-11, 29-31). They had to *"let nothing of it remain until the morning." "Its head* (mind) *with its legs* (walk) *and with the inwards thereof* (heart)*"* had to be eaten. Those who take into their being all that Christ is and does through faith in the promises are passed over by the curse of sin and death. *(Ex.12:23) For <u>the Lord will pass through to smite the Egyptians;</u> and <u>when he seeth the blood</u> upon the lintel, and on the two side-posts, <u>the Lord will pass over</u> the door, and <u>will not suffer the destroyer to come in unto your houses to smite you.</u>* Contrary to popular opinion, it was the Lord who passed over the Israelites who lived under the blood and slew the

133

Egyptians. The <u>destroyer was on His leash</u>. The moral of the story is fear the Lord and live under the blood through faith. *(Ps.91:1) He that dwelleth in the secret place of the Most High shall abide under the shadow of the Almighty.*

(Ps.111:10) The fear of the Lord is the beginning of wisdom. If we are obedient, we need not fear. Fear is only a means to an end. When we are willfully disobedient, we need the fear of God. Sins of ignorance (Rom.5:13; 7:8,9) and sins of failure (Rom.7:19-25) are under the blood. However, we cannot claim the sacrificial benefits if we walk in premeditated sin. *(Heb.10:26) For if we <u>sin willfully</u> after that we have received the knowledge of the truth, there remaineth no more a sacrifice for sins, (27) but a <u>certain</u> fearful expectation of <u>judgment</u> ....* Jesus bore all sin; He also <u>bore the penalty for all sin, except willful disobedience</u>. Notice that there is *"no more a sacrifice"* for that sin. We should have *"a <u>certain</u> <u>fearful</u> expectation of judgment."* Many have been lied to about the cleansing of the blood. *(1 Jn.1:7) But if <u>we walk in the light</u>, as he is in the light, we have fellowship one with another, and the blood of Jesus his Son cleanseth us from all sin.* The blood cleanses the one who walks in the light of the Word, not in the darkness of willful disobedience.

For willful disobedience, we are promised certain judgment. <u>We pay the penalty for this sin here and now</u>, as in the following verses: *(Mt.18:34) And his lord was wroth, and <u>delivered him to the tormentors</u>* (demons)*, till he should <u>pay all that was due</u>. (35) So shall also my heavenly <u>Father do unto you</u>, if ye forgive not every one his brother from your hearts.* God will use the demons to make us pay for a sin of the will. *(Mt.5:25) Agree with thine adversary quickly, while thou art with him in the way; lest haply the adversary deliver thee to the judge* (God)*, and the judge deliver thee to the officer* (demon)*, and thou be <u>cast into prison</u>. (26) Verily I say unto thee, thou shalt by no means come out thence, till thou have <u>paid the last farthing</u>.* The prison here is spiritual bondage to sin and the curse, administered by the demons. Jesus came *"... to proclaim liberty to the <u>captives</u>, and the <u>opening [of the prison] to them that are bound</u>" (Isa.61:1)*. Willful disobedience throws us back into the prison from which Jesus delivered us.

David sinned willfully with Bathsheba. When he repented, Nathan the prophet said, *"The Lord also hath put away thy sin,"* but he also said, *"The <u>sword shall never depart from thy house</u>."* In other words, I forgive you but you will have to pay the penalty. This proved true, for David lost three sons and many people. His own son Absalom won the sympathy of the people and usurped the kingdom. David had to flee for his life. We do not spank our children for failure or mistakes, but for willful disobedience. Paul said, *"For the good which I would I do not: but the evil which <u>I would not</u>* (willed not), *that I practice. But if what <u>I would not</u>* (willed not), *that I do, it is <u>no more I that do it, but sin which dwelleth in me</u>" (Rom.7:19,20)*. Paul was failing God in a sin that his will was against. Notice that he hated the sin and was not accounted guilty; the old sin nature was guilty. When we are against the sin, God takes our side against the sin. He takes the side of the spiritual man against the old man. In this state, Paul cried out to the Lord. *(24) Wretched man that I am! who shall deliver me out of the body of this death?* Then he accepted God's promise of deliverance by faith. *(25) I thank God through Jesus Christ our Lord.* Jesus bore the curse of the sin for a person who, like Paul, is repentant.

(Lk.14:33) So therefore whosoever he be of you that <u>renounceth not all that he hath</u>, he cannot be my disciple. Jesus did not say that we have to sell everything that we have, but we do have to renounce everything that we have. That is different. We have to renounce ownership. We are no longer an owner or ruler of our rights, will, or property; we are now stewards. Our commitment to God needs to be total. We need to put everything into God's hands and let Him tell us what to do with it. I believe that is what Ananias and Sapphira's story is about.

(Acts 5:1) But a certain man named Ananias, with Sapphira his wife, sold a possession, (2) and kept back [part] of the price, his wife also being privy to it, and brought a certain part, and laid it at the apostles' feet. (3) But Peter said, Ananias, why hath Satan filled thy heart to lie to the Holy Spirit, and to keep back [part] of the price of the land? (4) While it remained, did it not remain thine own? and after it was sold, was it not in thy power? How is it that thou hast conceived this thing in thy heart? <u>thou has not lied unto men, but unto God</u>. In a time when the church was giving up all luxuries in order to meet the needs of the brethren, these two acted as though they were doing likewise. They thought that they were lying to man, but they were lying to the Lord. *(Mt.25:40) … Inasmuch as ye did it unto one of these my brethren, [even] these least, ye did it unto me.* Their commitment to the body was not what they wanted people to believe. As a result, God struck them dead. *(Acts 5:5) And <u>Ananias hearing these words fell down and gave up the ghost</u>: and great fear came upon all that heard it.* Then Sapphira came in. *(9) But Peter [said] unto her, How is it that ye have agreed together to try the Spirit of the Lord? behold, <u>the feet of them that have buried thy husband are at the door, and they shall carry thee out. (10) And she fell down immediately at his feet, and gave up the ghost</u>.* God, through Peter, spoke a prophetic word that gave authority to Satan to kill them.

I am convinced that this is happening today. Since people see only natural reasons for death, they do not think that God is responsible, and therefore do not fear. God uses natural methods. Who knows what killed Ananias and Sapphira? Maybe they died from heart attacks. Some in the church today get sick and die for the same reason, lack of honest commitment to God and the body of Christ. Their sin is defiling the body. Their death may not be as dramatic as that of Ananias and Sapphira. In those days, God was honoring and defending a pure church; not so today. Many tares came into the Church as Jesus said would happen. "Church" means "called-out ones."

It is not a building full of uncommitted people. A great fear came upon the church of Ananias' day. They saw the hand of God on hypocrites trying to falsely join those who were separated from the world. *(11) And great fear came upon the whole church, and upon all that heard these things.* Even the lost feared God and His people. They had enough respect not to join them without Christian commitment. *(13) But of the rest durst no man join himself to them: howbeit the people magnified them; (14) and believers were the more added to the Lord, multitudes both of men and women.* The Church in these last days through tribulation will once again be holy; God will defend her from the pollutions of the worldly. Many will be added to the Lord.

Some who were coming together for the Lord's Supper in Corinth were disrespecting the body, living after the lusts of their flesh. They filled themselves up on the bread and getting drunk on the wine while the poor brethren did without (1 Cor.11:20-22). Paul had to remind them that this was not just a ceremony. *(1 Cor.11:26) For as often as ye eat this bread, and drink the cup, ye proclaim* (show forth) *the Lord's death till he come.* When we eat the bread and drink the cup, we are saying, "We are partaking in the body and blood of Christ. We are partaking in His death and life." When they claimed to be under this commitment, but their greedy actions proved the opposite, God brought judgment upon them. *(27) Wherefore whosoever shall eat the bread or drink the cup of the Lord in an unworthy manner, shall be guilty of the body and the blood of the Lord. (28) But let a man prove* (examine) *himself, and so let him eat of the bread, and drink of the cup. (29) For he that eateth and drinketh, eateth and drinketh <u>judgment unto himself, if he discern not the body</u>. (30) <u>For this cause many among you are weak and sickly, and not a few sleep</u>* (died). They were being chastened and some died. They were not truly being an example of the Lord's death while their flesh was so obviously alive. They were neither considering the body of Christ nor their conscience. *(31) But if we discern ourselves, we should not be judged. (32) But when we are judged, we are chastened of the Lord, that we may not be condemned with the world.* Most of the Church considers sickness and death torments of the devil rather than chastening from the Lord, therefore, they have no reason to repent.

God is just as able to defend those who are obedient. He prepared a spiritual ark in Zion when the enemy came in like a flood and conquered Israel and Judah (2 Ki.18:11,13). Just as in the case of Noah, a remnant escaped to repopulate God's land. *(2 Ki.19:30) And the remnant that is escaped of the house of Judah shall again take root downward, and bear fruit upward. (31) For out of Jerusalem shall go forth a remnant, and out of mount Zion they that shall escape: the zeal of the Lord shall perform this.* Those who were in this ark were safe from the rushing of the floodwaters. The things that have been are the things that will be (Eccl.1:9). History must repeat so get in the ark of safety. *(5) And it came to pass that night, that the angel of the Lord went forth, and smote in the camp of the Assyrians a hundred fourscore and five thousand: and when men arose early in the morning, behold, these were all dead bodies.* The Lord killed 185,000 who did not know Him. That is not even a big city today. Oklahoma City grieved over the deaths of less than 200 people, in a city with a population of over 500,000. We look at this as a terrible thing, and it is. But the Lord is right when He does this, as right as He was in Noah's day. Those in the Murrah Building or the World Trade Center Towers who abided in the ark of Christ could not die. Some just changed addresses! Heaven is not bad, folks. Those people are happy in the arms of Jesus. *(Ps.116:15) Precious in the sight of the Lord is the death of his saints.* Some in those catastrophes escaped physically as those in Zion or the ark. They were warned not to go or miraculously escaped. This will happen for many who are not under the curse through faith in the promises.

Many have had dreams or visions of cities and nations being nuked. Over sixteen million people live in the greater New York area for example. Many will one day be killed in the first real world war. *(Jer.25:32) Thus saith the Lord of hosts, Behold, <u>evil shall go forth from nation to nation</u>, and a great <u>tempest</u> shall be raised up from the <u>uttermost parts of the earth</u>. (33) And the <u>slain of the Lord</u> shall be at that day <u>from one end of the earth even unto the other</u> end of the earth: they shall not be lamented, neither gathered, nor buried; they shall be dung upon the face of the ground.* Notice that the Lord takes credit for cleansing the earth of the wicked.

(Rev.5:1) And I saw in the right hand of him that sat on the throne a book written within and on the back, close sealed with seven seals. (2) And I saw a strong angel proclaiming with a great voice, <u>Who is worthy to open the book, and to loose the seals thereof</u>? These seals are the seals of judgment that will wipe out much of mankind. *(3) And no one in the heaven, or on the earth, or under the earth, was able to open the book, or to look thereon. (4) And I wept much, because no one was found worthy to open the book, or to look thereon: (5) and one of the elders saith unto me, Weep not; behold, the <u>Lion that is of the tribe of Judah, the Root of David, hath overcome to open the book and the seven seals thereof</u>.*

The Book of Revelation prophesies about judgments that will kill a quarter of mankind (Rev.6:8), and later a third of mankind (Rev.9:15,18), and still later all of the wicked (Rev.20:7-9,15). In Revelation 5, John was crying because no one had been found worthy to open the seals of judgment. Then he was told that Jesus, the Lion of the tribe of Judah, had overcome and was found worthy to loose the seals of judgment. Why is it so important to kill so many? It is because of the world's treatment of God's people. *(Rev.6:9) And when he opened the fifth seal, I saw underneath the altar the <u>souls of them that had been slain for the Word of God</u>, and for the testimony which they held: (10) and <u>they cried</u> with a great voice, saying, <u>How long,</u>*

O Master, the holy and true, dost thou not judge and avenge our blood on them that dwell on the earth? At this time, the earth will have become polarized and there will be an orgy of persecution against the saints. The saints themselves will be pleading for God to wipe out this worldwide beast who will be making war on His people.

In 1 Samuel 4, the Israelites and the Philistines were at war. The Lord showed me that this is a type for our lives. The Philistines represent the carnal or fleshly man, and the Israelites represent the spiritual man. These two men are constantly at war. *(Gal.5:17) For the flesh lusteth against the Spirit, and the Spirit against the flesh; for these are contrary the one to the other; that ye may not do the things that ye would.* In 1 Samuel 4:11, the Philistines captured the Ark of the Covenant. The Israelite is the rightful possessor of the Ark of the Covenant. If we are saved, our "Ark of the Covenant" is our spirit because inside our spirit is the presence of God. In this war, the Philistines captured the Ark. The five Philistine lords tried to park the Ark in each of their five leading cities. In every city to which they took the Ark, the curse of God would fall on the people, and the people would get tumors and die. When our carnal (fleshly) man takes the Ark of the Covenant where he wants, instead of where our spiritual man should take it, the judgment of God falls on us. Sometimes even death! This is the curse of sin and death. *(1 Sam.5:6) But the hand of the Lord was heavy upon them of Ashdod, and he destroyed them, and smote them with tumors, even Ashdod and the borders thereof.* It is God's hand and His curse that He uses to turn us from going our own way instead of following the Ark. Everywhere that the carnal man took the Ark of the Covenant, the curse of God was evident. *"The way of transgressors is hard."*

(Rom.8:13) For if ye live after the flesh, ye must die. (14) For as many as are led by the Spirit of God, these are sons of God. When the Ark leads us, we are sons, and when we lead

it, we are cursed. The Ark led Israel through the wilderness, just as we are to be led through this world. God uses the carrot and stick method. The five lords of the Philistines represent the five senses that rule the carnal man. When we walk after the flesh, we are walking after our carnal senses instead of our spiritual senses. *(2 Cor.5:7) For we walk by faith, not by sight.* The Bible teaches us that maturity is having our *"senses exercised to discern good and evil" (Heb.5:14).* This is what Jesus called having eyes to see and ears to hear. There are brethren in the kingdom of heaven of all spiritual ages. When you came to the Lord, you were so eager to find out about Him. It was God when you woke up and God when you went to bed. It was God who was on your mind all day long. Right! That intense desire to know and serve God is never supposed to leave us. That is walking <u>after</u> the Spirit. Your interest is God. In this type, the curse on the carnal man for taking dominion over the spirit eventually brought repentance. *(1 Sam.5:10) And it came to pass, as the ark of God came to Ekron, that the Ekronites cried out saying, They have brought abut the ark of the God of Israel to us, to slay us and our people. (11) They sent therefore and gathered together all the lords of the Philistines, and they said, Send away the ark of God of Israel, and <u>let it go again to its own place, that it slay us not,</u> and our people. For there was a deadly discomfiture throughout all the city; <u>the hand of God was very heavy</u> there. (12) And the men that died not were smitten with the tumors; and the cry of the city went up to heaven.* Notice that the *"hand of God"* was against the carnal man who took authority over the Ark of God. We are the temple of God. We are not to take His temple where He does not want to go or do with it as we like. They sent the Ark back with a sin offering for the five lords and the carnal men of the five cities that they ruled over. Then the curse was lifted.

Remember how we saw that God used Satan to move David to number Israel? *(2 Sam.24:1) And again the <u>anger of the</u>*

***Lord** was kindled against Israel, and **he moved David against them**, saying, Go, number Israel and Judah.* Then God brought judgment for the sin that He moved David to do. *(15) **So the Lord sent a pestilence upon Israel** from the morning even to the time appointed; and there died of the people from Dan even to Beersheba seventy thousand men.* Christians have thought that putting good men over them would in many ways keep them from judgment. When God was angered with Israel, He moved David, *"a man after His own heart,"* to bring them into a place of judgment where God killed 70,000 Israelites. There is no possible way we can insulate ourselves from judgment if we need it. If God can use a good man, just think what He can do with the apostate leadership the Church has now! The leadership in this land is here to bring us into judgment. They are putting people to sleep with their prosperity, all fly away, and once-saved-always-saved doctrines. They are here to keep people pacified until they fall off the edge, having never become disciples of Jesus. Everyone who is deceived by these leaders will be without excuse because they have had the Book. If we trust in man, we are in trouble.

God judges those who take credit for His work. *(Acts 12:21) And upon a set day Herod arrayed himself in royal apparel, and sat on the throne, and made an oration unto them. (22) And the people shouted, saying, The voice of a god, and not of a man. (23) And immediately **an angel of the Lord smote him**, because he gave not God the glory: and he was eaten of worms, and gave up the ghost.* As I was meditating on these verses, I came to the conclusion that our priorities are messed up. Herod had killed John the Baptist and James, and now he was persecuting the Church. God did not kill Herod for these seemingly very good reasons. Herod was killed for taking the glory that belongs to God. God's purpose was fulfilled in these deaths and persecutions. God does not get angry when His purpose is fulfilled. Jesus said that we have to lose our life to gain our life. This losing of our old life can be the death of the flesh as we live or the death of the flesh when we physically die. *(Ps.116:15) Precious in the sight of the Lord is the death of his saints.* God is not going to cry over the death of the flesh in His saints. He is going to rejoice to now have perfect fellowship with them in the kingdom because the flesh is dead. Jesus used the term *"enter into life" (Mt.18:8)* concerning the death of the saints. It is so foolish to question God when we do not see the big picture as He does. *(Isa.57:1) The <u>righteous perisheth</u>, and no man layeth it to heart; and merciful men are taken away, none considering that the righteous is taken away from the evil [to come]. (2) He <u>entereth into peace</u>; they rest in their beds, <u>each one that walketh in his uprightness</u>.*

The most important death to us is the death of the carnal man, who is the enemy of God (Rom.8:7). The spiritual man is being released from bondage as he dies. God let Herod live while he was crucifying the flesh of His saints. He killed him because he glorified himself instead of God. In another way, death is the enemy of the spiritual man while we live. Those who are born again but walk after the flesh will spiritually be *"twice dead, plucked up by the roots" (Jude 1:12)*. You have to be twice born to be twice dead. These people in their falling away *"<u>crucify to themselves the Son of God afresh</u>" (Heb.6:6)*. How can we crucify Jesus again? It says *"to themselves."* In us the spiritual man is *"Christ in you."* Christ is put to death in us when we give life to the carnal man by obeying him. *(Rom.8:13) For <u>if ye live after the flesh, ye must die</u>*. Whichever man we obey we strengthen. Have you ever heard of the black dog–white dog scenario? If you feed the white dog (spirit), he whips the black dog (flesh), but if you feed the black dog (flesh), he whips the white dog (spirit).

While Paul was preaching to the proconsul, a false prophet called Elymas was withstanding him. *(Acts 13:9) But Saul, who is also called Paul, filled with the Holy Spirit, fastened his eyes on him (10) and said, O full of all guile and all villainy, thou son of the devil, thou enemy of all* *righteousness, wilt thou not cease to pervert the right ways of the Lord? (11) And now, behold, the <u>hand of the Lord is upon thee</u>, and <u>thou shalt be blind</u>, not seeing the sun for a season. And immediately there fell on him a mist and a darkness; and he went about seeking some to lead him by the hand. (12) Then <u>the proconsul, when he saw what was done, believed</u>, being astonished at the <u>teaching of the Lord</u>.* The proconsul received a *"teaching of the Lord"* by seeing Elymas struck blind for standing in the way of the Gospel. We do not <u>get any teaching of the Lord, if we think that the devil is responsible</u>. The *"hand of the Lord"* was upon Elymas. This teaching convinced the proconsul to not resist the Gospel for himself or those under his authority, and the Gospel prospered.

Who makes people dumb or deaf or blind? God picked Moses, who according to his own confession was not a man of eloquent words. But God assured him that He was the one who made his mouth and that He could make it work. *(Ex.4:11) And the Lord said unto him, Who hath made man's mouth? Or <u>who maketh a man dumb, or deaf, or seeing, or blind? Is it not I, the Lord</u>?* God takes credit for making people dumb, deaf, seeing, or blind. If we steer around these Scriptures, we end up not only with a different God but also without the necessary fear of Him. With this thinking, God's people get more stiff-necked, or hardened to God's chastening. Ultimately, false teachers and the curse ruin their lives.

If you or someone you know has one of these infirmities and are tempted to be angry with God because of this revelation, remember that God works all things together for our good. We all have things to overcome; these things can make us both humble and strong. Some have spiritual difficulties while others have physical difficulties. Muscles gain strength by resistance. Conquering these curses by faith will make us strong. We have to overcome the thinking that it is the will of God to keep these infirmities. God made Moses' mouth, and He would make it speak for him. *(Ps.34:19) Many are the* *afflictions of the righteous; But the <u>Lord delivereth him out of them all</u>.* We must have the same Jesus as we see in the Word. *(Heb.13:8) Jesus Christ [is] the same yesterday and to-day, [yea] and for ever.* Jesus healed these infirmities in the Gospels, and He heals them today. My wife and I were both healed of eye infirmities. Several in our assembly no longer wear glasses.

(Lev.14:33) And the Lord spake unto Moses and unto Aaron, saying, (34) When ye are come into the land of Canaan, which I give to you for a possession, and <u>I put the plague of leprosy in a house</u> of the land of your possession; (35) then he that owneth the house shall come and tell the priest, saying, There seemeth to me to be as it were a plague in the house. In Leviticus 14:49-53, a sacrificial atonement is made for this leprous house that is the same as the atonement for a man with leprosy in Leviticus 14:4-7. That lets us know that this house symbolizes the natural man that we live in. The Scriptures elsewhere teach that men need atonement or covering for sin which is what leprosy symbolizes. Leprosy corrupts a man much like sin. The owner of the house would have to call a priest to inspect the house. The infected stones were removed and thrown in an unclean place without the city. New stones were put in and the whole house was scraped (verses 40-42). The house was then reinspected. If the leprosy had spread, the entire house ultimately was torn down and all the stones discarded (verse 45). Does that sound like something God might do with the unfaithful who have been taken over by sin? First, we have to confess the sin in our house and deal with it. Then the bad stones need to be replaced with new stones. Finally, the mortar of the house was scraped inside and out to make sure there was no trace of the leprosy. We need to do likewise. *(2Cor. 7:1) Having therefore these promises, beloved, let us <u>cleanse ourselves from all defilement</u> of flesh and spirit, perfecting holiness in the fear of God.*

The scrapings of sin were discarded in an unclean place <u>without the city</u>. Later, if the priest reinspected and found the leprosy (sin) throughout the house, the only way to finally get rid of the leprosy (sin) was to <u>destroy the whole house</u> and dump it in the unclean place <u>without the city</u>. Some obvious verses come to mind. *(Rev.22:14) Blessed are they that <u>wash their robes</u>, that they may have the right [to come] to the tree of life, and may enter in by the gates <u>into the city</u>. (15) Without are the dogs, and the sorcerers, and the fornicators, and the murderers, and the idolaters, and every one that loveth and maketh a lie. (Mt.7:26) And every one that heareth these words of mine, and doeth them not, shall be likened unto a foolish man, who built his house upon the sand: (27) and the rain descended, and the floods came, and the winds blew, and smote upon <u>that house; and it fell: and great was the fall thereof</u>.* This is all God's plan to prove who will be counted worthy of the kingdom. Those who truly believe the Word will use it to be sanctified and will keep His commandments.

(Mt.13:37) … He that soweth the good seed is the Son of man; (38) and the field is the world; and the good seed, these are the sons of the kingdom; and the tares are the sons of the evil [one]. We are likened to seeds sown in the world. The dirt of this world represents corruption, and yet it is Jesus' carefully tilled soil, created to kill the husk of the seed so that the life within will come forth. All the dirt is involved in God's plan, including the wicked. Those who insult us and persecute us are part of this dirt. Even the people that fall away are part of God's plan because they are an example and a warning to the righteous.

(Lam.3:25) The Lord is good unto them that <u>wait for him</u>, to the soul that seeketh him. (26) It is good that a man should hope and <u>quietly wait</u> for the salvation of the Lord. We should patiently wait under the dirt of many adverse situations, for the time will come that the Lord will save us if we walk by faith. *(27) It is good for a man that he bear the yoke in his youth.* When we are young in the Lord, we tend to act more impulsively instead of patiently enduring the yoke of the dirt

146

of corruption around us. *(28) Let him sit alone and keep silence, because <u>he hath laid it upon him</u>.* Let us not fight with the dirt. God has put this yoke upon us for the seed to bear fruit. *(29) Let him put his mouth in the dust, if so be there may be hope.* In other words, let us speak humbly so that there may be hope of deliverance from the yoke of the corruption around us. *(30) Let him give his cheek to him that smiteth him; let him be filled full with reproach.* Many are not cooperating with God's plan; they are disobedient to Jesus' commands to *"resist not him that is evil"* and to *"turn the other cheek."* This is part of God's plan, to humble us and crucify the old nature in us. It is part of the yoke. *(31) <u>For the Lord will not cast off forever</u>.* There are times when it seems like the Lord has forgotten us. Yes, but we would not want him to dig us up before we sprout!

(Lam.3:32) For though <u>he cause grief, yet will he have compassion</u> according to the multitude of his loving kindnesses. (33) For <u>he doth not afflict willingly</u> (Hebrew: "from the heart")*, nor grieve the children of men.* God is not taking pleasure in the judgment of the wicked or the chastening of His children. God is doing many things that pain Him, but He is doing them to bring about the necessary end. When we see God taking the credit for all these things, do not think that God is hard. If we do, it is because our understanding is still incomplete.

He takes no pleasure in the creation or destruction of the wicked, but He does take credit for both. *(Pr.16:4) The <u>Lord hath made everything for its own end</u>* (Some manuscripts say: *for His own purpose*.)*: Yea, <u>even the wicked for the day of evil</u>.* The wicked are necessary to be examples of God's righteous judgment and to chasten the elect in the *"day of evil."* To God, the few who are righteous are worth far more than a whole world full of the wicked. The Bible says, *"The wicked are a ransom for the righteous."* A ransom is the price that must be paid for someone's freedom. God has determined that the creation of the wicked is a price that must be paid to bring the righteous out of bondage. *(Mt.24:9) Then shall they deliver you up unto tribulation, and shall kill you: and ye shall be <u>hated of all the nations</u> for <u>my name's sake</u>.* We are hated so that the name (Greek: "character and authority") of the Lord may be manifest in us. This is exactly what God did to the Egyptians' hearts in order to separate Israel from them. *(Ps.105:25) <u>He turned their heart to hate his people</u>, to deal subtly with his servants.* God will cause the world to hate us for His *"name's sake."* God's nature is manifest in those who are separated from the world through tribulation. When He is through doing this work in our life, He delivers us. *(Ps.106:10) And <u>he saved them from the hand of him that hated them</u>, and redeemed them from the hand of the enemy.*

(Job 5:17) Behold, happy is the man whom <u>God correcteth</u>. Therefore despise not thou the <u>chastening of the Almighty</u>. (18) <u>For he maketh sore. And bindeth up; He woundeth, and his hands make whole</u>. Our God is sovereignly, intimately involved in our upbringing. He has not left us to the "free will" of evil. He works all things together for our good. Correction in the form of making sore or wounding comes from His loving hands, and after we have been corrected, He will bind up our wounds and make us whole. Happy is the man who will be corrected easily, by God's Word instead of His chastening. *(Pr.29:19) A servant will not be corrected by words; for though he understand, he will not give heed.* The foolish will not be corrected and will continue to bring destruction on themselves. God must turn us in our short lives and before we wreak havoc on ourselves and others. For lack of repentance many must sadly be taken out. God sent the curse, and God sent Jesus to deliver us. These are two hands of the same loving Father. *(Ps.90:3) <u>Thou turnest man to destruction, And sayest, Return, ye children of men</u>.*

Many churches teach that God uses wounds and judgment to bring people to a place of humbleness, but that is where

148

they stop. They leave the poor chastened person without hope of deliverance. What father chastens without end? And if he does, it is because there is no repentance. *(Ps.34:17) [The righteous] cried, and the Lord heard, And <u>delivered them out of all their troubles</u>. (18) The Lord is nigh unto them that are of a broken heart, and <u>saveth such as are of a contrite spirit</u>. (19) Many are the afflictions of the righteous; but <u>the Lord delivereth him out of them all</u>.* If we believe that the Lord delivers from all troubles, then in this regard we are justified or reckoned righteous.

Justification or righteousness is by faith. *(Rom.4:3) For what saith the scripture? And Abraham believed God, and it was reckoned unto him for righteousness.* Abraham believed that God would give him a son. Did that have anything to do with salvation? No! God called him righteous because he believed His promise. That was it. God justifies or accounts us righteous for believing His promises. People have tied this justification only to initial salvation rather than the continual deliverance of the soul from corrupt thinking. We need to be justified in all areas of our life, which is what the promises cover. Justification concerning a promise is necessary in order to have it fulfilled. *(Rom.4:18) Who in hope believed against hope, to the end that he might become a father of many nations … (20) yet, <u>looking unto the promise of God, he wavered not through unbelief, but waxed strong through faith</u>, giving glory to God, (21) and <u>being fully assured that what he had promised, he was able also to perform</u>. (22) <u>Wherefore also it was reckoned unto him for righteousness</u>.* What God promised, Abraham believed and therefore was entitled to. God spoke through Elizabeth to Mary.

(Lk.1:45) And <u>blessed [is] she that believed; for there shall be a fulfillment of the things which have been spoken to her from the Lord</u>. None of the promises will be fulfilled if we do not believe them. Justification has to come first. *(Rom.5:1) Being therefore <u>justified by faith</u>, we have peace with God through our Lord Jesus Christ; (2) through whom also we*

have had <u>our access by faith into this grace</u> wherein we stand. Faith in the promises gives us access to grace for salvation, healing, provision, or deliverance from the curse. Anytime we are standing in the grace, we are there because we are justified by our faith. When we agree with the Word of God, even before we see it come to pass, God calls us justified or righteous, therefore, we get the blessing of the righteous. *(Gal.3:13) <u>Christ redeemed us from the curse of the law, having become a curse for us</u>; for it is written, Cursed is every one that hangeth on a tree: (14) that upon the Gentiles might come the blessing of Abraham in Christ Jesus; that we might receive the promise of the Spirit through faith.* It does not honor God for us to bear a curse that He says was put on Jesus. It angers God that many self-righteously keep a curse because of a false humility, therefore, Jesus suffered their curse for nothing. Those with true humility believe the promises.

(Ex.15:26) And he said, If thou wilt diligently hearken to the voice of the Lord thy God, and wilt do that which is right in his eyes, and wilt give ear to his commandments, and keep all his statutes, <u>I will put none of the diseases upon thee, which I have put upon the Egyptians</u>: for I am the Lord that healeth thee. The condition for divine health is being humble to God's Word. God is taking credit for the diseases that the Egyptians get as well as the Israelites. Yet, much of the Church is saying sickness is not from God. They have a one-handed God of blessing only. They reason that Jesus *"went about doing good and healing all that were oppressed of the devil; for God was with him" (Acts 10:38)*, which is true. The devil has a legal right to oppress the sinner and the unbelieving "Christian," but Jesus has a legal right to deliver the repentant believer. The curse is to motivate us to listen to God's Word and keep the commandments. We cannot pick and choose verses if we want the truth. We have to believe them all and fit them together.

God shares with us what it is to be a good Father. His tough love approach brings pain to the flesh, which causes us to count the cost and to turn before it is too late. *(Pr.22:15) Foolishness is bound up in the heart of a child; But <u>the rod of correction</u> shall drive it far from him. (Pr.13:24) <u>He that spareth his rod hateth his son</u>; But he that loveth him chasteneth him betimes. (Pr.23:14) Thou shalt beat him with the rod, And shalt <u>deliver his soul from Sheol</u>.* The "He" in verse (Pr.13:24) can be speaking of God or of us. The one who avoids chastening his children *"hateth"* them. The chastening curse is God's love toward us. When we are carnal, love does not motivate us, and when we are ignorant, fear does not motivate us. If pain is the only thing that motivates us to stop sinning and start believing, then that is what is necessary, considering that the alternative is damnation.

Jesus, hearing of Lazarus' death said, *"This is not unto death, but for the glory of God" (Jn.11:4)*. God always does things for more than one reason. The primary reason for Lazarus' death was "for the glory of God," so that the works of God might be seen. We see the purpose that is right under our noses, but God has other, higher motives. *(Jn.9:1) And as he passed by, he saw a man blind from his birth. (2) And his disciples asked him, saying, Rabbi, who sinned* (Greek: "who was sinning") *this man, or his parents, that he should be born blind?* They were suspecting a specific sin that these people were doing that would cause this man to be born blind. Do you know what the religious leaders said to this man after he was healed? *(34) They answered and said unto him, <u>Thou wast altogether born in sins</u>, and dost thou teach us? And they cast him out.* Did they think that because they were Pharisees or Sadducees, they were not born in sin? No, they were not quite that arrogant.

What was different about this man that caused them to say, *"Thou wast altogether born in sins"*? Paul said, *"All have sinned and have come short of the glory of God."* Do you suppose it might have had anything to do with a sin that they knew was common to those born blind? It could be that they thought venereal disease caused most blindness. According to

151

Zondervan Encyclopedia of the Bible, "The blindness from birth spoken of in the Bible was probably opthalmia neonatorum (gonorrhea of the eyes). This has been the prime cause of infantile blindness for centuries." Listen to what Jesus said. *(3) Jesus answered, Neither did this man sin, nor his parents: but <u>that the works of God should be made manifest</u> in him.* Jesus was not saying this man and his parents were the first sinless family on earth, for *"there is none righteous, no, not one."* God's primary purpose for this man's blindness was not because of his sins but for people to see the miracles of God. The secondary purpose was sin.

Jesus commanded a lame man to take up his bed and walk. *(Jn.5:14) Afterward Jesus findeth him in the temple, and said unto him, Behold, thou art made whole: <u>sin no more, lest a worse thing befall thee</u>.* That does not sound like Jesus believed that sickness or the curse would come upon you if you had no sin. How can the curse of sin (Deuteronomy 28) come on a man that is not a sinner?

Some would argue that Job had not sinned because God called him *"a perfect and an upright man, one that feareth God, and turneth away from evil" (Job 1:8)*. Job also denied that he was guilty of any outward immorality, which was true. His three friends were wrong to accuse him because *"... they had found no answer, and yet had condemned Job" (Job 32:3)*. God rebuked them for not speaking the truth and commanded them to sacrifice (Job 42:7-9).

The fourth man Elihu addressed Job for six chapters and was never corrected by God (Job 32-37). His assessment of Job was that *"he justified himself rather than God" (32:2)*. To this, God Himself agreed in His address to Job. *(Job 40:8) Wilt thou even annul my judgment? Wilt thou condemn me, that thou mayest be justified?* God corrected Job for four chapters (Job 38-41). Job *"was righteous in his own eyes" (32:1)*.

How does Job's self-righteousness square with God's first opinion of him as an upright man? God was speaking faith about Job because of his right standing through blood sacrifice. *(Rom.4:17) … God, who giveth life to the dead and calleth the things that are not as though they were.* He declares the end from the beginning (Isa.46:10). God speaks faith about us as His method of creation. As we walk in the light we have, God calls us righteous because of the blood of Jesus. Job was walking in the light that he knew; that which he did not know was under the blood. Through tribulation, God reveals to us ugly things we did not know about ourselves. As we confess and renounce these, we are cleansed and continue to stay in right standing with Him (1 Jn.1:7-9). Job was being delivered of the sin nature by chastening. God's purpose is to use the chastening of the curse to glorify us in His eyes.

God uses the curse to glorify Himself and His Son in our eyes. Jesus taried two days when told Lazarus was sick. *(Jn.11:4) But when Jesus heard it, he said, <u>This sickness is not unto death, but for the glory of God, that the Son of God may be glorified there by</u>. (6) When therefore he heard that he was sick, he abode at that time two days in the place where he was.* Jesus arrived late (Jn.11:39) to serve God's purpose. *(Jn.11:40) Jesus saith unto her, Said I not unto thee, that, if thou believedst, thou shouldest <u>see the glory of God</u>?* This miracle glorified God, causing many to believe Jesus (Jn.11:43-45).

Chapter 9
God's Sovereignty Over Signs, Chance, and Confirmations

And the Pharisees and Sadducees came, and trying him asked him to show them a sign from heaven. But he answered and said ... Ye know how to discern the face of the heaven; but ye cannot [discern] the signs of the times. An evil and adulterous generation seeketh after a sign; and <u>there shall no sign be given unto it, but the sign of Jonah</u> (Mt.16:1-4).

There is a fairly large section of Christianity that believes asking God for signs is wrong. The reason is because they do not believe in the signs themselves. Matthew 16:1-4 is not Jesus' answer to everyone, but to an *"evil and adulterous generation."* They saw the signs and wonders that He did, yet they wanted another sign that He was who He said He was, so He gave them the sign of Jonah. What sign would benefit these people anyway? They rebuked Jesus and claimed that His signs were from Beelzebub. Their type says the same thing about signs today. The blind man, who had no seminary degree, but had been healed by Jesus, gave them a common sense answer. *(Jn.9:30) ... Why, <u>herein is the marvel, that ye know not whence he is, and [yet] he opened mine eyes</u>. (31) We know that <u>God heareth not sinners</u>: but if any man be a worshipper of God, and <u>do his will, him he heareth</u>. (32) Since the world began it was never heard that any one opened the eyes of a man born blind. (33) <u>If this man were not from God, he could do nothing</u>. (34) They answered and said unto him, Thou wast altogether born in sins, and dost thou teach us? And they cast him out.* So it is with signs done by Jesus through disciples today! According to this description, obedient servants sent by God do signs.

Honest hearts everywhere recognize signs are from God for the purpose of confirming His true Word. *(Jn.3:1) Now there was a man of the Pharisees, named*

Nicodemus, a ruler of the Jews: (2) the same came unto him by night, and said to him, Rabbi, <u>we know that thou art a teacher come from God; for no one can do these signs that thou doest, except God be with him</u>. Nicodemus recognized the signs of healings, deliverances, provisions, and miracles that Jesus had been performing proved He was from God. When Jesus was leaving, He told the disciples how to identify those who believed the gospel. *(Mk.16: 15) And he said unto them, Go ye into all the world, and preach the Gospel to the whole creation. (16) He that believeth and is baptized shall be saved; but he that disbelieveth shall be condemned. (17) These <u>signs shall accompany them that believe</u>: in my name shall they cast out demons; they shall speak with new tongues; (18) they shall take up serpents, and if they drink any deadly thing, it shall in no wise hurt them; they shall lay hands on the sick, and they shall recover.* Notice that Jesus was not speaking of the signs of the disciples but rather of the signs of those who would believe their testimony. Only later did He speak of the signs done through His first disciples. *(20) And they went forth, and preached everywhere, the Lord working with them, and <u>confirming the word by the signs that followed</u>. Amen.* Since it is not the experience of many to have their words confirmed by signs, they tend to change the doctrine of Jesus to a modern gospel that affirms their new methods. *(Heb.13:8) Jesus Christ [is] the same yesterday and to day, [yea] and forever.* God still confirms His Word with signs through those who believe the true Gospel. If we change the Word we will not see signs because God confirms His Word, not ours. Jesus is the only one Who can give us the criteria of a believer. *(Jn.14:12) … <u>He that believeth on me, the works that I do shall he do also</u>; and greater [works] than these shall he do; because I go unto the Father.* The only criterion to have signs is to truly believe on the Jesus of the Bible.

Some who reject the supernatural parts of discipleship today reject all signs. *(Isa.7:10) And the Lord spake* *again unto Ahaz, saying, (11) <u>Ask thee a sign of the Lord thy God</u>; ask it either in the depth, or in the height above* (In other words, ask for a sign anywhere.) *(12) But <u>Ahaz said, I will not ask, neither will I tempt the Lord</u>. (13) And he said, Hear ye now, O house of David: Is it a small thing for you to weary men, that ye will <u>weary my God</u> also? (14) Therefore <u>the Lord himself will give you a sign</u>: behold, a virgin shall conceive, and bear a son, and shall call his name Immanuel.* The evil Ahaz's excuse for disobeying the Lord concerning a sign was so that he would not tempt the Lord. Does that sound ludicrous? Never more than today! The people who say you should not ask the Lord for a sign *"weary my God."* All through the Bible, God's people ask for signs and get them. God wants us to know correct direction and to confirm His words to those that hear.

I will speak more on signs of healings, deliverances, miracles, and provisions in a later chapter. For now I would like to deal with signs for knowledge, wisdom, warning, and direction for our lives. In Acts 2:17, we are told that in the <u>last days</u> God's Spirit would bring forth prophecy, dreams, and visions. Job 33:14-18 says that God speaks in dreams or visions to open men's ears, seal their instructions, withdraw them from wrong purpose, deliver man from pride, keep his soul from the pit, and keep him from perishing by the sword, but man regards it not! To a large extent these signs and confirmations are being ignored today. Sometimes dreams and visions are literal. Sometimes they are parables and need interpreting in the light of Scriptures. Joseph, Daniel, and Jacob, to name a few, were great examples of men that God used to interpret these signs.

There are five signs given in dreams in Matthew 1 and 2 in which God spoke to give wisdom, direction, warning, and to fulfill prophecy. Joseph was told by an angel in a <u>dream</u> to not fear to take Mary for his wife. The sign of the star led the wise men to Jesus. They were then warned in a <u>dream</u> to not return to Herod who wanted the location of Jesus so that he could kill Him. Joseph was then warned by an angel in a <u>dream</u> to take Jesus and flee to Egypt. Later he was told by an angel in a <u>dream</u> to return for Herod was dead. He was then told in a <u>dream</u> where to settle in order to fulfill prophecy that called Jesus a Nazarene.

The New Testament is replete with these kinds of signs and the disciples acted upon them as direction from God. *(Acts 16:9) And a <u>vision</u> appeared to Paul in the night: There was a man of Macedonia standing, beseeching him, and saying, Come over into Macedonia, and help us. (10) And <u>when he had seen the vision</u>, straightway we <u>sought to go forth</u> into Macedonia, concluding that <u>God had called us to preach</u> the Gospel to them.* The disciples saw a <u>vision</u> of Jesus glorified on the mountain. Zacharias saw Gabriel in a <u>vision</u>. Angels appeared to women in a <u>vision</u> telling them that Jesus was alive. A <u>vision</u> brought Paul to the Lord (and many in our day). A <u>vision</u> brought Ananias to Paul to heal and fill him with the Holy Spirit. Ananias' coming was confirmed to Paul in a <u>vision</u>. An angel appeared to Cornelius in a <u>vision</u> sending him to Peter for the knowledge of salvation. Meantime Peter was given a <u>vision</u> that was interpreted by him to mean that the Gentiles would be saved. The Lord comforted Paul in a <u>vision</u> telling him to not fear but preach boldly for the sake of many who would believe. John was given the <u>vision</u> of Revelation.

When I was a very young disciple, I asked the Lord concerning opposing views of the rapture. I was in my living room, with the Scriptures before me, praying to God for understanding. I was having trouble fitting together what appeared to be opposing Scriptures. Suddenly understanding flooded my mind in what I knew later was the Word of Wisdom. The Scriptures suddenly all fit together. I jumped up very excited and ran into the kitchen to tell my wife what had happened. I had never received such an obviously supernatural revelation, and since it was not one that I had ever heard before, <u>I asked</u>

the Lord to give me a sign. The sign that I asked of Him was that He would send someone to me who would tell me exactly what He had shown me.

For about a week, I told my friends at the local assembly of my revelation. I was told more than once that I had missed God. Then a minister showed up at a school dedication that the assembly was having on a Friday night. Some of the more "mature" brethren drew the minister aside to convert him to their way of thinking. I left that evening not knowing what had happened but was later contacted by brethren who told me that this minister had told them the exact thing that I had been telling them.

I invited the minister, whose name was Bolivar, to my house along with some of the brethren. When Bolivar heard my name he was excited, and began to share with me recent happenings that brought him to our assembly. When he was in Opelousas, Louisiana, he was given a vision of Route 61. In the vision he saw a sign on Route 61 that said, "Three miles to three L's." He found Route 61 on a map and followed it to Baton Rouge where we lived, but he still did not understand the vision. He looked in the phone book for an assembly to visit. Even though our denomination was his last preference because of its narrow-minded sectarianism, he felt impressed to go. Our city had many churches, but he ended up at ours on this Friday night. After he had been to my house and had realized that my name was Eells (sometimes pronounced "L's") and that there were three of us, he decided to check the odometer. He found that it was exactly three miles from Route 61 to my driveway! A sovereign God can get you where He wants you. Bolivar shared the same revelation that the Lord had given me a week before. Notice that the confirmation was given through a literal sign.

There were three brethren at the Bible study that day who were looking for a confirmation to a revelation, myself included. Don Robertson, a close friend from my youth and the man who witnessed to me, was there. He had received a vision some years before in which he saw a brown-skinned man, dressed in a particular way, sitting before him telling him the truth about the rapture. When he came in that day, he recognized Bolivar to be that man, even dressed the same as in his vision. The Lord said, "There he is, sit down, and listen." Another friend, Skip Chenevert, had a revelation on the sons of God, which Bolivar confirmed. He also told Mary and me that one day we would move to Florida, which happened.

The lot is a very important sign in the Scriptures. It can be a very useful tool to ask God for a confirmation, a direction, or to give peace between people. Be advised, the lot is not a tool for fortune telling, nor can it be used for anything other than righteous endeavor. Suppose that you think you have the mind of the Lord in an instance and someone else thinks they too have the mind of the Lord, but you are contrary to one another. The lot is a way to decide. *(Pr.18:18) The lot causeth contentions to cease, and parteth between the mighty.* My oldest daughter and another man's daughter had gotten into some trouble when they were children. He and his daughter were blaming my daughter. My daughter was saying the opposite, and I wanted the truth. I cast a lot, and the Lord told me very plainly that he was wrong and his daughter was lying, which eventually proved to be true.

Some people say the lot is not spiritual in these days. What is spiritual about being contrary to one another? If you are in a group of people, who may not trust what you are saying but will trust in the Lord, and you need a decision, the lot can decide. But the lot can fail. We saw in Ezekiel 14 that He would deceive one who put an idol before their face and then asked direction of the Lord. If you have an ulterior motive, it doesn't matter whether the answer comes from a prophet, the Word of God, your own thinking, or the lot, you are asking to be deceived. Repent and commit your way to the Lord and then ask.

In Leviticus 16, we find the law for the annual atonement. The priest would take two goats and would cast a lot to see which goat would be sacrificed and which would be the scapegoat, which would be set free. In this case, two stones were used, a black stone and a white stone. The white stone was called "the lot of the Lord," and the black stone was called "the lot of Azazel (scapegoat)." In this case, it is really talking about the Lord and us. He was the sin sacrifice for us to be set free. The high priest would reach in his bag and pull out a stone, which would be either black or white. That sign would indicate what would happen to the goat standing in front of the high priest.

Let me relate a little bit of history. According to the Talmud, 240 years before Jesus, there was a high priest who was called Simon the Righteous. Simon the Righteous was known to be a faithful and honorable high priest. He started his ministry 240 years before the birth of Jesus, and continued for forty years. When Simon reached into his bag, he came out with the lot of the Lord every time for forty straight years. This came to be known as a sign of God's approval of their sacrifice. Simon also wore a crimson cord into the holy of holies for forty years. Every time Simon wore that cord into the holy of holies, it turned white. This probably symbolized the cleansing of the blood.

Simon also had a vision every time he was about to enter the holy of holies. He saw a man dressed in white enter in with him. Then when he came out, he saw a vision of the man coming out with him. On the last day of Simon's ministry, a man dressed in black went in with him but did not come back out. Simon himself correctly interpreted this to mean he would die. On that day he died. For the next 200 years, there was no sign. The stone came up as would be commonly expected, fairly split between the lot of the Lord and the lot of Azazel. That led us up to the time of the crucifixion. Then there was another forty years from the crucifixion to the destruction of the temple. During that period, every time the high priest reached into his bag, he came out with the black stone. Of course, they considered that a sign of God's disapproval of their sacrifice. When they rejected Jesus, God rejected their sacrifices. The chance against this happening for forty straight years was 1 trillion, 100 billion, to 1. This sign of the lot proved the sovereignty of God in the New Testament and Jesus as the Messiah.

Many today, because they do not believe in the sovereignty of God, believe in what they call luck, chance, gambling, or fate. There is no such thing as any of that. That is a fiction of their imagination. Sometimes it is a deception by a demon spirit. *(Gal.6:7) Be not deceived; God is not mocked: for whatsoever a man soweth, that shall he also reap. (Jn.3:27) John answered and said, A man can receive nothing, except it have been given him from heaven.* We are actually making our own future by believing or disbelieving the promises of God and by sowing our own seed and reaping a harvest, good or bad.

(Pr.16:33) <u>The lot is cast into the lap; But the whole disposing thereof is of the Lord</u>. The Lord decides which way the lot comes up. It does not matter how you do it, whether you are using stones or flipping a nickel or asking God for a sign, just so you are asking God for direction by faith. In faith, God will give you an answer. I have proved this in my own life, time after time. Is that the way we should lead our lives? No, I think we should learn to hear the Holy Spirit, but let us face the facts here; we are not sure of what we hear sometimes and would like a confirmation.

There were other signs according to the Talmud that happened in the forty years after Jesus' crucifixion. The western lamp of the menorah in the holy place would go out every night. They went through a lot of pain to make sure that the menorah never went out, because it was a symbol of the life of Israel. They had vessels that emptied into the menorah to make sure that it never ran out of oil. The priest's job was to make sure that it never ran out of oil. The light of God's people was never supposed to go out, but it did every night for forty straight years. The chance, if you believe in such, against that happening is beyond reason. This was a clear sign that God was reprobating Israel. Also, the door to the holy of holies would open seemingly by itself every night, despite the efforts of the priests to stop it. This was a sign from God for us to enter into the holy of holies (presence of God) through faith in Jesus Christ (Heb.10:19,20). Another sign that proved this is that the veil in front of the holy of holies was rent in two from top to bottom when Jesus was crucified (Mt.27:51). There was no reason for the priests to make a false report concerning this, because it certainly was not a good sign to them. God is sovereign in signs.

Can you imagine that God would have such control that He could make the lot choose one offender out of a ship full of people? In Jonah 1, Jonah rebelled and ran from the Lord. While in a ship, a great storm came up and the men feared exceedingly that they would sink. *(Jnh.1:7) And they said every one to his fellow, Come, and let us cast lots, that we may know for whose cause this evil is upon us. So they cast lots, and <u>the lot fell upon Jonah</u>.* What are the chances, of casting lots on that ship and coming up with Jonah? They are phenomenal! God is sovereign, and those pagans knew it better than most Christians today. Maybe they did not know what God they were praying to, but they knew whoever He was, He was sovereign. They knew that someone in the boat was causing a curse to befall everyone and they believed the lot would reveal who it was. Their wisdom puts the Church to shame. God through Paul commanded the Corinthians to put the wicked people out of the Church for that reason (1 Cor.5).

For several years, Mary and I had been receiving visions and dreams about moving from the Baton Rouge, Louisiana area to Pensacola, Florida. One time, as we were talking about it, I went to the Lord and asked, "When are these visions and dreams going to come to pass?" I went to my Bible and opened it. As I looked down, my eyes fell immediately on Habakkuk 2:3 which states: ***For the vision is yet for the appointed time, and it hasteth toward the end, and shall not lie: though it tarry, wait for it; because it will surely come, it will not delay***. That was God's sign to us. It was specific and to the point. At that time Mary and I were impatient and wondering when we were going to move. We watched almost no TV, but I walked over and turned it on and there was Charles Stanley speaking the words, "They that wait upon the Lord." We knew that those words were a sign for us to be patient. Then I walked over to this little breadbox with the Scripture cards in it. I picked out a card and without looking at it showed it to Mary. It said, "They that wait upon the Lord." That was three confirmations in a row. The Lord wanted us to rest and wait, for He was going to bring it to pass in His time. If we believe in God's sovereignty to speak through signs and confirmations, He can give such peace in the midst of trials!

Mary had a dream while she was pregnant. *In the dream she saw a big boy and a little girl. As she was waking up a voice said, "Justin Joseph and Jennifer Joy."* We both thought surely we are going to have twins. In the course of time, Mary gave birth in our home to a 7lb.15oz. normal-size boy, but no girl. This surprised us because we were used to having our dreams come true. Mary's thinking was that the dream would be fulfilled later with twins. I said to her, "No, Mary, this is Justin Joseph. He was bigger in your dream because he was to be born first, and Jennifer Joy was smaller because she will be born later." She was not at all convinced and we needed to know what to name this boy. I pulled three quarters out of my pocket. I told her, "Let's ask God to give us a sign. I am going to flip these and they are all going to come down heads, because this is Justin." After we prayed, I flipped the quarters, and they all came down heads. She still was not convinced. I said, "I am going to do it again, and they are all going to come down heads." I did, and they all came down heads again. She said, "Well, I don't know, David." I said, "OK, I am going to do this one more time, and then we are not going to tempt the Lord any more." You guessed it! They all came down heads. What are the "chances" of nine heads in a row? Mary was convinced. *(Pr.18:18) The lot causeth contentions to cease, And parteth between the mighty.* Two years and three months later, our little girl Jennifer Joy was born. Justin Joseph means "just increaser," and Jennifer Joy means "pure joy." Their names, given by the Lord, fit their attributes.

The birth of Jennifer was a sign of God's timing to us that we were about to move to Pensacola. About five years before her birth, Mary had a dream that we were walking through a house in Pensacola, and I had a baby girl on my hip. (This was perfectly fulfilled at the time we moved.) Also, in the dream, she knew that the Interstate was completed from Baton Rouge to Pensacola. This stretch of interstate had been notoriously under construction for many years but was completed by the time we moved. The value of these signs to know that you are in the perfect Will of God cannot be measured. Without respect for Scriptural signs Christians many times go their own way to their detriment. The Word does not tell us when or where to move, who to marry, or where to work, but it does demonstrate the signs that God uses to give such direction.

When Jennifer was about sixteen months old, we knew we were about to move to Pensacola because she was now the size she was in the dream. At this time, I had asked some brethren to agree with me that God would give us a house and give us a car in Pensacola. We agreed according to the Word. *(Mt.18:19) Again I say unto you, that if two of you shall agree on earth as touching anything that they shall ask, it shall be done for them of my Father who is in heaven.* A week after this prayer of faith, my wife Mary and daughter Deborah were in a car wreck, driving down <u>Florida Boulevard</u> in Baton Rouge. I emphasize <u>Florida Boulevard</u> because this was <u>a sign</u> that this wreck played an important part in putting us on the interstate boulevard to Florida. They had come to a stop behind a Cadillac. A man in a Lincoln was looking at the sights and rear-ended our Toyota, driving it into the Cadillac, totaling our car and slightly injuring them. While they were using the "jaws of life" to open the car, a man came and told Mary, "Don't worry, he has good insurance," which she thought was strange. The man who drove the Lincoln was very remorseful. He told us he was the president of a large warehouse corporation and that his company was self-insured. He had 100/300/100 insurance on his car. He told us that he would speak to his insurance representatives on our behalf. What are the "chances" of being hit by someone like that? The insurance people were very generous with us, as you might expect. God chose this method to answer my prayer that God would give us a house and car. They replaced the wrecked car with a better one. With the settlement money, we were able to replace our larger family car with a new one and purchase our house, and all with non-taxable money. This settlement ties in with another story.

Rick Knight was a young friend of ours when we lived in the Baton Rouge area. About five years before the wreck, Rick had a dream. *He had been gone from our neighborhood for a while and had come for a visit to our neighbor Bruce's home. In the dream, Bruce told him to look towards our home. When he did, he saw a moving van backed up to our place. We were moving to Pensacola. When he came over to help us load up the van, I showed him some papers that had the word "pension" written on them. I told him, "I am never going to work for man again."*

The Spirit convinced me of Rick's dream when I heard it. I told people where I worked that I was about to retire and move to Pensacola. Of course, they all told me that at 37 there is no way they would offer me retirement. They were all proven wrong. The Exxon refinery decided they wanted to replace some of their employees that had expensive benefits with contract labor. They offered retirement to anyone who had worked over fifteen years. When this was offered, I did not have to think about it because I had my signs. Several people came to me and recounted that I had told them that this was going to happen. It was a witness to them that God can tell us of the future.

We had not seen Rick for a few years, but the weekend that we were moving, he showed up at Bruce's house. Bruce pointed him toward our home. What he saw was what he had seen in the dream; we had a moving van backed up to our place. As Rick excitedly helped us to load the van, I shared with him about my pension. I had received a one-year severance pay with a small retirement when I reach retirement age, should Exxon still be solvent and the Lord tarry that long. The year's pay came in at the same time as the first of two installments of insurance money from the wreck. This was enough for our house in Pensacola and enough to live on for a year. The second installment was settled and came after we gave our car to a mission in Pensacola. Then we were able to buy a new car. The sign of the dream was perfectly fulfilled.

You might think, "How could he never work for man again with that kind of pension?" A few months before leaving Baton Rouge, the Lord gave me another sign. In a vision, I suddenly appeared before an immense palace that I believe represented the New Jerusalem. A large door opened and the Lord was standing there dressed as a King. He ushered me inside and showed me a tower that was built of logs like a log cabin but narrowing toward the top, where there was a place to stand. He revealed to me that this represented my ministry. He also showed me a payment book with a certain amount per month in it. He said, "I want you to have this," meaning the tower and the payment. We have lived on an average of that amount per month, coming miraculously from many directions, since

1986. Although we had lean months and fat months to try us, over the year it averaged what the Lord said per month. We have had to walk by faith to receive it. This sign gave me faith that God would supply my needs without some visible means of support.

After this, in another vision, I was caught up high above the Baton Rouge area, where I lived. As I looked toward Florida, I saw that tower in Pensacola. A few months later, God had miraculously bought us a house and car in Pensacola, Florida, where we now live. The Lord gave me some insight to the meaning of the tower. The individual logs are the saints who are likened to trees in many Scriptures. At the corners where they united, crosses were formed. God's people coming together in unity bearing their own cross would create a tower of safety from their enemies. The Israelites built towers like this in their cities and sometimes among their flocks to protect them from invading enemies (Jdg.9:46,51). *(Pr.18:10) The name* (Hebrew: "character and authority") *of the Lord is a strong tower; the righteous runneth into it, and is safe.* Truth builds of us a tower of the character and authority of Jesus to defend us from enemies. Very hard times and many enemies are coming. Get behind the high walls of spiritual Zion, the *"tower of the flock"* (Mic.4:8).

Many times in my experience, the Lord has used the lot as a sign to prove God's sovereignty and direction to others. I was asking the Lord what to do with our mobile home when we knew we were about to move to Pensacola. Mary was asking me if we should sell it. As I prayed about it, the Lord impressed me to give it to a Christian couple named Mike and Karen Burley whom we knew in Houston, Texas. So I contacted them only to find out that they had just lost their job and their company house. When I told Mary what the Lord told me, she was not sure. I wanted the Lord to confirm to Mary that giving away our home was indeed God's direction. So to give her peace of mind, I suggested that we ask of the Lord a sign.

I asked God to confirm this decision with six heads in a row, and that is exactly what we got. What is the "chance" of six heads in a row coming up? It convinced Mary. Without telling them what the Lord had said, I invited them to move in with us temporarily. Mary reminded me that Karen had a dream some years before that we had left our area and returned some time later to find someone else was living in our home. We did not think to ask her at the time if she knew who it was. When they moved in, I reminded them of the dream. Then I said to Karen, "I think I know who it was that was living in our home. It was you, wasn't it?" Karen said, "Yes, it was." (She wisely did not tell us when she first told us the dream because she did not want it to be a self-fulfilled prophecy.) I said, "Well then it's your home." Of course, they were exited to see how God had provided for them even before their need. A couple of months later, God provided us a house and car in Pensacola. The occurrences after the lot certainly proved the sign and the sovereignty of God. You try it sometime. I am not telling you to lead your life by the lot, but I am talking about confirmations and directions. As a sign agrees with your spirit, it teaches you to be more confident that it is the Lord who is speaking to you. We do not need six heads for proof. The more confident we become, the less proof we need that it is God who is speaking.

The children of Israel by the lot decided who got what part of the Promised Land. By the lot, they decided who was going to war first. The lot left no room for argument. There are times when it is needed because even spiritual people do not always agree, nor can you get them to always believe you. In 1 Samuel 10:1, Samuel secretly anointed Saul to be king. Later, he had to prove this direction of the Lord to the people. *(1 Sam.10:19) But ye have this day rejected your God, who himself saveth you out of all your calamities and your distresses; and ye have said unto him, Nay, but set a king over us. Now therefore present yourselves before the Lord by* *your tribes, and by your thousands. (20) So <u>Samuel brought all the tribes of Israel near, and the tribe of Benjamin was taken</u>. "Was taken"* means that when they cast the lot, out of the twelve tribes, the tribe of Benjamin was taken. *(21) And he brought the tribe of Benjamin near by their families; and the family of the Matrites <u>was taken</u>: and Saul the son of Kish <u>was taken</u>.* The lot narrowed it down to the one who was already anointed to be king. Of all Israel, it came down to Saul. We have the same sovereign God in the New Testament. There is no such thing as chance. Why did not Samuel say, "The Lord told me the king is Saul, and I have already anointed him"? Why did not Samuel anoint Saul in front of others, so that they would know it? God did not want there to be an argument, or a division in Israel over picking a king. After all was said and done, and Saul fell away and made foolish mistakes, God did not want the people to come back and blame Samuel for having picked the wrong king. The only ones that did not respect the lot were called "worthless fellows." *(1 Sam.10:27) But certain <u>worthless fellows</u> said, how shall this man save us?*

Jonathan asked a sign from the Lord. *(1 Sam.14:6) And Jonathan said to the young man that bare his armor, Come, and let us go over unto the garrison of these uncircumcised* (Philistines)*: it may be that the Lord will work for us; for <u>there is no restraint of the Lord to save by many or by few</u>. (7) And his armor bearer said unto him, Do all that is in thy heart: turn thee, behold, I am with thee according to thy heart. (8) Then said Jonathan, Behold, we will pass over unto the men, and we will disclose ourselves unto them. (9) If they say thus unto us, Tarry until we come to you; then we will stand still in our place, and will not go up unto them. (10) But if they say thus, Come up unto us; then we will go up; for the Lord hath delivered them into our hand: and <u>this shall be the sign unto us</u>.* He had faith that the Lord would honor his sign and put these thoughts and words in the Philistines. He also did not believe the devil could give him a wrong answer. God is faithful and wants us to ask of Him a sign so that He can prove Himself to us and give us victory over our enemies. Jonathan got the sign that he asked and knew that God had given the Philistines into his hand. As soon as Jonathan wiped out about an acre's worth of Philistines, there was an earthquake to cause the rest to flee. While the Philistines were fleeing, Saul took advantage of the situation to kill as many on the run as possible. *(1 Sam.14:24) … Saul had adjured the people, saying, Cursed be the man that eateth any food until it be evening, and I be avenged on mine enemies.* Jonathan, unaware of the oath, used his cane to take honey and ate. Then the others told him of the oath.

(1 Sam.14:36) And Saul said, Let us go down after the Philistines by night, and take spoil among them until the morning light, and let us not leave a man of them. And they said, Do whatsoever seemeth good unto thee. Then said the priest, Let us draw near hither unto God. (37) And Saul asked counsel of God, Shall I go down after the Philistines? Wilt thou deliver them into the hand of Israel? But he answered him not that day. I have found that the Lord does not always want to answer us. Job had to endure a tremendous trial without an answer from the Lord until the end. He had to trust the Lord. Sometimes the Lord wants us to leave Him a way out. A simple yes or no could be wrong on both counts. The true answer could be a "yes, but not now," or a "no, but yes later." I felt the Lord showed me when casting lots, to use two coins. I feel the reason is so that I could get two heads for a "yes" and two tails for a "no" or a head and a tail meaning, "I do not want to answer you in this way or at this time." I always felt in my heart that God wanted this way out.

The time I cast a lot for our home, I used two coins and each time they came up double heads. When I was young in the Lord, I got many answers this way, and they were confirmed. The older I got in the Lord, the less He wanted me to rely on the lot. The lot and other signs helped me to be sure I was hearing the voice and direction of the Lord. He wants to wean us away from the necessity of having signs as we become surer of His voice. There are still times that I use the lot. God does not want us to ask for signs of what He clearly tells us in His Word. What the Word says is final. God does not have to confirm to you that what He said is true. A few years ago my oldest son had been asked by a local motorcycle dealer to come and apply for a job. I asked the Lord by lot if he was going to get the job and the answer was "yes." Later, I asked the Lord to show me a verse concerning the job. I opened the Bible, and the verse I saw implied that they were going to be less than truthful with him. So I thought, "Does this mean 'yes, he will get the job, but they won't tell the truth'?" As it turned out they told him he could have the job in December but it was January when he actually got it. Exactly the way the Lord showed me.

(1 Sam.14:24) Saul had adjured the people, saying, Cursed be the man that eateth any food until it be evening, and I be avenged on mine enemies. His son Jonathan did not hear when this curse was pronounced and ate some honey. Saul wanted an answer from the Lord, whether to go down against the Philistines. But the Lord was not answering Saul, and he suspected sin in the camp was hindering. *(1 Sam.14:38) And Saul said, Draw nigh hither, all ye chiefs of the people; and know and see wherein this sin hath been this day. (39) For, as the Lord liveth, who saveth Israel, though it be in Jonathan my son, he shall surely die. But there was not a man among all the people that answered him. (40) Then said he unto all Israel, Be ye on one side, and I and Jonathan my son will be on the other side. And the people said unto Saul, Do what seemeth good unto thee. (41) Therefore Saul said unto the Lord, the God of Israel, Show the right. And Jonathan and Saul were taken by lot; but the people escaped. (42) And Saul said, Cast lots between me and Jonathan my son. And Jonathan was taken. (43) Then Saul said to Jonathan, Tell me what thou has done.*

171

And Jonathan told him, and said, I did certainly taste a little honey with the end of the rod that was in my hand; and, lo, I must die. (44) And Saul said, God do so and more also; for thou shalt surely die, Jonathan. (45) And the people said unto Saul, Shall Jonathan die, who hath wrought this great salvation in Israel? ... So the people rescued Jonathan, that he died not. (46) Then Saul went up from following the Philistines; and the Philistines went to their own place. Out of all Israel, Jonathan was revealed by the lot to be the cause of God's silence. We have the same sovereign God! Saul did not continue to go after the Philistines when they spared Jonathan. God did not give Saul direction because the curse that he had spoken was not fulfilled. Without an answer from the Lord, he would not go even though they could have destroyed the Philistines. Many are moved by opportunity and reason today, but those led by the Spirit are the sons of God.

The Apostles were giving thought to replacing Judas. *(Acts 1:20) For it is written in the book of Psalms, Let his habitation be made desolate, and let no man dwell therein: and, his office let another take. (21) Of the men therefore that have companied with us all the time that the Lord Jesus went in and went out among us, (22) beginning from the baptism of John, unto the day that he was received up from us, of these must one become a witness with us of his resurrection, (23) And they put forward two, Joseph called Barsabbas, who was surnamed Justus, and Matthias. (24) And <u>they prayed, and said, Thou, Lord, who knowest the hearts of all men, show of these two the one whom thou hast chosen</u>, (25) to take the place in this ministry and apostleship from which Judas fell away, that he might go to his own place. (26) And <u>they gave lots for them; and the lot fell upon Matthias; and he was numbered with the eleven apostles</u>.* We are told by most of the church that a mistake was made in this situation, because the twelfth apostle should have been Paul. The reason for this being the accepted doctrine is that there were only to be twelve apostles. Because of this doctrine, the Greek word "apostolos" in the New Testament is not translated apostle in most cases. However, we have no right to believe it should be translated any other way than apostle. Using the same exact Greek word *apostolos*, there are at least twenty-five apostles listed in the New Testament. We still have apostles today. God chose Matthias, by the lot, to take Judas' place as the twelfth apostle. They also say that Matthias is not mentioned later in the Scriptures, but most of the other apostles are not mentioned later either. Isaiah 53 tells of the sacrificial life and death of Jesus. In this chapter, there has been discovered in the Bible code skip sequence the names of Jesus and twelve apostles including Matthias and excluding Judas and Paul. It was written since the time of Isaiah that Matthias would take Judas' place. The Jewish apostles, who used the lot all their life, trusted it for important decisions because they believed in a sovereign God Who answers prayer.

God chose Gideon to lead Israel against the Midianites, Amalekites, and the children of the East. Gideon was worried because he knew he did not have much of an army, and he had no self-confidence. He wanted the confidence of the Lord. *(Jdg.6:36) And Gideon said unto God, If thou wilt save Israel by my hand, as thou hast spoken, (37) behold, I will put a fleece of wool on the threshing-floor; <u>if there be dew on the fleece only, and it be dry upon all the ground, then shall I know that thou wilt save Israel by my hand, as thou has spoken</u>. (38) And it was so; for he rose up early on the morrow, and pressed the fleece together, and wrung the dew out of the fleece, a bowlful of water. (39) And Gideon said unto God, Let not thine anger be kindled against me, and I will speak but this once: let me make trial, I pray thee, but this once with the fleece; <u>let it now be dry only upon the fleece, and upon all the ground let there be dew</u>. (40) And God did so that night: for it was dry upon the fleece only, and there was dew on all the ground.* That is being pretty specific with the Lord. Gideon wanted a sign that could not naturally occur. Naturally speaking, a fleece would soak up any moisture around. In this case, the fleece was dry and the ground was wet. God has no problem doing these signs for us if we need an answer.

Once, years ago, I was preaching to a man on the verge of conversion. He had many questions, but also a problem believing that God loved him individually. I suggested that he ask God for a sign. I said, "Ask God to let it rain while the sun is shining if you love me." That man was totally joyous the next day, for that is exactly what happened. He knelt down by his bed, and after praying that prayer, looked out the window; the sun was shining and it was raining. He needed this. It convinced him of a personal God and Savior.

Another time when I was teaching a class, I suggested to everyone that they put God first in the morning and seek the Lord in the Word for an hour before coming to work. When we got to this point, I put a sign before them. I said, "If you don't believe God wants you to meet with Him first in the morning before work, set your alarm for the time that you normally get up. Then ask God to wake you up an hour before your alarm goes off. When you wake up, turn your head and look at your clock." Almost everyone in the class came back lit up like a light bulb. They said things such as, "I woke up, turned to my clock, and it was exactly an hour before the alarm was to go off." They saw and were impressed with God's sovereignty and to know that it was His Will for them to meet with Him early in the morning. These things impress people with God's personal love and interest in them.

The children of Israel had gone to war against the Philistines, and the Philistines had captured the Ark of the Covenant. They carried their prize to Philistia, then from city to city. The curse of God would fall upon every city that received the Ark, for the people would get tumors and die. Soon they would demand the lords of the Philistines to move the Ark out of their city. When they placed the Ark next to Dagon, their god, he fell over on his face and broke off his head and hands.

The Philistine lords began to fear the God of the Hebrews. They were being reminded of what this God did to Egypt and Pharaoh to set Israel free. The priests and diviners gave them advice to ask a sign of God to see if this was indeed His judgment upon them. *(1 Sam.6:7) Now therefore take and prepare you a new cart, and two milch kine (<u>milk cows</u>), on which there hath come <u>no yoke</u>; and tie the cows to the cart, and <u>bring their calves home</u> from them; (8) and take the ark of the Lord and lay it upon the cart; and put the jewels of gold, which ye return him for a trespass-offering, in a coffer by the side thereof; and send it away, that it may go. (9) And see; <u>if it goeth up by the way of its own border to Beth-shemesh, then he hath done us this great evil: but if not, then we shall know that it is not his hand that smote us; it was a chance that happened to us.</u>* <u>The flesh can believe in chance against all odds.</u> Cows that had never drawn a cart before because they had never been yoked would naturally go home the way their calves went. They would not go away from their calves into a country they have never been to. It was totally impossible that the cows would go the way they did without God having total sovereignty over those cows' minds. *(1 Sam.6:10) And the men did so, and took two milch kine* (milk cows), *and tied them to the cart, and shut up their calves at home; (11) and they put the ark of the Lord upon the cart, and the coffer with the mice of gold and the images of their tumors. (12) And the <u>kine took the straight way by the way to Beth-shemesh</u>; they went along the highway, <u>lowing as they went</u>, and <u>turned not aside to the right hand or to the left</u>* .... It did not appear that those cows even liked bringing the Ark back to Israel, the way they moaned about it. The Philistines knew this was God and even sacrificed to Him. They made it impossible for this sign to naturally occur. They asked God to do something that is not normal. You can do that, too, and you will never forget it or the Philistines around you.

I was reminding the Lord some years back about my two oldest boys, who were raised in the Lord but were doing their

175

own thing. I had prayed and put them into God's hand by faith, but since it seemed to be taking a long time, I asked the Lord to give me a word concerning them. I flipped my Bible open and stuck my finger down, and it said, *"**Thy prayers and thy alms are gone up for a memorial before God**" (Acts 10:2)*. A memorial is that which keeps alive the memory of someone. So God was continually remembering my request. I did it again, and my finger came down on *"**It is finished**" (Jn.19:30)*. In other words, God was saying, "You prayed about it. I heard the prayer. Now it is done; just believe it." Jesus said, *(Mk.11:24)* *"**Therefore I say unto you, All things whatsoever ye pray and ask for, believe that ye receive them, and ye shall have them**."*

Once I was having much pain and passing a lot of blood. I had peace concerning this, probably because Christ had consistently healed us for many years. The thought had come to me that I had cancer, but I told no one except a friend, Mike Burley, who agreed with me in faith. Shortly after this, I saw two sisters who said they had been praying for ministers they knew, including me. They said the Lord had spoken to them that I was going to have a battle with cancer, but I was going to win. I thanked them and told them I had suspected as much. I went home and asked the Lord to give me a word concerning this. I flipped open my Bible and without looking stuck my finger right on *"**Thou shalt die, and not live**" (2 Ki.20:1)*. I said, "I don't accept that Lord. That is not what your Word promises me. You told me, *"**By whose stripes ye were healed**"* and *"**When you pray believe you have received**."* I asked God to give me another word. I opened my Bible and stuck my finger down right on, *"**I shall not die, but live**" (Ps.118:17)*. The exact opposite! The only two verses like that in the Scriptures. Think about the sovereignty of God to cause the page to stop at the exact spot and then control my finger to fall on the exact portion of the exact verse. Awesome God that He is! God was trying me to see if I was going to believe the Scripture. If you do not ever receive what is contrary to the

Word, you will be blessed. The symptoms gradually decreased until they were gone.

A sister we knew, who lived a few hours from us, had a tumor so big that it looked as though she were several months pregnant. She called me, and I cursed it in Jesus' name. She called right back and said that it had gone down like a balloon that had let its air out. Later, it started growing again. I asked the Lord to give me a word concerning this sister. <u>Five times in a row</u>, I flipped my Bible open, stuck my finger down, and read a verse concerning the resurrection of the dead. I wrote them all down. I asked the Lord, "What are you saying to me? Are you going to raise her from the dead, or are you speaking of raising her at the resurrection of the dead?" The sign God gave me was prophetic and came to pass even though it was not God's best that she died. Doctors were afraid to operate on her. She looked nine months pregnant. Her family pressured her to go to Mexico for treatments. I knew she wavered a lot in her faith toward the end of her trial because she said so. I am not condemning her for that. She was a good faithful woman of the Lord who had been healed by the Lord most of her Christian life. Her husband decided that they were not necessarily seeking the Will of God so much as their own desire when they believed for her to be healed. Of course, Jesus and the disciples prayed for people who had their own desires to be healed and <u>God healed them all</u> (Mt.4:24; 8:16; 9:35; 12:15; Acts 5:16) <u>through their faith</u>. *(Ps.103:3) **Who forgiveth all thine iniquities; Who healeth <u>all</u> thy diseases.*** The minute they gave up their faith to heal her, and prayed, "Lord, if it be Thy Will," that sister fell dead. Her husband and the doctors were shocked because she showed no signs of dying. He told me that the moment those words came out of their mouths in prayer, she fell dead. He told me, "David, we were holding her here by faith." I thought, "Yeah, that is what we are supposed to do."

We told Pauline Warner, a sister in our assembly, the sad news. She said it really upset her because she thought they were holding to their faith. She said it scared her to think that faith could fail. As she was thinking on this in her car, <u>a verse was spoken to her</u>, "Acts 5:1." Pauline called me on her cell phone and told me the verse. Since she did not know what it said, she wanted me to read it to her. *(Acts 5:1) But a certain man named Ananias, with Sapphira his wife, <u>sold a possession</u>.* At first I told her that I did not see how it fit because they were faithful with their finances. Suddenly it came to me that a man and his wife had *"sold a possession."* Healing is our possession by blood covenant. It is the *"children's bread"* according to Jesus. "If it be Thy Will" should never be prayed when the Scripture clearly reveals the Will of God (1 Pet.2:24; Ps.103:3). Jesus and the apostles never prayed that prayer for healing, deliverance, or provision. From this we see that we can accept a lie in exchange for a promised possession. This verse that was spoken to Pauline and the "if it be Thy Will" prayer helped many to understand that we should *"hold fast the confession of our hope that it waver not; for he is faithful that promised" (Heb.10:23).*

Here is a sign that is still impressing people with God's sovereignty. *(2 Ki.20:1) In those days was Hezekiah sick unto death. And Isaiah the prophet the son of Amoz came to him, and said unto him, Thus saith the Lord, Set thy house in order: for thou shalt die, and not live. (2) Then he turned his face to the wall, and prayed unto the Lord, saying, (3) Remember now, O Lord, I beseech thee, how I have walked before thee in truth and with a perfect heart, and have done that which is good in thy sight. And Hezekiah wept sore. (4) And it came to pass, before Isaiah was gone out into the middle part of the city, that the word of the Lord came to him, saying, (5) Turn back, and say to Hezekiah the prince of my people, Thus saith the Lord, the God of David thy father, I have heard thy prayer, I have seen thy tears: behold, I will heal thee; on the third day* *thou shalt go up unto the house of the Lord. (8) And Hezekiah said unto Isaiah, <u>What shall be the sign that the Lord will heal me, and that I shall go up unto the house of the Lord the third day?</u>* We may ask, "Why did he not believe the Lord?" For one thing, Hezekiah was talking to Isaiah the prophet. The Bible tells you to try the prophet (1 Jn.4:1). Many times in personal prophecy, something will be shared that only you knew. This is a sign that this prophecy is not merely from the mind of the prophet. Other times, key events leading to the fulfillment of a prophecy will be shared so that as they come to pass, you will know that this is the Lord. *(Lam.3:37) Who is he that saith, and it cometh to pass, when the Lord commandeth it not?* This gives you a way to prove if the one in question is really a prophet.

There are a lot of prophets with spirits of divination. These spirits do not control the future, therefore, these prophets have a low percentage of fulfillments. Those who go to these false prophets do not realize that these spirits are telling them what they themselves plan to bring to pass, but God does not always permit them. *(9) And Isaiah said, This shall be the <u>sign</u> unto thee from the Lord, that the Lord will do the thing that he hath spoken: <u>shall the shadow go forward ten steps, or go back ten steps</u>? (10) And Hezekiah answered, It is a light thing for the shadow to decline ten steps: nay, but <u>let the shadow return backward ten steps</u>. (11) And Isaiah the prophet cried unto the Lord; and he brought the shadow ten steps backward, by which it had gone down on the dial of Ahaz.* Hezekiah did not know it, but *"it is a light thing"* for God to back the sun up ten degrees. He thought he was making this sign hard on God.

When Elijah did not know what to answer Elisha, he left the answer up to the Lord by a sign. *(2 Ki.2:9) And it came to pass, when they were gone over, that Elijah said unto Elisha, Ask what I shall do for thee, before I am taken from thee. And Elisha said, I pray thee, let a double portion of thy spirit be upon me. (10) And he said, Thou hast asked a hard thing: nevertheless, if thou see me when I am taken from thee, it shall be so unto thee; but if not, it shall not be so. (11) And it came to pass, as they still went on, and talked, that, behold, there appeared a chariot of fire, and horses of fire, which parted them both asunder; and Elijah went up by a whirlwind into heaven. (12) And Elisha saw it* …. In this case, Elijah did not know if God was going to give a double portion of the Spirit to Elisha or not. He thought that Elisha had possibly asked for too much. After all, Elijah was the greatest miracle worker since Moses. Elijah left it up to the Lord to confirm by a sign, and He honored that. Elisha received a double portion, and went on to do twice as many miracles.

God is sovereign over history in order to use people and events for signs to us. *(1 Cor.10:11) Now these things happened unto them by way of example* (Greek: "figure, type, or shadow"); *and they were written for our admonition, upon whom the ends of the ages are come.* According to Deuteronomy 21:17, the double portion was the portion of inheritance for the firstborn son. Elisha, the second-born son, got a double portion of the Spirit that Elijah, the firstborn son, should have had. He got a double portion of what the Father God gave as an inheritance. The second-born son of the Father received the firstborn's inheritance, just like Ephraim and Manasseh, Jacob and Esau, Isaac and Ishmael, or Abel and Cain. Each of these pairs is a type of the two sons of Father God. God said, *"Israel is my son, my firstborn" (Ex.4:22)*. The Church is His born again or second-born son. As Jesus said, *"So the last shall be first and the first last" (Mt.20:16)*. The Church was last born but is first with God in anointing, inheritance, and position.

Each of these pairs of sons gives us a revelation of the difference between the natural firstborn and the spiritual second-born sons. Ephraim was the second son of Joseph, who was the clearest type of Jesus in the Bible. Ephraim received the double-portion inheritance that should have been given to firstborn Manasseh (Gen.48:17-19). Ephraim

180

was called a *"multitude* (Hebrew: fullness) *of nations,"*because he represented the Church of all nations. The Church is the Father's second-born (born again) son who received the double-portion that Israel, the firstborn, should have received but rejected.

Esau, in like manner, sold his double-portion birthright *"for one mess of meat."* In other words, he walked after the flesh. We are Jacob, the second-born, only if we accept the New Testament double-portion anointing sold by natural Israel. What they rejected from Jesus we must accept and not a modern powerless gospel. Many of the Church are proving themselves to be like Esau, not accepting their double-portion. Receive your double-portion anointing and be filled with the Spirit and New Testament gifts.

Paul warns the Church not to be Ishmaels (firstborn), children of the handmaid who were in bondage to the Law and religion (Gal.4:21-31). He exhorts us to be Isaacs (second-born), children of the freewoman and of promise. We must have new life through believing and acting on the promises. *"The righteous shall live by faith"* in these promises. Being born of the promises is to be a partaker in the life, benefits, and work of Christ through faith. The great promise that empowers us to come into all that God has promised is *"the promise of the Father."(Acts 1:4) … he* (Jesus) *charged them not to depart from Jerusalem, but to wait for the promise of the Father, which, [said he], ye heard from me: (5) For John indeed baptized with water; but ye shall be baptized in the Holy Spirit not many days hence. (8) But ye shall receive power, when the Holy Spirit is come upon you: and ye shall be my witnesses....* The Holy Spirit is that double-portion inheritance given by Jesus after His death and resurrection.

Corporately, firstborn natural Israel preceded the second-born spiritual Israel or the Church. Individually, we are all like those two sons, we are born of the flesh before being born of the Spirit. *(1 Cor.15:45) So also it is*

181

written, The first man (firstborn) *Adam became a living soul. The last* (second-born) *Adam [became] a life-giving spirit. (46) Howbeit* <u>*that is not first which is spiritual, but that which is natural; then that which is spiritual. (47) The first man is of the earth, earthy: the second man is of heaven.*</u> *(48) As is the earthy, such are they also that are earthy: and as is the heavenly, such are they also that are heavenly. (49) And as we have borne the image of the earthy, we shall* (Greek: "let us") *also bear the image of the heavenly.* We have all been born of the firstborn Adam, we also must be born again of the second-born Adam, Jesus. The finished creation of God was the second-born Son Jesus and all those in the Church who abide in Him. Most of natural Israel had an opportunity to be a part of this but sold their birthright. They get one more chance in the coming days.

The Church, which is made up of Jews and Gentiles who believe, is first with God, not an afterthought. Jesus spiritually fathered the twelve patriarchs of the Church just as Jacob naturally fathered the twelve patriarchs of Israel. The Church took Jesus' name as the body of Christ, or Christians. Israel took Jacob's name "Israel," which was given to him by God (Gen.32:28). Jacob was clearly a type of Jesus. He married two wives, daughters of one father who was a type of "the" Father. These two wives represented natural Israel and the Church, or spiritual Israel. Jacob, as Jesus, loved the second-born daughter Rachel, who represents the Church, with all his heart. However, he was forced to marry the firstborn daughter Leah, who represents natural Israel, first (Gen.29:26). Jesus loved the Church first because she is like Him, born from above, not from the earth. Except for the faithful elect, natural Israel loved the world and God divorced her (Jer.3:8; Isa.50:1; Hos.2:2-4).

Another interesting fact is that when Jacob crossed the Jordan with his two families to return to the Promised Land, a type of heaven, he declared himself to be two companies.

(Gen.32:10) … I passed over this Jordan; and now I am become two companies. Israel had become two companies, firstborn natural Israel and born again spiritual Israel, the Church. Crossing Jordan represents death and resurrection. Then, as you might expect, in heaven they saw the face of God. *(30) And Jacob called the name of the place Peniel: for, [said he], I have seen God face to face, and my life is preserved* (Hebrew: "to snatch away").

Both Leah and Rachel had handmaids who bore more children to Jacob (as Jesus) than they did. Paul, speaking of the handmaid, said, *"More are the children of the desolate than of her that hath the husband" (Gal.4:27).* This is clear that there are more of the seed of the Lord in both Israel and the Church who are in bondage than are free to have a full bride relationship with Him. Much of the Church is in bondage to sin, religion, or legalism and are not free to follow the Spirit as every son must do (Rom.8:14). Bondage makes us servants while freedom makes us sons. *(Jn.8:31) Jesus therefore said to those Jews that had believed him, If ye abide in my word, [then] are ye truly my disciples; (32) and ye shall know the truth, and the truth shall make you free. (34) … Every one that committeth sin is the bondservant of sin. (35) And the bondservant abideth not in the house forever: the son abideth forever.* Paul confirms this, saying, *"Cast out the handmaid and her son: for the son of the handmaid shall not inherit with the son of the freewoman" (Gal.4:30).* In the following chapters, there is good news that we do not have to live in bondage.

All must be born from above to enter the kingdom. *(Jn.3:3) Jesus answered and said unto him, Verily, verily, I say unto thee, Except one be born anew* (Greek: "from above"), *he cannot see the kingdom of God.* They *"cannot enter into the kingdom of God" (Jn.3:5).* According to Jesus, the righteous from the Old Testament went to Abraham's bosom (Lk.16:22). At death when Jesus descended into the lower parts of the earth, He preached to the spirits in that prison who believed the Gospel and were born from above. He then led those captives to heaven (Epe.4:8,9; 1 Pet.4:19). Therefore the righteous from among Israel of the Old Testament are now in the Church. A remnant of natural Israel will be born from above in the future and join spiritual Israel, the Church (called-out ones).

This shows the sovereignty of God to give signs to the Church in all the types and shadows of Scriptures, and the error of believing that the Church was an afterthought to God when Israel failed. The Church is the crowning creation of God though not all will attain status of Bride. Later chapters explain the double-portion inheritance.

Chapter 10
The Sovereignty of God Through Us

I have been crucified with Christ; and it is <u>no longer I that live, but Christ living in me</u>: and that [life] which I now live in the flesh I live in faith, [the faith] which is in the Son of God, who loved me, and gave himself up for me (Gal.2:20).

I am learning that it is not I, living the Christian life and doing the works of Christ, but it is I accepting my death so that Christ may live and do His works through me. Jesus gave up a natural body in order to take up a corporate body so that He could continue on a much larger scale His deliverance of this fallen creation. *(1 Cor.12:27) Now <u>ye are the body of Christ</u>, and severally members thereof.* We are not the body of *"another Jesus,"* a weak and worthless Jesus. We are the body of the same Jesus, Who walked in that first body, exercising God's power to set the captives free. *(Heb.13:8) <u>Jesus Christ [is] the same yesterday and today, [yea] and forever.</u>* It is sad that most do not agree that Christ's plan is to continue exercising the sovereignty that He had in His first body in His second. *(Amos 3:3) <u>Shall two walk together, except they have agreed</u>?* This chapter will be devoted to bringing us into agreement with the Word so that Christ may walk in us and exercise His sovereignty through us. A king's sons are princes who grow up to inherit his authority and exercise his sovereignty. *(Ps.45:16) Instead of thy fathers shall be thy children, whom <u>thou shalt make princes in all the earth</u>.*

The mind of the flesh is the enemy of God and cannot be subject to Him (Rom.8:7). In Adam we all died and were made useless to God; by abiding in Christ, Who is the Word, we become vessels of His reigning authority. *(1 Cor.15:22) As <u>in Adam all die</u>, so also <u>in Christ shall all</u>*

be made alive. (Rom.5:17) For if, by the trespass of the one, death reigned through the one; much more shall they that receive the abundance of grace and of the gift of righteousness reign in life through the one, [even] Jesus Christ. We were meant to accept God's grace and *"reign in life."* As the Adamic man dies in us, the spiritual man comes to life. *(2 Cor.4:16) Wherefore we faint not; but though our outward man* (the Adamic, nature of self) *is decaying, yet our inward man* (Christ in you) *is renewed day by day.* As we read the Word and repent of our carnal thinking and life to accept Christ's thinking and life, He is able to reign through us.

(2 Cor.4:11) For we who live are always delivered unto death (to self) *for Jesus' sake, that the life also of Jesus may be manifested in our mortal flesh.* Through death to self, we can expect the life of Jesus to be manifested in our human bodies. The life of Christ here is not only His fruit but also His ministry, as we shall see. Those who teach that we cannot expect the life of Christ in this life are deceivers. Those who preach that as long as we are in this body we will always be in bondage to sin are deceivers. *(2 Jn.1:7) For many deceivers are gone forth into the world, [even] they that confess not that Jesus Christ cometh in the flesh.* When Jesus physically comes again, He will have a glorified body but He is coming now in the flesh of His body of believers. Those who preach that our ultimate hope here is only to be forgiven and not transformed are deceivers. Paul explained that he was revealing a mystery with the words *"Christ in you, the hope of glory" (Col.1:27).* He said that the wisdom in this mystery was to *"present every man perfect* (complete or mature) *in Christ" (28).* Christ in you has power over sin and the curse around us. As we come to realize the purpose of Christ is to live in us, our faith in what He can do in us and through us grows exponentially. *(Phm.1:6) That the fellowship* (Greek: "sharing in common") *of thy faith may become effectual, in the knowledge of every good thing which is in you, unto Christ.*

As we accept the mind of Christ, which is the Word of God, it transforms us. *(Rom. 12:2) And be not fashioned according to this world: but <u>be ye transformed by the renewing of your mind</u>, and ye may prove what is the good and acceptable and perfect will of God.* If we do not repent (Greek: "change our mind") when we read the Word, we do not accept the transformation to the life and work of Christ. The first thing we must believe is the Gospel. *(Gal. 2:20) I have been crucified with Christ; and it is no longer I that live, but Christ living in me....* The old me died at the cross and now Jesus lives in me. Faith in this justifies us and entitles us to the power to bring it to pass. Because many do not understand this, they believe we have no hope but to continue in sin and count on God's grace for forgiveness. *(Rom. 6:1) ... Shall we continue in sin, that grace may abound? (2) God forbid. <u>We who died to sin, how shall we any longer live therein</u>?* Notice that because of grace we do not have to live in sin. *(3) Or are ye ignorant that all we who were baptized into Christ Jesus were baptized into his death? (4) We were buried therefore with him through baptism unto death: that like as Christ was raised from the dead through the glory of the Father, <u>so we also might walk in newness of life</u> ....* When we were baptized, the old sinner died and was buried so now we can walk in new life. *(5) For if we have become united with [him] in the likeness of his death, we shall be also [in the likeness] of his resurrection.* By faith at baptism we both die and resurrect. Neither a dead man nor a resurrected man can sin. *(6) Knowing this, that <u>our old man was crucified with [him]</u>, that the body of sin might be done away, <u>that so we should no longer be in bondage to sin</u>.* Through faith we died, and now Jesus lives in us. We were *"delivered out of the power of darkness" (Col. 1:13).* This is the <u>real</u> good news.

We are only free from the power of sin if we believe it. We can now use these promises as a two-edged sword to destroy corruption in our lives. *(2 Cor. 7:1) <u>Having therefore these promises, beloved, let us cleanse ourselves from all defilement of</u>*

flesh and spirit, perfecting holiness in the fear of God. We are responsible to cleanse ourselves by faith in the promises.

Those who believe the promises will bear fruit. As a type, Mary believed the promise that she was to bear the fruit of Jesus in her mortal body (Lk.1:31-35). Jesus said, *"My mother and my brethren are these that hear the word of God, and do it" (Lk.8:21).* In a type, we who bring forth the fruit of Jesus are His mother. In the parable of the sower, Jesus sowed the seed (Greek: *sperma,* "sperm") of the Word in our heart. Since the Word is the spiritual sperm of Jesus, it can only bring forth His fruit. No word from man or religion can do this. Only one of the four types that received the Word bore fruit 30, 60, or 100-fold. Mary was told, *"Blessed [is] she that believed; for there shall be a fulfillment of the things which have been spoken to her from the Lord" (Lk.1:45).* Because she believed the Word, she bore the fruit of Jesus. The Word must be believed for it to be fulfilled in us. *(Heb.4:2) For indeed we have had good tidings* (Gospel) *preached unto us, even as also they: but the word of hearing did not profit them, because it was not united by faith with them that heard.* We can hear the Gospel but make it ineffective by our own unbelief, as Israel did. By bearing the fruit of the same Jesus, we are proving who the true believers are. Jesus said, *"Ye shall know them by their fruits,"* not by who they say they are.

Paul showed us how to exercise this faith with our renewed imagination. *(2 Cor.3:18) But we all, with unveiled face beholding as in a mirror the glory of the Lord, are transformed into the same image from glory to glory, even as from the Lord the Spirit.* If our face is truly unveiled, then we see by faith the finished work of God in the mirror, which is *"Christ in you, the hope of glory."* Only seeing the Jesus of the Word in the mirror will transform us into the image of God. The Jesus we see must be the One Who has power over sin and the curse around us. Most Christians would think us proud to look in the mirror by faith and see Jesus, but in truth these are the only ones who are humble to the Word. <u>The one who sees his</u> <u>natural face in the mirror will have no power to obey.</u> *(Jas.1:23)* *For if any one is a <u>hearer of the word and not a doer</u>, he is like* *unto a man <u>beholding his natural face in a mirror</u>.* These are the ones who do not unite faith with the Gospel so that it can be fulfilled in them.

(Rom.6:11) Even so <u>reckon</u> (consider it done) <u>*ye also*</u> <u>*yourselves to be dead unto sin, but alive unto God*</u> *in Christ* *Jesus. (12) <u>Let not sin therefore reign in your mortal body</u>, that* *ye should obey the lusts thereof.* Notice that the way to not let sin reign is to reckon yourself to be immune to it because you are dead. It is to believe that Jesus took away your sin and that you are free to obey God. God gives power to save from sin to those who believe the true Gospel. *(Rom.1:16) For I am not* *ashamed of the <u>Gospel</u>: for it <u>is the power</u> of God unto salvation* *to every <u>one that believeth</u>* .... Those who do not accept their power over sin by faith will prove themselves tares and not wheat when they do not bear fruit. *(Rom.6:17) But thanks* *be to God, that, whereas <u>ye were servants of sin</u>, ye became* *obedient from the heart to that form of teaching whereunto ye* *were delivered; (18) and being <u>made free from sin</u>, ye <u>became</u>* <u>*servants of righteousness*</u>. The true teaching, believed and acted on by the heart, sets us free from sin. Jesus said, *"And ye* *shall know the truth and the truth shall make you free."* If our truth is not setting us free, either it is not THE TRUTH or we do not really believe it. If you have not had victory, study the truth, not religion.

I recently received a "woe is me" email from a friend who was grieved over his inability to overcome a certain sin. I highlighted in his letter phrases like the following: "I couldn't resist; I'm hooked; my flesh is weak; they really got me; I have no hope; no will power; I'm defeated," and "I'm licked," and sent it back to him with this following note: "Just because you fail, that does not mean you give up faith. You were delivered of this sin 2,000 years ago. <u>Compare what you have believed</u>

189

in these phrases with what you should believe. (I sent him the Gospel message of our deliverance from sin.) You have a lot of faith to stay in bondage. Even in your failure, you must walk by faith in order to get out of bondage."

My friend's will was against the sin so it was not a willful disobedience. His failure was in his faith. He believed everything he should not have and that robbed him of power. Faith that fizzles out at the finish had a flaw in it from the first. If we sin, there are some steps we should take to lay a foundation for our faith. If we say we have no sin, in other words, justify self, we are deceived (1 Jn.1:8). If we confess our sins, we will be forgiven and cleansed from all sin (9). We should first confess our sins. Then, as the Israelites who had been bitten of the serpents turned and set their eyes on the sacrificial serpent on the pole, seeing their sin and curse on Him, we should turn and confess the sacrifice of Jesus (Num.21:8). From then on, we should believe that our sin has been put on Him and we are delivered. As John the Baptist said, *"Behold the lamb of God that taketh away the sin of the world."* God's complaint about the Old Testament Law was that it could not *"make perfect them that draw nigh" (Heb.10:1). (4) For it is impossible that the blood of bulls and goats should take away sins. (14) For by one offering he hath perfected forever them that are sanctified.* The Old Testament had a blood covering and forgiveness but could not deliver from the sin nature. Many today are preaching only what that covenant offered leaving those that believe them in bondage to sin. Many of you, upon coming to the Lord, experienced total deliverance from certain sins. What the real Gospel teaches is that God wants to continue that process.

I hear it commonly preached that we are just sinners saved by grace. It may surprise you to know that there is no such saying in the Bible. Sinner saved by grace is an oxymoron. A man is either a sinner or he is saved from sin by grace. Jesus always made a distinction between His followers and sinners.

(Mt.26:45) … The Son of man is betrayed into the hands of <u>sinners</u>. (Lk.6:33) And if ye do good to them that do good to you, what thank have ye? for <u>even sinners</u> do the same. (34) And if ye lend to them of whom ye hope to receive, what thank have ye? <u>even sinners lend to sinners</u>, to receive again as much.

It has been said that Paul as a disciple claimed to be the chief of sinners. False! He said that he was the chief of those that Jesus came to save from sin. *(1 Tim.1:15) Faithful is the saying, and worthy of all acceptation, that Christ Jesus came into the world to <u>save sinners</u>; of whom I am chief:* (God was showcasing Paul as an example of His power to save anyone.) *(16) howbeit for this cause I obtained mercy, that in me as chief might Jesus Christ show forth all his longsuffering, for an ensample of them that should thereafter believe on him unto eternal life.* Paul had just said that his sins were <u>in his past by God's enabling power</u> and that he was now counted among the faithful. *(12) I thank him that <u>enabled</u> me, [even] Christ Jesus our Lord, for that he counted me <u>faithful</u>, appointing me to [his] service; (13) though <u>I was before</u> a blasphemer, and a persecutor, and injurious: howbeit I obtained mercy, because <u>I did it</u> ignorantly in unbelief.* Paul included himself when he said that <u>we were sinners</u> but we were made righteous. *(Rom.5:8) But God commendeth his own love toward us, in that, <u>while we were yet sinners</u>, Christ died for us. (19) For as through the one man's disobedience the many <u>were made sinners</u>, even so through the obedience of the one shall the many be <u>made righteous</u>. (Gal.2:17) But if, while we sought to be justified in Christ, we ourselves also were <u>found sinners</u>, is Christ a minister of sin? God forbid. (1 Cor.6:9) Or know ye not that the <u>unrighteous shall not inherit the kingdom of God</u>? Be not deceived: neither fornicators, nor idolaters, nor adulterers, nor effeminate, nor abusers of themselves with men, (10) nor thieves, nor covetous, nor drunkards, nor revilers, nor extortioners, shall inherit the kingdom of God. (11) And such <u>were some of you</u>: but <u>ye were washed</u>, but <u>ye were sanctified</u>,* *but ye were justified in the name of the Lord Jesus Christ, and in the Spirit of our God.*

The Lord through Paul said that Jesus is separated from sinners. *(Heb.7:26) For such a high priest became us, holy, guileless, undefiled, <u>separated from sinners</u>, and made higher than the heavens.* Those who justify themselves in their sin by saying that we are all just sinners saved by grace will not obtain mercy through our High Priest. *(Pr.28:13) He that covereth his transgressions shall not prosper: But <u>whoso confesseth and forsaketh them shall obtain mercy</u>.* David said that sinners would be <u>separated</u> from among the righteous and would be judged. *(Ps.1:1) Blessed is the man that walketh not in the counsel of the wicked, Nor standeth in the <u>way of sinners</u>, Nor sitteth in the seat of scoffers. (5) Therefore the <u>wicked shall not stand in the judgment</u>, Nor <u>sinners in the congregation of the righteous</u>.*

If we believe the deceiver's gospel that we are always going to be sinners instead of *"<u>made free from sin</u>,"* then that is what we will have. Jesus said, *"As thou hast believed, [so] be it done unto thee"* and *"According to your faith be it done unto you."* It is important that we believe exactly what the Word says. It is important that we see the Biblical Jesus in the mirror and not *"another Jesus"* of man's making (2 Cor.11:4). If in the mirror, we are looking at the humanistic Jesus preached most often today, then that is the only image we can come into. This is a Jesus who has no power. Does the Jesus in your mirror have power over sin and the curse? Does He have power to minister healing, deliverance, and provision? If so, then that is what He will be able to do through you.

(Col.1:21) And you, being in time past alienated and enemies in your mind in your evil works, (22) yet <u>now</u> hath he <u>reconciled</u> (Greek: "exchanged") *in the body of his flesh through death, <u>to present you holy</u> and without blemish and unreprovable before him: (23) <u>if so be that ye continue in the faith</u>, grounded and steadfast, and <u>not moved away from the hope of the Gospel</u>*

which ye heard (the original Gospel). We are <u>now</u> reconciled because of the cross <u>if</u> we continue in the faith, unwavering from the true Gospel. The Greek word translated "reconciled" here means "exchanged." On the cross, Jesus exchanged His life, blessings, and power for our old life, curse, and weakness. Our old life and its penalty, the curse, are on the cross, and now Christ lives in us. God exchanges us to present us holy and without blemish, to deliver us from our past evil works. The Christ, Who is blessed with righteousness and power, will exercise sovereignty through us because He lives in us. We are now ministers of this reconciliation (2 Cor.5:18-21). In other words, it is our job to administer the exchange to those who believe so that people are saved from sin, healed, delivered, and provided for.

The curse is enumerated in Deuteronomy 28, and it covers everything bad that happens to man as a result of breaking God's laws. Jesus bore this curse so that we would have authority over it, both in our own lives and in the lives of others who believe. *(Gal.3:13)* <u>*Christ redeemed us from the curse of the law,*</u> <u>*having become a curse for us*</u> *... (14) that upon the Gentiles might come the blessing of Abraham in Christ Jesus ....* Jesus became the curse, and now we who believe have the *"blessings of Abraham."* He was blessed in *"all things" (Gen.24:1)*. The exchange was accomplished at the cross but will be manifested as we apply the Gospel by faith to the curse. Before the fall, Adam lived in the Garden of Eden with no sickness, corruption, or lack of any kind. Look around you. The curse is manifested in all of the creation because of the fall. In His life and in His death, Jesus destroyed the curse. He passed on this ministry to His disciples, and they were commanded to pass it on to their disciples, and on down to us (Mt.28:19,20). Eventually this Gospel was totally corrupted by religion so that what was passed on was a form of godliness that denies the power thereof (2 Tim.3:5).

The Holy Spirit empowers those who have received Him to come into all that Christ is. Paul prays in Ephesians, *"That he would grant you, according to the riches of his glory, that ye may be strengthened with <u>power through his Spirit</u> in the inward man; <u>that Christ may dwell in your hearts</u> through faith; to the end that ye, being rooted and grounded in love, may be strong to <u>apprehend</u> with all the saints what is the <u>breadth and length and height and depth</u>, and to know the love <u>of Christ</u> which passeth knowledge, <u>that ye may be filled unto all the fullness of God"</u> (Epe.3:16-19).* The full scope of Christ, His breadth, length, height, depth, and love, was provided to us through faith. Christ is to be *"<u>apprehended</u>"* by faith as we are empowered by God's Spirit, *"<u>that ye may be filled unto all the fullness of God</u>."* Does it seem too good to be true? "Gospel" means "good news." I did not write the Word, I just believe it. Do not let religion stop you, brothers and sisters.

Notice the phrase *"<u>the fullness of God</u>."* If, as Genesis 1 says, each seed brings forth after its own kind, then what seed has been sown in us? First, by our parents, we were all born of the seed of fallen humanity. Then, according to the parable of the sower, we receive the seed (Greek: *sperma*, "sperm") of the Word (Jesus) and are born again from above. That seed of the Word is not the seed of man, but God. *(Jn.1:1) …The <u>Word was God</u>. (Jn.3:6) That which is born of the flesh is flesh; and <u>that which is born of the Spirit is spirit</u>. (7) Marvel not that I said unto thee, Ye must be born anew* (Greek: "from above"). When Jesus told the Jews that He was the Son of God, they tried to stone Him, saying, *"Thou, being a man, makest thyself God" (Jn.10:29-33).* They knew that if God had a son, He would be God, also. *(Jn.10:34) Jesus answered them, Is it not written in your law, 'I said, ye are gods'? (35) If <u>he called them gods, unto whom the word of God came (and the scripture cannot be broken) (36)</u> say ye of him, whom the Father sanctified and sent into the world, Thou blasphemest; because I said, I am [the] Son of God?* In the original language, there were no capital or lower case letters for words such as "gods" or "spirit." Jesus was saying that the Jews who had received the Old Testament Word of the letter were by position gods. How much more then are we who have received the New Testament Word of the Spirit? We are gods, not in the flesh for that is the seed of man, but in the spirit for that is the seed of God. Jesus said, *"The words that I have spoken unto you are spirit."* Since each seed brings forth after its own kind, the son of a dog is dog, the son of a man is man, and the son of God is god. The more of God's seed that we give good earth to, the more God manifests Himself in us. *(Rom.1:3) concerning his <u>Son</u>, who was born of the <u>seed of David</u> according to the <u>flesh</u>,* (Jesus was Son of man in the flesh.) *(4) Who was declared [to be] the <u>Son of God</u> with power, according to the <u>spirit</u> of holiness* (Son of God in the spirit), *by the resurrection from the dead; [even] Jesus Christ our Lord.* We, as Jesus, are son of man in the flesh but son of God in the spiritual man. *(Heb.2:17) Wherefore it behooved him <u>in all things to be made like unto his brethren</u> ....* Jesus was made like us in everything. *(18) For in that he himself hath suffered being tempted, he is able to succor* (Greek: "come to the aid of") *them that are tempted.* As Son of man, Jesus knew temptation and is therefore able to help us. Our Jesus is the *"only begotten* (born) *Son of God,"* and we are reborn sons of God through Him.

(Epe.4:11-13) And he gave some [to be] apostles; and some, prophets; and some, evangelists; and some, pastors and teachers (The Nicolaitan error [Rev.2:6,15] teaches that some of these ministries are done away with, but the Word says no such thing.); *for the <u>perfecting of the saints</u>, unto the work of ministering, unto the building up of the body of Christ: <u>till we all attain</u> unto the unity of the faith, and of the knowledge of the Son of God, unto a <u>full-grown man</u>, unto the <u>measure of the stature of the fullness of Christ</u>.* The fullness of Christ, all of His righteousness and ministry, are provided for us. The apostate church tells us that this stature is unattainable because they count on man's ability,

195

not God's. They are saying that God is unable or unwilling to completely save us from the power of sin and corruption. *(Heb.7:25) Wherefore also he is able to save to the uttermost* (Greek: "completely") *them that draw near unto God through him, seeing he ever liveth to make intercession for them.*

I can hear some say, "Dave, I do not see any of these people around. How can this be?" First of all, without a mind completely renewed by the Word, we could not discern them. Jesus was discerned by very few as being in the fullness of God. The leaders of Israel did not recognize Him. Even His disciples questioned Him: Peter rebuked Him, and Thomas doubted Him. Secondly, He has saved the best wine for last. *(2 Thes.1:10) When <u>he shall come to be glorified in his saints</u>, and to be <u>marvelled at in all them that believed (because our testimony unto you was believed) in that day</u>.* Paul believed there was a day coming when the saints would have grace to believe His teaching and manifest Jesus. This declares that the Lord would come when this happens. His crop has come to maturity, ready for the harvest. *(11) To which end we also pray always for you, that our God may count you worthy of your calling, and <u>fulfill every desire of goodness and [every] work of faith, with power</u>; (12) that the name* (Greek: "character and authority") *of our <u>Lord Jesus may be glorified in you</u>, and ye in him, according to the grace of our God and the Lord Jesus Christ.* God's grace, through the faith of the saints, will manifest the character and authority of Jesus in preparation for His work and His coming.

The prophet Joel declares full restoration of all that the curse and religion has taken from God's people. *(Joel 2:23) Be glad then, ye children of Zion, and rejoice in the Lord your God; for he giveth you the former* (or early) *rain in just measure, and he causeth to come down for you the rain, the <u>former rain and the latter rain</u>, in the first [month]. (24) And the floors shall be full of wheat, and the vats shall overflow with new wine and oil* (bearing much fruit). *(25) And <u>I will restore</u>*

to you the years that the locust hath eaten, the canker-worm, and the caterpillar, and the palmer-worm, my great army which I sent among you. These insects represent the curse on God's crop or His people. God said the early and latter rain would restore His people from the years of devastation. This rain was identified in Joel 2:28,29 as the outpouring of the Spirit on God's people.

Peter quotes Joel 2:28,29, declaring that the outpouring of the Spirit on Pentecost was a fulfillment of this prophecy. *(Acts 2:16) But <u>this is that which hath been spoken through the prophet Joel</u>: (17) And it shall be <u>in the last days</u>, saith God, <u>I will pour forth of my Spirit</u> upon all flesh: And your sons and your daughters shall prophesy, And your young men shall see visions, And your old men shall dream dreams.* The *"former rain"* of the Spirit came *"in the last days"* of the Old Testament people of God, and the *"latter rain"* will come in *"the last days"* of the New Testament people of God. This former rain came to the Jews that believed, to restore them after a great falling away, and then it was passed on to the Gentiles. Those disciples who received that power of the Spirit walked as Jesus walked and did His works. The pagans called them "Christians," meaning "Christ-like." There is little evidence to convict many of that today, but the story is not over. For almost 2,000 years, only a few have been partakers of the former rain. The latter rain will come to believers, to restore the fallen Church to Christ-likeness, and then it passes on to the Jews.

When will the latter rain come? Both the Jews and the Church have fallen away from what was given in the Gospels and Acts for 2,000 years. The Spirit of God says, *(Hos.5:15) "I will go and return to my place, till they acknowledge their offence, and seek my face: <u>in their affliction</u> they will seek me earnestly."* This is clear that the Lord left Israel and the Church to their own self-will and false leadership. In the midst of affliction, which has already begun, there will be repentance. His people will say, *(Hos.6:1) "Come, and <u>let us return unto</u>*

the Lord; for he hath torn, and he will heal us; he hath smitten, and he will bind us up. (2) After two days will he revive us: on the third day he will raise us up, and we shall live before him. (3) And let us know, let us follow on to know the Lord: his going forth is sure as the morning; and he will come unto us as the rain, as the latter rain that watereth the earth." The Lord will come as the latter rain. The Holy Spirit will manifest in those who receive Him, Jesus Christ. We see on the morning of the third day the latter rain outpouring will come to empower and restore after a two-day (2,000 year) falling away period.

What are these two days, and when is the morning of the third day? *(2 Pet.3:8) But forget not this one thing, beloved, that one day is with the Lord as a thousand years, and a thousand years as one day.* Having read the writings of the early Church fathers, I can tell you that they commonly believed in the 1,000-year prophetic day and that after six of these days from the beginning, the end time would come. The Hindus, Muslims, and the Jews also believed this. Gibbon in *The Rise And Fall of The Roman Empire* said that the early Christians believed this. I have found in Scripture over a dozen astounding revelations using the 1,000-year days pointing to this time in which we live. The Bible is laid out in seven prophetic 1,000-year days. These days are always numbered from the creation of the first Adam or the birth of the "last Adam" (1 Cor.15:45), Jesus Christ. There were 4,000 years, or four days, between the Adams. Since the days of Jesus, the calendar was tampered with extensively, but most believe we have come to the morning of the third day, or beginning of the third 1,000 years from the last Adam's birth. It is also the morning of the seventh day, or the beginning of the seventh 1,000 years from the first Adam. This is when the end time begins, and God finishes His work. *(Gen.2:2) And on the seventh day God finished his work, which he had made; and he rested on the seventh day from all his work, which he had made.* According to this type, God is about to finish His new creation work on this morning of the seventh day, also called the third day in some types, and rest. This soon coming latter rain outpouring will restore the true believers to the holiness, power, and ministry of Jesus.

As Solomon said, *"That which hath been is that which shall be; and that which hath been done is that which shall be done"* ... *(Eccl.1:9)*. What happened with the former rain in Acts will also happen in the latter rain acts of our day. The apostate people of God will fight against this move of the Spirit and be rejected. The persecuted, Spirit-filled remnant will by signs and wonders bring revival to lovers of truth worldwide. The former rain was first offered to Israel, but as many blasphemed, it was given to the Gentiles. The latter rain will first be given to the Church, but when many blaspheme, it will be given to a remnant of Israel. I thank my God that by His grace I was not stubborn but received His early rain. It has given to me a miraculous life of God's provision, but the latter rain will be far greater.

Do all believers have the former or early rain of the Holy Spirit? Jesus said to His disciples, *"Ye who have followed me in the <u>regeneration</u> ..." (Mt.19:28)*. Regeneration comes from the Greek word meaning "new birth." The disciples were born again but did not have the Holy Spirit because Jesus told them, *"He abideth <u>with you</u> and <u>shall be in you</u>" (Jn.14:17)*. He later told them, *"But ye shall receive power, when the Holy Spirit is come upon you: and ye shall be my witnesses ... unto the uttermost part of the earth" (Acts 1:8)*. When the Spirit comes, we receive the power needed to be witnesses of Jesus. The disciples were called Christians by the lost because they did the works of Jesus.

The apostate church of our day has separated many from this infilling power by saying that all who are born again automatically have the Holy Spirit. Obviously, Jesus did not teach this, nor did the disciples teach it later. Paul did not believe it. *(Acts 19:1) ... Paul ... found certain <u>disciples</u>: (2) and he said unto them, <u>Did ye receive the Holy Spirit when ye</u>*

believed? And they [said] unto him, <u>Nay</u>, we did not so much as hear whether the Holy Spirit was [given]. These disciples had not experienced the infilling of the Spirit. *(6) And when Paul had <u>laid his hands upon them</u>, the <u>Holy Spirit came on them</u>; and they spake with tongues, and prophesied*. Why would believers need prayer to receive the Spirit if it was automatic? As with every New Testament case, they knew when they received the Spirit from the signs and gifts.

(Acts 8:14) Now when the apostles that were at Jerusalem heard that Samaria <u>had received the word</u> of God, they sent unto them Peter and John: (15) who, when they were come down, <u>prayed for them, that they might receive the Holy Spirit</u>: (16) for as yet <u>it was fallen upon none of them: only they had been baptized</u> into the name of the Lord Jesus. (17) Then laid they their hands on them, and they received the Holy Spirit. <u>Baptized believers</u> did not receive the Holy Spirit until the Apostles came and prayed for them.

Our spirit must be born again before the Holy Spirit will come to dwell in it. The lost cannot receive the Spirit for Jesus said, *"The Spirit of truth whom <u>the world cannot receive</u>"… (Jn.14:17)*. The promise of the covenant is clear that those who have *"a new spirit"* can have *"My Spirit." (Eze.36:26) A new heart also will I give you, and <u>a new spirit will I put within you</u>; and I will take away the stony heart out of your flesh, and I will give you a heart of flesh. (27) <u>And I will put my Spirit within you</u>, and cause you to walk in my statutes, and ye shall keep mine ordinances, and do them*. When God's Spirit comes to dwell in our born again spirit, He will empower you to obey the Word.

Jesus had two spirits, a born again, human spirit and the Holy Spirit, or Spirit of God. When we are saved, we receive a born again spirit in His image called the *"Spirit of Christ."* Only then are we capable of receiving the *"Spirit of God"* into the holy, born again temple for power. Notice the clear difference in these two states. *(Rom.8:9) But ye are not in the* *flesh but in the Spirit, if so be that the <u>Spirit of God</u> dwelleth in you.* (The Spirit of God empowers us to be spiritual.) *<u>But if any man hath not the <u>Spirit of Christ</u>, he is none of his.</u>* If we do not have the Spirit of Christ we are not born again. *(10) And if Christ is in you, the <u>body is dead</u> because of sin; but the <u>spirit is life</u> because of righteousness.* The Spirit of Christ does not empower our fallen body but gives us His Spirit of life. *(11) But if the Spirit of him* (God) *that raised up Jesus from the dead dwelleth in you, he that raised up Christ Jesus from the dead shall give <u>life also to your mortal bodies</u> through his Spirit that dwelleth in you.* When we receive the Spirit of God, He empowers and gives life to our bodies as He did with Jesus. *(Mk. 5:30) And straightway Jesus, perceiving in himself that the <u>power [proceeding] from him</u> had gone forth, turned him about in the crowd, and said, Who touched my garments?* This is the power of the Spirit of God coming out of Jesus' body to heal.

(Acts 5:32) And we are witnesses of these things; and [so is] the <u>Holy Spirit, whom God hath given to them that obey him</u>. Obey, dear friend, and receive. If you are born again, ask God for His Spirit. *(Lk.11:13) If ye then, being evil, know how to give good gifts unto <u>your children</u>, how much more shall [your] heavenly Father <u>give the Holy Spirit to them that ask him</u>?* God only gives the Holy Spirit to those who belong to Him. *(Acts 2:18) Yea and on my servants and on my handmaidens in those days Will I pour forth of my Spirit; and they shall prophesy.*

With this power of the latter rain, God is going to completely destroy the curse of sin and death in the most faithful of His people. *(1 Cor.15:51) Behold, I tell you a mystery: We all shall <u>not sleep</u>, but <u>we shall all be changed</u>, (52) in a moment, in the twinkling of an eye, at the <u>last trump</u>: for the trumpet shall sound, and the dead shall be raised incorruptible, and we shall be changed.* Notice that we shall all be changed at the last trump, which is at the end of the tribulation when God takes over the world. *(Rev.11:15) And the <u>seventh</u>*

angel sounded (last trumpet)*; and there followed great voices in heaven, and they said, The kingdom of the world is become [the kingdom] of our Lord, and of his Christ: and he shall reign for ever and ever.* Who are these people who will not die but be changed at the last trumpet? All that sin will die. *(Eze.18:4,20) The soul that sinneth, it shall die* …. Jesus told His disciples that they would have to lose their life to find life. *(Mt.16:25) For whosoever would save his life* (soul) *shall lose it: and whosoever shall lose his life* (soul) *for my sake shall find it.* The Greek word for "life" in this verse is *psuche* or "soul." Our soul is our mind, will, and emotions. Jesus was saying we must lose our fleshly mind, will, and emotions to gain our spiritual mind, will, and emotions.

Even though all of God's elect will lose their lives, all will not physically die. Some will be changed without dying because they have already put their old life to death. *(Rom.8:6) For the mind of the flesh is death; but the mind of the Spirit is life and peace.* Those with the mind of the flesh must die so that the mind of the Spirit can live. Everyone who has not overcome sin in the mind, will, and emotions must die. *(Rom.6:23) For the wages of sin is death* …. Sin must be overcome before physical death can be overcome. Jesus died to empower us to lose our old life, to gain His life, and to have a blood covering so we would be accepted during the process. This process can be finished in a fruit-bearing disciple at physical death should he not completely crucify the old life while still alive. This process can also be finished in this life as we die to self through faith in what Jesus did at the cross. There is no curse of death in the Bible on those who do not sin. Enoch and Elijah symbolize these people who will not die because they walk by faith in God. Jesus overcame in His first body so that He could do it in His second body, which is made up of those believers who take up their crosses. He abolished all of the old life, even the last enemy, death. *(2 Tim.1:10) … Jesus, who abolished death, and brought life and immortality to light through the Gospel.* After God abolishes the rule of the beast, harlot, and the old life over His people, death will be abolished. *(1 Cor.15:24) Then cometh the <u>end</u>, when he shall deliver up the kingdom to God, even the Father; <u>when he shall have abolished all rule</u> and all authority and power. (25) For he must reign, till he hath put all his enemies under his feet. (26) The last enemy that shall be abolished is death.*

One enemy in power that rules over God's people is the old life of flesh. *(Rom.8:7) Because the <u>mind of the flesh</u> is <u>enmity</u>* (enemy) *against God; for it is not subject to the law of God, neither indeed can it be.* Jesus conquered these enemies for us at the cross, but we must walk by faith to see it manifested. The resurrection and rapture, both which abolish death, are at <u>the end</u>, when He will have abolished <u>all other rule</u> over His people, not seven years before the end while these reign. Jesus said, *"I will raise him up in the last day" (Jn.6:44)*, or *"at the last day" (39)*. There is one more resurrection of the righteous dead at the end so all are included (Rev.20:4; 1 Cor.15:22-24). The rapture happens at that time (1 Thes.4:15-17).

(Jn.11:25) Jesus said unto her, I am the resurrection, and the life: he that believeth on me, <u>though he die, yet shall he live</u> (resurrection)*; (26) <u>and</u> whosoever <u>liveth and believeth on me shall never die</u>.* If the first part of this sentence is speaking of physical death, certainly the last part is. In order to prove the power of God's salvation, He will restore in these last days the faith to believe that Jesus abolished sin and death. Then some will escape death. *(Heb.11:5) <u>By faith</u> Enoch was <u>translated that he should not see death</u>; and he was not found, because God translated him: for he hath had witness borne to him that before his translation he had been well pleasing unto God.* The faith to be an overcomer will be restored by the latter rain. *(2 Thes.1:10) When he shall come to be <u>glorified in his saints</u>, and to be marveled at in all them that believed (<u>because our testimony unto you was believed</u>) in that day.*

When will these things happen? Jesus gave us a clear clue in a type and shadow. *(Mt.16:28) there are <u>some of them that stand here</u>, who <u>shall in no wise taste of death</u>, till they <u>see the Son of man coming</u> in his kingdom.* Notice He said that some who stand *"here"* will not die till they see the coming of the Lord. Where is *here*? In type, they stood before the end of six days, or 6,000 years, which is proven by the next verse. *(Mt.17:1) And <u>after six days</u> Jesus taketh with him Peter, and James, and John his brother, and bringeth them up into a high mountain apart: (2) and <u>he was transfigured</u> before them; and his face did shine as the sun, and his garments became white as the light.*

Some alive today will see the coming of the Lord because we just passed the end of six days, or 6,000 years. We are now *"<u>after six days</u>,"* on the morning of the seventh day, when Peter, James, and John saw the coming of the Lord in His glorified body. In type, three disciples saw the coming of the Lord without dying. Peter, James, and John, who were the <u>closest disciples to the Lord</u>, also prefigured *"<u>we that are alive, that are left until the coming of the Lord</u>"* (1 Thes.4;15). The two witnesses represent the martyrs who are resurrected at the last trump (Rev.11:12,15). These two groups account for the resurrection and rapture at the coming of the Lord, fulfilling the Word.

Chapter 11
The Last Adam Restored Our Dominion

The last Adam became a life giving spirit (1 Cor.15:45).

The sovereignty of God is manifested through those who believe the Gospel and let Jesus in them exercise dominion over this fallen creation. Some say that Jesus had dominion because He was the Son of God, therefore we cannot hope to do the same. That is not what Jesus said, as we shall see. It is true that Jesus was the Son of God (spiritual man) dwelling in and empowering the son of man (natural man, Rom.1:3). Jesus usually called Himself *"the son of man."* They did not have the New Testament when Jesus was administering God's salvation; they had the Old Testament. Jesus always did things to fulfill the Old Testament *"so the scripture might be fulfilled."* He called Himself *"the son of man."* I am sure that the Jews caught on to what He was saying. They had heard that phrase, *"the son of man,"* in the Old Testament. Jesus said of Himself, *"and he gave him the authority to execute judgment because he is a son of man" (Jn.5:27).* Jesus did not have authority to execute judgment because He was the Son of God, but because He was a son of man. This authority was given to man. Adam and his children were given this authority, and the devil usurped it. *(Gen.1:26) ... And God said "Let us make man in our image after our likeness, and let them have dominion over the fish of the sea, over the birds in the heavens, of the cattle, and over all the earth, and over every creeping thing that creepeth upon the earth." (27) And God created man in his own image ... (28) ... God said unto them "Be fruitful and multiply and replenish the earth and subdue it"* (to have dominion over it).

Adam was created in the image of God, which included having dominion. Adam and his children were to have dominion over all the earth. Adam lost that dominion for himself and his children. He actually gave it away. *(Rom.6:16) ... Know you not that to whom you present yourself as servants unto obedience <u>his servants you are whom you obey</u>*. Adam, through Eve, obeyed the devil and gave to him his own dominion. He obeyed and became the servant of sin and the devil. The devil ruled over him, the curse ruled over him, and the devil, through the curse, ruled over him. But the first Adam failed when tempted, and the last one did not. Speaking of Jesus, Paul said, *"The <u>last Adam</u> became a life giving spirit" (1 Cor.15:45)*. Jesus said, *"The words that I have spoken unto you are spirit, and are life."* His words recreate His spirit in us who believe them. Jesus, Who is called the last Adam, is the spiritual father of the spiritual man creation. The last Adam did not fall when tempted of the devil and so took back dominion for Himself and His children.

(Heb.2:5) For <u>not unto angels did he subject the world to come</u> (Greek: "inhabited earth") *... (6) ... What is man that thou art mindful of him?* He did not put the inhabited earth under the authority of the angels, but man. Jesus came down here and took on the likeness of sinful flesh. Any angel had power and ability unlimited by flesh. Jesus was limited by flesh. The Bible says that He got tired, He hungered, and He thirsted. He was *"tempted in all points, like as we"* but did not give in to sin. One reason that Jesus had to come in the likeness of sinful flesh and become a man is because God wanted Him to have this dominion and to pass it on to His spiritual children. *(Ps.115:16) <u>The heavens are the heavens of the Lord</u>; But the <u>earth hath he given to the children of men</u>*.

(1 Cor.15:21) ... As <u>in Adam all died</u>, so also <u>in Christ shall all be made alive</u>. When Adam died, all the seed of mankind was in his loins; and they died, too. When the last Adam died and was resurrected, all the seed of the sons of God were in Him because He is the Word of God, the seed (Greek: *sperma*) that the sower went forth and sowed. So the seed of all His children was in Him when He was resurrected. Everyone

who abides in Christ, or the Word, is resurrected above sin and the curse. What we are finding out through tribulation is who among the many called were chosen in Him before the foundation of the world. His children are His seed, the Word. They are the Word in flesh. *(Rom.5:17) For if, <u>by the trespass of the one</u>* (Adam)*, <u>death reigned</u> through the one; much more shall they that receive the abundance of grace and of the gift of righteousness <u>reign in life</u> through the one, [even] Jesus Christ* (last Adam). Adam put us under the dominion of death and the curse, but Jesus restored us. Those who have the gift of grace and righteousness are to *"<u>reign in life</u>"* through Christ.

(Heb.2:6) (Quoting Psalm 8) *... one has somewhere testified saying "what is <u>man</u> that thou art mindful of him, or <u>the son of man</u> that thou visiteth him?"* When Jesus kept relating to the Jews that He was the son of man, a few of them had to catch on that He was applying Psalm 8 to Himself. This was spoken to both Adams and those who were in them. God gave authority to Adam and to his children. Man and the <u>son of man</u> are mentioned here. *(Gen.1:26) ... Let us make man in our image, after our likeness, and let <u>them</u> have <u>dominion</u>.* Adam lost it for himself and for his children when he fell under the dominion of the devil. The last Adam overcame and took back dominion. Jesus passed on His same authority to His disciples, who were sons of man and sons of God. They were not born sons of God; they had to be reborn sons of God through receiving the living Word. The <u>Son of God was living in and empowering the sons of men</u>.

(Heb.2:7) (Quoting Psalm 8) *Thou madest him a little lower than the angels, <u>thou crownedst him with glory and honor and didst set him over the works of thy hands</u>, (8) <u>Thou didst put all things in subjection under his feet</u>.* This clearly means that man was meant to be a prince on this earth and rule for God over His creation. This address is to the Hebrew Christians, children of the new creation Adam. The works of God's hands here means the elements, not just things that occur in nature.

Even the things that man makes are made of God's elements. By God's grace I have commanded cars, washing machines, refrigerators, air conditioners, microwaves, boat motors, lawn mowers, and many other things to be repaired and seen it happen. Yet it was *"not I but Christ"* living in me through the Word. The reason that many do without this dominion is because they refuse to accept the Word.

Proof that the authority that the last Adam had was passed on to His children is seen in such statements as the following: *"As the Father hath sent me so send I you"*; *"What you bind on earth is bound in heaven and what you loose on earth is loosed in heaven"*; *"I give you authority over all the power of the enemy"*; *"All things whatsoever you ask in prayer believing you shall receive"*; and *"Whosoever shall say unto this mountain, be thou taken up and cast into the sea, and shall not doubt in his heart … he shall have it."* This is the kind of authority that Jesus passed on to all of His disciples until this day.

(Heb.2:8) Thou didst put all things into subjection under his feet. (Everything was put under the feet of Jesus and His body, for we are in Him.) *For in that, he subjected all things unto him and he left nothing that is not subject to him.* This statement puts all things under the dominion of *"man"* and *"the son of man"* in Hebrews 2:6. Compare this statement that all is under His feet with another witness given in Ephesians. Jesus was promoted *(Epe.1:21)* " *… Far above all rule and authority and power and dominion and above every name that is named, not only in this world but in the world that is to come; (22) and he put all things in subjection under his feet, and he gave him to be the head over all things to the church, which is his body, the fullness of him which filleth all and in all."* Notice that Jesus is the head of the body, the Church; but God put all things under the feet of the body. We can see that even if we are the lowest members of the body, the feet, we have dominion over all things. This dominion is ours when we are abiding in the body, submitted to the head. *(Jn.15:7) If ye abide in me* and

my words abide in you, ask whatsoever ye will and it *shall be done* unto you. *(8) Herein is my Father glorified, that you bear much fruit, and so shall ye be my disciples.* Disciples are those who bear fruit through answered prayer because the Word abides in them. Christians who do not abide in the body in this way, and the lost who have not yet come into the body of the resurrected Christ, lost their dominion when the first Adam lost his. We have this dominion only because we abide in Him and the Word lives in us.

(Epe.1:22) And he put all things in subjection under his feet, and he gave him to be the head over all things to the church, which is his body, the fullness of him which filleth all and in all. Not only is everything put under the authority of the lowest member of the body, the feet, but also there is a historic view to this verse. In Daniel 2:31-45, we see a vision of the antichrist kingdom from the time of Daniel to today. This image was of a man whose head, breast and arms, belly, thighs, legs, and feet represented different world ruling empires. The head was said to be the Babylonian Empire (verses 37,38) of Daniel's day. The feet represent the last world empire of antichrist in our day. The feet of Christ or "historic view" also represent the end time body of Christ. In other words, the feet of antichrist will do battle in these days with the feet of Christ.

What Daniel knew, but most do not, is that we win! *(Dan.2:34) Thou sawest till that a stone was cut out without hands, which smote the image upon its feet that were of iron and clay, and brake them in pieces. (45) Forasmuch as thou sawest that a stone was cut out of the mountain without hands ....* The mountain here is the kingdom of God. The stone made of it is Christ in His end time faithful remnant, which is not made with hands, meaning they are not the work of men or religion but God. This stone will smite the end time antichrist body or feet and destroy it. Daniel declares this to be true in another vision of the end time antichrist system. *(Dan.7:26) But the judgment shall be set, and they* (end time saints) *shall take away*

209

his dominion, to consume and to destroy it unto the end. (27) And the kingdom and the dominion, and the greatness of the kingdoms under the whole heaven, shall be given to the people of the saints of the Most High .... The kingdom of antichrist was destroyed in Egypt in order to bring God's people out of that type of the world. Pharaoh was told, *"Knowest thou not yet that Egypt is destroyed?" (Ex.10:7)* The same judgments are spoken in Revelation for the same reason. As always these judgments are spoken through the saints.

Returning to Hebrews: *(Heb.2:8) Thou didst put all things in subjection under his feet, For in that he subjected all things unto him, he left nothing that is not subject unto him. But now we see not yet all things subject to him.* All things have now been made subject, though we do not see this authority manifested except in small ways in a few who believe the Word in this regard. Soon, because of the latter rain and because their lives will depend upon it, saints will begin to stretch forth their faith for signs and wonders. Soon a wilderness experience is going to thrust many into a position of need where they are going to be fellowshipping with disciples with different revelations and experiences. God is going to destroy man-made religion by bringing His people into fellowship with others who have exercised their faith in these areas. Dominion will come forth because the need will be so great, God will pour out His Spirit. The saints (sanctified ones) are going to believe the Word. However, we do not have to wait because God said that He did not leave anything that was not subject to the lowest member of the body now. We can be among God's first fruits like Moses, Aaron, Joseph, Elijah, Jesus, or the man-child of the end time in Revelation 12.

(Jn.15:7) If ye abide in me, and my words abide in you, ask whatsoever ye will, and it shall be done unto you. Many believe we cannot act in faith when we do not know the Will of God. If the Word is in us and we abide in Christ through faith, then *"ask whatsoever ye will, and it shall be done."* God's Word is His

Will. When the Word is in us, we know His Will and should act on it. God gave us this dominion to use it to <u>glorify Him</u>. *(8) <u>Herein is my father glorified</u>, that ye bear much fruit, and <u>so shall ye be my disciples</u>.* Answered prayer, signs and wonders, healings, deliverances, and provisions all glorify God; this is how we are disciples (Greek: "learners and followers") of Jesus. No one who exercises this dominion is perfect, except by faith. We walk by faith in Jesus and are counted righteous. We are sons of God through Jesus, sons of man through Adam. We have no authority outside of God but through believing Jesus Christ. *(Jn.14:12) Verily, verily, I say unto you, <u>he that believeth</u> on me, <u>the works that I do shall he do also</u>; and greater [works] than these shall he do; because I go unto the Father. (13) And <u>whatsoever</u> ye shall ask in my name, that will I do, that the Father may be glorified in the Son.*

True believers do the works of Jesus according to His Word. The condition to exercise dominion over everything is faith, not maturity. Baby Christians have simple yet powerful faith.

Chapter 12
Vessels of Dominion Through Faith

Verily I say unto you. <u>Whosoever</u> shall say unto this mountain, Be thou taken up and cast into the sea; and shall not doubt in his heart, but shall believe that what he saith cometh to pass; he shall have it (Mk.11:23).

The word "whosoever" includes you and me. We are called to exercise dominion through the spoken word of faith. When we exercise dominion in ministry, it is by command as Jesus and His disciples did. Did you ever notice that when they ministered to others, they did not ask God to heal, deliver, or provide for them? They commanded these things because they knew that God already guaranteed them to His covenant people. *(Phl.4:19) And my <u>God shall supply every need of yours</u> according to his riches in glory in Christ Jesus.* They saw these things as already accomplished at the cross and God's promises as our authority to minister them. *(2 Pet.1:3) Seeing that <u>his divine power</u> <u>hath</u> <u>granted unto us all things</u> that pertain unto life and godliness, through the knowledge of him that called us by his own glory and virtue; (4) whereby he hath granted unto us his precious and exceeding great promises; that through these ye may become partakers of the divine nature ....*

The Lord still reigns through those who have renewed their minds with the Word. *(Rev.5:9) Worthy art thou to take the book and to open the seals thereof: for thou wast slain, and didst purchase unto God with thy blood [men] of every tribe, and tongue, and people, and nation, (10) and madest them [to be] unto our God a kingdom and priests; and <u>they reign upon the earth</u>.* Before the judgment seals of the tribulation are opened, the saints of God are said to be reigning on earth. We have the authority to reign as Jesus reigned because He lives in us through the Word that we put in our heart. The more of His Word we accept, the more He can live through us because He is the Word. He says, *"They reign upon the earth."* Jesus gave us an example of the dominion that the Son of God could manifest through the son of man. He gave us an example of what man was sent to do with God's Word and Spirit in him. Then He equipped the early disciples with these and sent them out to repeat this process.

(Mt.28:19) Go ye therefore, and make disciples of all the nations ... (20) teaching them to observe all things whatsoever I commanded you: and lo, I am with you always, even unto the end of the world. The apostles were to make disciples and give them the same authority and commands that they had received, and in turn, those disciples were to do the same right on down to us. We all should have received from our teachers the same authority, commands, and gifts given to the first disciples. What happened? The apostate religious traditions of men happened! Obedience to Jesus' command would have made a geometric progression from His day to our day that would have shaken the world. Jesus said that He would be with the disciples in this endeavor *"unto the end of the world."* Since the first disciples were not around that long, He, obviously, was talking to us, also.

Then what were they commanded so that we can know what we are commanded? Jesus commanded us to walk in His steps. *(Jn.20:21) ... As the Father hath sent me, so send I you. (Mt.10:8) Heal the sick, raise the dead, cleanse the lepers, cast out demons, freely you have received, freely give.* We have received the same authority as Jesus and the early disciples to do the same work. *(Jn.14:12) He that believeth on me, the works that I do shall he do also; and greater works than these shall he do; because I go unto the Father.* Those who believe will be vessels of God's sovereign dominion in the earth. We have to obey all these commands that Jesus gave them. The great commission has been passed on to us from the Lord. When we

213

make disciples, we must also pass on the command to do these things. *(Mk.16:15) And he said unto them, Go ye into all the world, and preach the Gospel to the whole creation*. Again, this could not have been spoken to only the first disciples because they neither went into the entire world nor preached to the whole creation. Disciples will finish this work in our day.

Please notice that in the following verse Jesus is telling His apostles how to identify those who believed their Gospel. *(16) He that believeth and is baptized shall be saved; but he that disbelieveth shall be condemned. (17) And these signs shall accompany them that believe* (believers have signs): *in my name shall they cast out demons; they shall speak with new tongues; (18) they shall take up serpents, and if they drink any deadly thing, it shall in no wise hurt them; they shall lay hands on the sick, and they shall recover.* These signs were not spoken of the first disciples but of those who came after and believed their Gospel. So the doctrine that all these signs passed away with the apostles is clearly a lie that has made many of God's people powerless. *(2 Tim.3:1) But know this, that in the last days grievous times shall come. (2) For men shall be … (5) holding a form of godliness, but having denied the power thereof, from these also turn away.* We are commanded to leave the powerless, unscriptural, religious institutions of men.

Some think that these things only happen for people with gifts of healings or miracles or faith. Jesus said, *"Whosoever shall say … and shall not doubt … he shall have it" (Mk.11:23)*. Whosoever commands without doubt shall have it. This obviously includes every believer in the true Gospel. The apostle Paul said that he preached *"in the power of signs and wonders, in the power of the Holy Spirit; so that from Jerusalem, and round about even unto Illyricum, I have fully preached the Gospel of Christ" (Rom.15:19)*. Fully preaching the Gospel is demonstrating its power to deliver from the curse. The world is tired of hearing that Jesus saves. They want to see it. Some think that these things only happen for the super mature saints. Maturity is to become as a child, simply accepting the Word of our Father. Young faith is powerful. *(Ps.8:2) … Out of the mouths of <u>babes and sucklings</u> have thou <u>established strength</u>, because of thine adversaries, that thou mightest still the enemy and the avenger.* God uses the spoken words of babes to still His enemies and ours. Both spiritual and physical little children with a little knowledge will see signs and wonders and put the principalities and powers in their place. Jesus told His grown disciples, *"Except ye turn, and become as <u>little children</u>, ye shall in no wise <u>enter into the kingdom</u> of heaven. Whosoever therefore shall humble himself as this little child, the same is the <u>greatest</u> in the kingdom of heaven (Mt.18:3,4)*. Only the childlike will enter and partake of the kingdom, but what is the kingdom? The kingdom is where God's will is perfectly done and there is no curse. *(Mt.6:10) Thy kingdom come. Thy will be done, as in heaven, so on earth.* He uses our prayers to bring the kingdom of heaven on earth. There is no curse in heaven. *(Mt.10:7) And as ye go, preach, saying, The <u>kingdom of heaven</u> is <u>at hand</u>* (Greek: "near"). *(8) <u>Heal the sick, raise the dead, cleanse the lepers, cast out demons: freely ye received, freely give</u>*. Being near those who exercise dominion over the curse, we are near the kingdom. *(Lk.11:20) But if I by the finger of God <u>cast out demons</u>, then is the <u>kingdom of God come upon you</u>*. Having been delivered from the curse, the kingdom has come upon us and we can partake of the kingdom, passing it on to others who believe.

Once my wife complained to me that the washer had stopped working. I turned to my children and told them to go lay their hands on it and command it to run. They obeyed with childlike faith and immediately it started. Several times, while driving in a rainstorm, I told them to point their fingers at the sky and command the rain to stop. Children are not proud and do not mind looking foolish to others. They commanded, God honored their faith, and the rain stopped, sometimes immediately.

When we first moved to Florida, my children found a squirrel in the road with a broken back. They came to me wanting to keep it and take care of it. I told them that we were not going to mess with that squirrel; they should just go command it to be healed. They did, and it ran up a tree. A couple of years later, they did the same thing for another squirrel that had fallen from an oak tree in our yard. They prayed for Mary and me many times with power.

One hot day, I got the mower out to cut the grass. I pulled and pulled trying to start it until I was sweating profusely. Then I checked the spark and found none. I did not feel up to looking for the problem, so I called my boys over to agree with me. We commanded the mower to run. I do not know if that mower ever got any spark, but it did run.

Once when I noticed a lone shoe on my front porch, I called the children together to scold them. I said, "I told you not to leave your shoes on the porch because a dog will pack one of them off and the other one won't be worth anything." I realized later that I got exactly what I had loosed with my tongue. The children and I scoured the yard and the neighbor's yard with no success. I said, "Let's pray and agree that God will put it in that dog to bring the shoe back." Children always have faith so easily. So we joined hands and agreed. The next day we were looking out of the picture window, and what do you think we saw? A stray dog came across the yard with that shoe in his mouth and dropped it right in front of the porch. Hallelujah! Teach your children simple faith, and do not let any theologians around them.

In spite of our own failures and weaknesses, we should receive this authority from our Lord like little children. By the grace of God, I have commanded eyes restored, bones mended, cancers gone, diseases gone, bleeding stopped, blood pressure normal, demons out, dead resurrected, those in comas to come out, water pumps to stop leaking, alternators to have new bearings, smoking engines to stop using oil, hurricanes to stop or change directions, property protected, storms to stop and back up, moles to get out of my yard, mole crickets to die, gas in my tank, engines to start, to name a few. None of the above was without witnesses. Yet it was *"not I but Christ"* living in me through the Word. God has not left us without help. We have left Him without help. He desires to use us as vessels to do His work. *(Phl.4:13) I can do all things in him that strengtheneth me.*

God wants us to command and not doubt. I was preaching in a mission church in Pensacola. A girl came forward and was saved. She indicated that she had a problem and wanted to talk. She was distraught because she had just killed her unborn baby. A man of another race who was an acquaintance of her husband had raped her. She was afraid that her husband would find out and get in trouble. Three days before this time she had been at the health unit where they had tested her with the heart monitor, a sonogram, and a sample of the fluid. They declared the baby to be dead and scheduled her to get a D&C.

As she was talking, I became impressed to ask her if there was anyone she had not forgiven. She said that there was a doctor that she thought purposely aborted one of her babies. I said to her, "Since you have just done the same thing, don't you think you had better forgive him?" She agreed, so I suggested she pray for him, which she did. I asked her if she wanted to be filled with the Holy Spirit. After a brief teaching on the baptism of the Holy Spirit, she agreed and we prayed. Although she was a very quiet girl, when she got filled she was exuberant and rejoicing. The next thing that came to my mind and out of my mouth was, "I believe the Lord wants to resurrect your baby." When I said that, the pastor, who was sitting next to me, his secretary, a deacon, and a few other ladies left the room. I paid no attention but continued. I asked Mary to put her hand on the girl's tummy, and we commanded the spirit of life to come back into that baby. I then instructed the girl how

217

to walk by faith and left the room. A door opened as I was walking down the hall, and the pastor coaxed me inside where I saw the others who had left the room. He said, "David, God is not going to do that for her." I said, "Why not?" He said, "She killed that baby." I said, "I don't think you understand grace. That is a new creature in there, and she is not guilty of what the old man did. Besides, if I want to believe it, why try to destroy my faith? Just let me believe it." Then I left the room. The girl stayed in the mission that night, but she called me the next day. She told me that she wanted to go to the health unit, but no one wanted to take her. I told her I would be glad to. On the way to the health unit, I reminded her to obey Jesus in Mark 11:24 and to believe that she had received what we prayed for. I also told her not to accept what people who walk by sight say. She was very simple and all this was new to her but she respected the Word.

At the clinic, they reproved her for not getting the D&C and told her she was endangering herself. She told the doctor that she wanted them to check the baby again. He agreed and sent her into another room with a technician. He put the sonogram and the heart monitor on her. He saw no signs of life, and the baby had not moved for four days. He told her, "Ma'am, you have got to have a D&C because your baby is dead." She said, "I just don't accept that." When she said that, the heart monitor began to register a beat and the baby moved energetically. The sonogram showed the baby alive. That unbelieving technician said, "That's a miracle." Now I don't know what God did, but she gave birth a few months later to a beautiful baby boy, who was obviously her husband's. Since she still had not told her husband about the rape, this was an answer to her prayers. This newborn Christian did not walk by sight but faith, and God confirmed His Word with a wonder. Praise God! When I tell this story, I get choked up and can hardly finish because of the awesome grace of God.

Here is a condensed version of a Bible study we had on the effect imagination has on our faith. Real faith is acted upon by the whole man. *(Rom.10:10) For with the <u>heart man believeth</u> unto righteousness; and with the <u>mouth confession</u> is made unto salvation.* It is fruitless for the heart to believe and the body to not react or for the body to act and the heart to not believe. The part of man that God designed to effectually connect the heart of man with his actions is the imagination. Our imagination should be renewed so that faith may have unhindered flow through us. Evil imaginations must be cast down if we want to win our battle with the flesh and the devil and to do the works of Jesus. *(2 Cor.10:4) For the weapons of our warfare are not of the flesh, but mighty before God to the casting down of strongholds), (5) <u>casting down imaginations</u>, and every high thing that is exalted <u>against the knowledge of God</u>, and bringing every thought into captivity to the obedience of Christ.* Cast down imaginations must be replaced with Biblical ones. For instance: *(2 Cor.3:18) But we all, with unveiled face <u>beholding as in a mirror</u> the glory of the Lord, are transformed into the <u>same image</u> from glory to glory ....* Notice that this renewed imagination of seeing Jesus in the mirror completes our faith, enabling us to come into His image and to do His works. This is the same faithful imagination that Paul had. *(Gal.2:20) I have been crucified with Christ; and it is <u>no longer I that live</u>, but <u>Christ living in me</u> ....* We are to believe, imagine and confess that Jesus lives in us. Jesus said that if we believe we will do His works and greater. *(Jn.14:12) ... He that believeth on me, the works that I do shall he do also; and greater [works] than these shall he do; because I go unto the Father.*

After this teaching, we were given opportunity to put this to work. At the very next Bible study, Pauline Warner asked prayer for Jacqui Kitts, whom she said would not be coming because her whole face was swollen with an abscessed tooth. My suggestion was that we would see Jacqui's swollen face in our imagination. Then we would speak to it commanding

219

her tooth to be healed and the swelling to go down. Then we would imagine her face returning to normal with a smile. With everyone's agreement we proceeded to act on this suggestion, and I vocalized our common command for her healing. This was a Biblical imagination because Jesus lives in Jacqui, and He is not abscessed or swollen. We are to accept the resurrected life of Christ. *(1 Jn.4:17) … As he is, even so are we in this world.* The Lord taught us to pray *"thy kingdom come. Thy will be done, as in heaven, so on earth" (Mt.6:10).* There is no sickness in God's kingdom. Jacqui was healed by the stripes of Jesus 2,000 years ago. The next morning, Jacqui called me and gave me the good report. She said that the night before, at about the time when we normally pray, the swelling suddenly went out of her face and her tooth was healed. We rejoiced and thanked the Lord together.

God quickly gave us several more opportunities to exercise our faith in this way. In a following Bible study, Bob Aicardi related that the water level in his swimming pool was dropping at about four to five inches a week. He inspected the liner and tested the plumbing for leaks and found none. The water bill was sizable. In frustration, Bob cried out to God, "Lord, there is no reason for this to be happening to this pool or to me. I belong to you, and I am not under the curse." When Bob asked for the prayer of agreement, we visualized the pool leaking and commanded it to stop. I said, "I command you pool not to leak one more drop in the name of Jesus." We then visualized the pool as repaired. The next day Bob watched the water level expecting God to act on his behalf and noticed that the leak had completely stopped. Isn't God awesome?

Bob then brought another prayer request to the study. He related that when he first moved into his house he walked around the property and asked God to put a hedge around it and his family. For 3-1/2 years there had been no roaches, bugs, or rodents. Now he faced mole crickets marching across his front lawn, devouring the roots of his grass. His neighbor was worried that they would get their lawn, too, so they suggested Bob use some poison. Bob wanted to exercise his faith instead, but he knew something had to happen quickly. When Bob asked for prayer, we visualized his lawn from his front porch with the mole crickets wiping it out. Bob prayed, "They would be turned into fertilizer." I commanded them to die and not take one more inch of that property in Jesus' name. In our various ways, we then visualized the crickets as dead. I suggested to Bob that he get a point of reference on his porch so that he could tell where the mole crickets were. Bob reported back that he had done that and not only had they not taken another inch but not even a sign of a single living mole cricket remained. They were all fertilizer. Glory to God! He gives authority to believers, and He wants to use us to continue to destroy the curse for His glory. Bob's place turned into a great testimony. He later had a problem with ant piles, and every time he commanded a pile to die, it did.

Chapter 13
Authority in Prayer

And <u>all things, whatsoever</u> ye shall ask in prayer, believing, ye shall receive (Mt.21:22).

Sometimes we cannot think of a verse on which to base a particular prayer request. That is where all encompassing promises such as this one come in. Jesus passed on His authority in prayer by the promises that He spoke. *(Mt.18:18) Verily I say unto you, <u>what things soever</u> ye shall bind* (forbid) *on earth shall be bound* (forbidden) *in heaven; and <u>what things soever</u> ye shall loose* (permit) *on earth shall be loosed* (permitted) *in heaven.* Should we think it dangerous for God to give such authority unto men? Not at all. Most Christians have not put enough Word in their heart to believe these promises. *"Faith cometh of hearing and hearing by the word."* A person has to have a renewed mind to believe this without being double-minded. If he has the renewed mind of Christ, he is totally dependable and subservient to Christ. Also, faith is a gift of God, and you will find that your faith will not go where God does not want you. *(Jn.15:7) If ye abide in me, and my <u>words abide in you, ask whatsoever ye will</u>, and it shall be done unto you.*

When I was a baby Christian, I loved the Word and was convinced that it was all true. Before any religious folks got to me to tell me that I could not believe these things, I started exercising them. When these people did speak to me, it was too late, I had discovered the power. So we do not have to be in the Lord for years to exercise faith. We must be convinced that what we read <u>once</u> is the word of a totally faithful God. Stay away from those leaders who have been "in the Lord," so called, for many years and still don't believe these verses. Many of these, *"ever learning, and never able to come to the knowledge of the truth,"* will stay double-minded all their powerless lives.

New Testament prayer should not be confused with Old Testament prayer. In the Old Testament, David prayed *"evening, and morning, and at noon"* and Daniel prayed *"on his knees three times a day,"* facing the temple in Jerusalem. We do not have to pray towards the temple; we are the temple. We carry the Lord with us in every place and situation, which is where prayer is needed. This is also why we are told to *"pray without ceasing"* *(1 Thes.5:17)*. We need to pray when we see the need and while the burden is upon us. Much of what is taught about prayer today is an Old Testament relationship with God. We should not wait legalistically until night or morning when we are tired and trying to remember what to pray for. This is not an *"effectual fervent prayer"* that *"availeth much"* *(Jas.5:16)*. This does not mean that we cannot take time out every day to concentrate only on prayer. God's plan for spiritual men who have the Holy Spirit is to be in constant communication with Him, otherwise, we treat Him as baggage, ignoring Him without ceasing. That is not why we became His temple. Prayer without ceasing necessitates us praying in our mind sometimes. He hears us just as well. *(1 Chr.28:9) ... The Lord searcheth all hearts, and understandeth all the imaginations of the thoughts: if thou seek him, he will be found of thee; but if thou forsake him, he will cast thee off forever.* In heaven thoughts are audible to the mind. We now can practice fellowship with God and pray about everything without ceasing. As the song says, "How much needless grief we bear, all because we do not carry everything to God in prayer."

Jesus gave us authority in three different kinds of prayer. We have examples in the Scriptures of the prayer of faith, the prayer of agreement, and the prayer of importunity.

The prayer of faith is the most common prayer for the mature Christian who prays without ceasing. Believing that you received is the key to the prayer of faith. *(Mk.11:24) Therefore I say unto you, All things whatsoever ye pray and ask for, believe that ye receive* (Greek: "received") *them, and ye shall have them.* If possible, be convinced of God's Word and pray the prayer of faith, believing you have received, because one day there may not be time to "pray through." *(Heb.11:1) Now faith is assurance* (or substance) *of [things] hoped for, a conviction of things not seen.* All prayer must be concluded with faith, because that is the substance from which the desired need is made. We give God the substance, and He gives us the answer.

The reason Jesus said, *"All things whatsoever ye pray and ask for, believe that ye receive* (Greek: "received") *them,"* is because all of our provision was accomplished at the cross. Notice in the following verses that all things have been received and that the only thing left is for us to believe it. Also notice the past tense of our sacrificial provision in the following verses: *(Epe.2:8) for by grace have ye been saved through faith; (1 Pet.2:24) who his own self bare our sins in his body ... by whose stripes we were healed; (Col.1:13) who delivered us out of the power of darkness and translated us into the kingdom of the Son of his love; (2 Cor.5:18) ... who reconciled us to himself; (Gal.2:20) I have been crucified with Christ, and it is no longer I that live, but Christ liveth in me; (Gal. 3:13) Christ redeemed us from the curse; (1 Pet.1:3) ... the Father ... begat us again ... by the resurrection of Jesus Christ; (Heb.10:10) We ... have been sanctified ...; (14) He hath perfected forever them that are sanctified; (Epe.1:3) ... who hath blessed us with every spiritual blessing,* and God *(2 Pet.1:3) hath granted unto us all things ...* . Jesus told us in His day which, of course, is also in the past that *"Now shall the prince of this world be cast out" (Jn.12:31); "but be of good cheer, I have overcome the world" (Jn.16:33); "It is finished" (Jn.19:30).* This is why we are to believe we have received. The devil and the curse were conquered. We were saved, healed, delivered, and provided for.

Redemption from the curse is truly finished! In fact, God's *"works were finished from the foundation of the world"*

(Heb.4:3), when He spoke the plan into existence. The only thing left is for the true sons of God to enter into those works by faith, believing they have received. Since the works are finished, we should believe and rest from our own works to save, heal, and deliver ourselves. *(Heb.4:3) For <u>we who have believed</u> do enter into that <u>rest</u>.* That is a spiritual Sabbath rest. *(Heb.4:9) There remaineth therefore a <u>sabbath rest</u>* (Greek: *sabbatismos*, "keeping of rest") *for the people of God.* This constant "keeping of rest" every day through the past tense promises is our New Testament spiritual Sabbath. *(10) For he that is entered into his rest hath himself also <u>rested from his works</u>, as God did from his.* This rest is to believe these past tense promises.

(Heb.4:1) Let us fear therefore, lest haply, <u>a promise being left</u> of <u>entering into his rest</u>, any one of you should seem to have come short of it. (2) For indeed we have had good tidings preached unto us, even as also they: but the word of hearing <u>did not profit them, because it was not united by faith</u> with them that heard. Our faith in each of these promises brings us into more of the rest. For example, if we believe that *"by his stripes you <u>were</u> healed,"* then we will not keep seeking a healing but will rest accepting that it <u>was</u> accomplished at the cross. This is true faith and always brings the answer. Through believing the promises, we enter into rest from our own works. For a child of God to say that they believe they have received and yet continue seeking to receive, usually through worldly methods, is to be double-minded. *(Jas.1:6) But let him ask in <u>faith</u>, <u>nothing doubting</u>: for he that doubteth is like the surge of the sea driven by the wind and tossed. (7) For <u>let not that man think that he shall receive anything of the Lord</u>; (8) a <u>doubleminded</u> man, unstable in all his ways.* Those who continue to work for what God has freely given believe in salvation by works. *(Heb.4:10) For he that is entered into his rest, hath himself also rested from his works. (Heb.3:19) And we see that they were not able to enter in because of unbelief.*

225

Since the promises of deliverance from the curse are past tense, when we believe them, we must stop working. It is an evil heart of unbelief to not rest. God was angry with Israel because they would not believe His Word in their trial in the wilderness (Heb.3:8-10). *(Heb.3:11) As I sware in my wrath, They shall not enter into my rest. (12) Take heed, brethren, lest haply there shall be in any one of you an* <u>*evil heart of unbelief*</u>*, in falling away from the living God .... (14) We are become partakers of Christ* (His health, holiness, and blessing) *if we hold fast the beginning of our confidence firm unto the end.* When we believe we <u>have received</u>, we are put in a position of <u>weakness</u> because we cannot do anything to bring the desired result to pass. This <u>weakness is our wilderness experience</u> because there is no help from Egypt or the world. Only God's power saves in the wilderness. God says, *"My power is made perfect in weakness" (2 Cor.12:9)*. Our weapon against our enemies who try to talk us out of our covenant rights is the two-edged sword of these past tense promises (Heb.4:11,12).

Let me share with you a good example of the power of the true Gospel through our <u>past provision</u>. A few years ago, I ran across a lady who had two large, inoperable tumors. She listed for me several famous preachers she had been to, who had prayed for her to be healed. She said to me, "David, I just don't understand why I have not been healed." I said, "You just told me why you have not been healed. You are looking in the wrong direction. Turn around and look behind you for *'by whose stripes ye* <u>*were*</u> *healed' (1 Pet.2:24)*. You are looking forward to a healing that happened behind you. You have little hope, but no faith. Faith *'calleth the things that are not,* (in this case healing) *as though they* <u>*were*</u>*' (Rom.4:17)*. Faith looks back at what was accomplished at the cross, but hope looks forward to what will be accomplished. Jesus said, *'All things whatsoever ye pray and ask for believe that ye* <u>*receive*</u> (Greek: "received") *them, and ye shall have them' (Mk.11:24)*.

That is the Gospel, sister, that you must believe." With these few words, I saw the light come on in her eyes, and her face brightened. I said, "Now we are going to pray one more time, but this time believe the Scriptures, and <u>believe you have received</u> whether you see an instant manifestation, or not." She agreed, so I rebuked the infirmity and commanded her to be healed in Jesus's Name. She instantly felt the tumors leave. We rejoiced and thanked God together. I said, "Sister, that is the first time you believed the true Gospel concerning your healing. If you would have done that when those other preachers prayed, you would have been healed."

Jesus guaranteed the Father's answer to the <u>prayer of agreement</u>. *(Mt.18:19) Again I say unto you, that <u>if two of you shall agree on earth as touching</u>* (Greek: "around") *<u>anything that they shall ask, it shall be done</u> for them of my Father who is in heaven.* The prayer of agreement is the most powerful prayer. *(Dt.32:30) <u>How should one chase a thousand</u>, and <u>two put ten thousand</u> to flight.* Combining our faith multiplies its power. For example, calling for the elders of the Church to pray the prayer of faith and to anoint with oil for healing (Jas.5:14,15) should always be a prayer of agreement. The one prayed for should be in agreement with the elders' faith that by the stripes of Jesus they were healed (1 Pet.2:24). Jesus gave us this example of seeking agreement when He tried to get words or actions of faith out of those that He then prayed for.

I often use the prayer of agreement to minister because it keeps faith in the mind of the person in need. There was a grieving man in a small congregation whose wife had left him and gone to live with another man. I called him to the front and asked him if he would agree with me according to Matthew 18:19 that his wife would be sitting right next to him the next time he assembled with the church. He was eager to do so, and we agreed. Sure enough, at the next assembly she was sitting next to him, and they were at peace. The man she was living with beat her up and threw her out with her belongings. God is bigger than our need and faithful to His Word!

(Mt.18:20) For where two or three are gathered together in my name, there am I in the midst of them. Small groups of Christians will see consistent, powerful answers to prayer no matter what they pray for with this method. Years ago, when I worked for the Exxon Refinery, men from many Christian backgrounds came together at noon, from all over the plant, to pray and study the Word. We did not have much time to dwell on prayer if we were to get into the Word and come to some agreement and maturity of understanding. One of the first things I taught was the prayer of agreement. We would share our prayer request in the simplest, shortest form possible. Then we would all agree that these needs were met, sometimes commanding them done but always thanking God and going on to study the Word. We certainly were not heard for our *"much speaking,"* but we <u>were</u> heard. At first, most of these brethren had never seen God answer prayer and did not have faith to ask. They were encouraged as they saw the power of combined faith and soon were eager to pray. We saw blind eyes opened, tumors and cancers disappear, all kinds of sicknesses healed, demons cast out, funds supplied, equipment repaired, marriages restored, souls saved, souls filled with the Spirit, etc. Even the lost passed requests to us for prayer. One of the biggest miracles was that many who attended began to believe on Jesus *"as the scripture hath said"* and were no longer nominal Christians. Many repented of dishonest practices such as taking tools home, exaggerating overtime hours, or cheating on taxes. My boss called me in one day very happy with the change in some of his employees who attended these meetings and tried to give me credit. I witnessed to him of our sovereign God.

Through the prayer of agreement, God changes hearts in our behalf. *(Pr.21:1) The king's heart is in the hand of the Lord as the watercourses: He turneth it whithersoever he will.* I cannot

228

tell you how many times that we have asked God to change the minds of men in order to give favor to His people in need. A brother in our assembly, Tony Nassef, has an environmental engineering firm. The owner of a large mall hired Tony's firm for a $1.9 million job. However, he was not satisfied with the time the job was taking, even though the tasks were being performed in record time. The owner, president, and vice-president had a conference call with Tony for an hour-and-a-half where they berated Tony, cursed, and threatened lawsuits if the work was not performed faster. During and after this conference, Tony prayed to God for favor and to help him control his anger with these men. Tony then contacted me, and we prayed the prayer of agreement that God would give Tony His favor and the favor of these men. We agreed that God would open these men's eyes to appreciate the speed and professionalism that God had provided through Tony's firm. Just 17 hours later, the vice-president called and said that the owner had asked him to contact Tony and apologize for him for what he had said and to ask if Tony would continue to work for them. He also related that the work performed was of a high caliber and that he had the utmost confidence in the work of Tony and his firm. He asked that Tony continue the work as he saw fit and not as he had directed. By God's grace the work was completed in a quarter of the typical time and saved the owner an additional $1.5 million. This is one of many times that God has given favor through men in answer to the prayer of agreement for Tony. He is no respecter of persons; He will do it for you, too.

Once when the family needed a break, we headed out toward Pensacola Beach. On the way I got their attention and we prayed the prayer of agreement. I said, "Father, we don't get to do this often, and we ask you to make the best of this day. We ask that you give us a nice <u>sunshiny</u> day, but <u>not too hot</u>. We ask that you give us a place on the beach <u>without a lot of naked people</u> around (meaning people in colored underwear, normally called swimsuits). We thank you for this in Jesus' name." Driving down the beach road, you cannot see the beach except sporadically because of the dunes, but we saw cars everywhere on the side of the road, which did not bode well for seclusion. We picked a spot and crossed the dunes to the beach. Looking in either direction for several miles there was nothing but people. I thought, "Lord, this is not what we asked for." After being there only a short time, we noticed a large black thunderstorm coming toward the beach from the direction of the mainland. For those who do not know, the beach is a very long island running parallel to the mainland but several miles from it. Again I thought, "Lord, this is not what we asked for." Little did we know that there were tornados jumping around in that storm. The closer it got, the more people left the beach.

Mary was saying to me that we had better go, but I was seeking to hold fast to our prayer and felt reluctance to leave. The leading edge of the storm was about to reach us and Mary was again saying that we had better leave. I looked up and down the beach for several miles in either direction, and there was not a single soul to be seen but us. It was then that the Lord spoke in my spirit and said, "Why don't you blow that storm back?" Being a little introverted, I did not want Mary and the children to see me blowing into the wind, so I walked down the beach a few yards and started blowing. The storm stopped very quickly and then started backing up. It backed up several miles and stayed there. I was awed at the Lord! Here we were having a beautiful sunshiny day, not too hot, and without any semi-naked people around just as we asked for the next two hours that we were there. On the way back, we came into the rain again in the middle of the first bridge so we knew that the people on Gulf Breeze and in Pensacola did not know the sun was shining on Pensacola Beach, which kept them away. God thinks of everything! As we returned to our house, we saw store awnings ripped off, trees down, and other obvious signs of a tornado. The children questioned what happened. I said that I must have blown too hard and they got a kick out of that. God was interested in blessing our day and giving us a testimony of His omnipotence to answer our prayers of faith and agreement.

Jesus gave us another guarantee for the prayer of importunity. *(Lk.11:8) I say unto you, Though he will not rise and give him because he is his friend, yet because of his importunity* (persistence) *he will arise and give him as many as he needeth. (9) And I say unto you, Ask, and it shall be given you; seek, and ye shall find; knock, and it shall be opened unto you. (10) For every one that asketh receiveth; and he that seeketh findeth; and to him that knocketh it shall be opened.* Jesus was adamant that we would receive an answer for persistent asking, seeking, and knocking. However there is a difference between importunity and vain repetition. *(Mt.6:7) And in praying use not vain repetitions, as the Gentiles do: for they think that they shall be heard for their much speaking.* Vain repetitions are attempts at salvation by works and do not end up believing that God will answer. Importunity should be used when we lack the faith to pray the prayer of faith. Importunity is a way to receive faith. Faith is His gift to give, and without it we do not have access to grace. *(Epe.2:8) For by grace have ye been saved through faith; and that not of yourselves, [it is] the gift of God.* The prayer of importunity cannot circumvent faith, for it must end up there. We must ultimately exercise faith to receive. *(Heb.11:6) And without faith it is impossible to be well pleasing [unto him]; for he that cometh to God must believe that he is, and [that] he is a rewarder of them that seek after him.* Every true believer has been given *"the measure of faith" (Rom.12:3)*, but we must learn to exercise it.

I share with you this example to compare the prayers of faith, agreement, and importunity. In 1984, I had plowed up the ground around our home to plant grass. Since it had been rainy, we had placed planks on blocks to make a walk to the house. My second son Nathan, who was then about three, and I were on this walk. Nathan stumbled, falling into the mud, when I caught his arm. His full weight was being thrown against his forearm at a right angle. I felt his arm snap in my hand, and he cried out. I knew his arm was broken as I gathered him into my arms. He was crying and holding his arm. I commanded his arm to be healed as I carried him to the door. I thought to myself, "I won't alarm Mary by telling her that he broke his arm." I believe God put that thought in me at that moment. As I handed him to her, I said, "He hurt his arm falling from the walk." She rocked him and prayed, as he cried. Soon he fell asleep, and she began to examine his arm. He cried out when she touched the break. She said to me "David, his arm is not hurt, it is broken!" I said, "Yes, I know, but God has always healed us before and He will heal us this time, too, won't He?" She agreed. When Nathan fell asleep, we put him in bed with us. I had prayed the <u>prayer of faith</u>, believing I had received and soon fell asleep. Mary, not yet at peace, prayed the <u>prayer of importunity</u> until about four a.m. Nathan cried several times during the night.

In the morning, we slipped quietly into the kitchen for coffee. Soon we heard Nathan so we took a peek. He saw us, grinned and scurried across the bed on all fours. I picked him up <u>by his arms</u>, tossing him in the air, as he laughed. He was totally healed! Praise God! Even though we had attacked the problem differently, we arrived at the same faith, essentially the <u>prayer of agreement</u> at four a.m. Friend, God will not fail you, but prayer must end at faith; the double-minded will not receive (Jas.1:6-8).

232

Chapter 14
Authority Over Demons

And these signs shall accompany them that believe: in my name shall they cast out demons ... (Mk.16:17).

Notice that the only condition for casting out demons is to be a true believer. Once again, <u>this verse was not spoken of the first disciples but of those that would believe their word, including us</u>. Probably a third of Jesus' ministry was casting out demons. The disciples were to carry on this ministry; they also were commanded of the Lord to make sure that their disciples did likewise, until the end of the world. *(Mt.28:19) Go ye therefore, and make disciples of all the nations ... (20) <u>teaching them to observe all things whatsoever I commanded you</u>: and lo, I am with you always, even unto the <u>end of the world</u>.*

It is a great joy to see people in bondage delivered. *(Lk.10:17) And the seventy returned <u>with joy</u>, saying, Lord, even the <u>demons are subject unto us in thy name</u>.* The seventy were the second group in an ever-increasing multitude of disciples to receive dominion over demons. In our day, ignorant religious leaders have condemned many to bondage, institutions, and death because they have not obeyed the Lord in this. *(19) Behold, <u>I have given you authority</u> to tread upon <u>serpents and scorpions</u>, and <u>over all the power of the enemy</u>: and <u>nothing shall in any wise hurt you</u>. (20) Nevertheless in this rejoice not, that the <u>spirits are subject unto you</u>; but rejoice that your names are written in heaven.* Having authority over the power of enemy spirits makes them completely subject to us, and they cannot harm us if we believe it. Familiarity with the Word and being filled with the Spirit will empower us and defend us against these deceivers.

The Lord divides these demons into two categories: *"serpents and scorpions."* Serpents, whose venom is in their <u>heads</u>, are

<u>mind</u>-deceiving demons. It was the serpent that deceived Eve by offering the forbidden fruit of the tree of the <u>knowledge</u> of good and evil (Gen.3:5,6). There are forbidden knowledge gifts that Satan bestows on his deceivers that sometimes mimic true gifts. *(Dt.18:10) There shall not be found with thee any one that maketh his son or his daughter to pass through the fire, one that useth divination* (fortune telling, false prophecy), *one that practiseth augury* (a soothsayer – interpreter of times and omens), *or an enchanter* (magician), *or a sorcerer* (witch), *(11) or a charmer* (hypnotist or caster of spells), *or a consulter with a familiar spirit* (a medium possessed with a spirit guide), *or a wizard* (psychic or clairvoyant), *or a necromancer* (a medium or spiritist who feigns consulting the dead). *(12) For whosoever doeth these things is an abomination unto the Lord ....* These false ministries have been given modern day names and in some cases are passing themselves off as Christian ministries. In Acts 16:16, there was *"a certain maid having a spirit of divination"* (Greek: "a spirit, a python"). This serpent, python spirit gifted the maid with divination, or false prophecy. The pastor of a church that I spoke in had this false gift of prophecy. I prayed for the congregation that God would reveal him. After this, one man had a dream of this pastor being a serpent speaking through a microphone, putting the congregation to sleep. Another woman saw him in a dream as a dragon, which is called in Rev.12:9 *"the old <u>serpent</u>."* She looked up this pastor's last name and found it meant "dragon."

Some of these serpent false ministries are like Pharaoh's wise men and sorcerers who counterfeited the signs and wonders given to Moses (Ex.7:11,22; 8:7). It is interesting that they could counterfeit some of the judgments (turning a staff into a serpent, the waters into blood, and multiplying the plague of frogs), but they could not remove them. Moses removed them, meaning God allowed them to magnify the curse, but not to deliver from it. It is still true today.

I have a friend who was mixed up in a ministry that was seeing many signs and wonders. As I watched, I noticed that these supernatural occurrences were not the gifts of provision as in the book of Acts or in 1 Corinthians 12 and 14. These signs and wonders seemed to be placebos to pacify a desire for the supernatural. They were flesh-pleasing signs that brought no practical, lasting deliverance from the curse. I perceived deceiving spirits involved and even saw some through the gift of discerning of spirits. When some tried to constrain them to stick to the Word, they would merely pass it off saying that God was doing a new thing.

Even though there may be new things to our own experience, Solomon said, *"There is no new thing under the sun."* We should find precedent in the Word for our signs and wonders. Paul warned of lying signs and wonders that come through Satan and his minions but are sent by God to deceive those who do not love truth (2 Thes.2:9-12). In concern for my friend whom I knew was gifted with dreams and visions, I prayed that the Lord would give her some to warn her of what was going on. The next time I saw her she related to me that she saw a vision in her church assembly. The ceiling disappeared, and she saw a great red dragon (*"the old serpent"*) stretched over the whole building. God was obviously saying that Satan was exercising dominion through deception there. Then she saw another vision: a Trojan horse was being wheeled through the back door. A voice told her, "Christians brought that in here." This symbolized a false gift in which the enemy was hidden in order to conquer them.

If the demons cannot keep you out of Christianity entirely, they have another strategy. There are religious spirits that specialize in keeping people in bondage to false, so-called "Christian" religions that do not teach the Word that sets free. There are many serpent spirits at work in the church today deceiving many with *"doctrines of demons,"* as Paul shared in 1 Timothy 4:1-3. Serpent spirits are manifest as false directions, doctrines, prophecies, and leadership to name a few. *(2 Cor.11:13) For such men are false apostles* (Greek: "one sent forth"), *deceitful workers, fashioning themselves into apostles of Christ. (14) And no marvel; for even Satan fashioneth himself into an angel* (Greek: "messenger") *of light* (truth). *(15) It is no great thing therefore if his ministers also fashion themselves as ministers of righteousness, whose end shall be according to their works.* The word "angel" in Greek is *angelos*, and is sometimes translated "messenger" when describing ministers who are sent by God or other ministers (Lk.7:24,27; 9:52). It is obvious that there are men who have infiltrated the ranks of ministers who are sent by Satan through their own ego and religious organizations. Both Jesus and Paul taught that these ministers were in the majority (Jn.10:8; 2 Cor.2:17).

Serpent spirits can also be mind-corrupting such as lust, greed, anger, bitterness, lying, homosexuality, alcoholism, idolatry, and uncleanness. Luke 8:35 shows insanity in various forms to be demonic. I was ministering to a group of elderly once when I was impressed to command a spirit out of a very sullen-looking woman with Alzheimer's. After I commanded the spirit to come out, her countenance changed and she smiled and said very intelligibly, "Thank you very much, I needed that." Most were shocked because they had never heard her speak. I knew then that Alzheimer's can be a demon.

There is indication that "spirits of infirmity" (Lk.13:11) are serpent spirits. When the Israelites sinned, God sent fiery serpents to bite them, and they were dying. The serpent bite clearly inflicted physical sickness through poison. When Moses prayed to the Lord for them, He had them make a brass serpent on a pole, and when they looked on it they were healed (Num.21:4-9). The serpent on the pole was said to be Christ (Jn.3:14) who became sin for us (2 Cor.5:21) and bore the curse of the serpent (Gal.3:13) so we could be healed (1 Pet. 2:24). The serpent on the pole has been hijacked by the medical establishment to symbolize their healing business.

Some sicknesses proven from the text of the New Testament to be caused by demons are crippled (Lk.13:11); dumb (Mt.12:22); blind and dumb (Mt.9:32,33; Lk.11:14); dumb and deaf (Mk.9:25); vexed with sickness (Mt.15:22,28); epileptic (Mt.17:15,18); and healed of evil spirits (Lk.8:2,36,42; Acts 10:38). There are other healings in the New Testament that appear to be deliverances which I did not list here. Beside these, I have seen cancers, coughs, rashes, diabetes, arthritis, allergies, insomnia, chronic pains, AIDS, restlessness, and many I do not recall that responded to deliverance. I am sure in the combined experience of Christians the list is longer. Some say these have natural causes. Almost all demons manifest natural causes.

The second category Jesus gave was <u>scorpion</u> spirits. The Greek word for "scorpion" is *scorpios* which means "scatter" or "to penetrate and put to flight." Scorpion spirits of fear, depression, manic depression, paranoia, worry, anxiety, suicide, guilt, condemnation, and dementia to name a few, penetrate the mind and cause one to flee from an enemy that they should be chasing. A scorpion's venom is in its tail just as a hornet. The hornet can put a large man to flight through fear. God sent the *"hornet"* to drive out the enemy from before the Israelites through fear (Dt.7:20; Josh.24:12; Ex.23:27,28). Jesus taught that he had already bound the strong man (Satan and his demons) and divided the spoils of his house (Lk.11:20-23). Concerning these spoils, Jesus said, ***He that gathereth not with me <u>scattereth</u>.*** The Greek word for "scattereth" here is *scorpizo*. If we are not gathering the spoils of Satan's house, the lost, for God's kingdom, we will be running from scorpion spirits. We must be vessels of God's sovereignty to conquer them and set the captives free.

A commonly taught false doctrine is that Christians cannot have demons. When Jesus sent His disciples to *"cast out demons,"* He told them, *"...<u>Go not into [any] way of the</u> <u>Gentiles</u> (lost), **and enter not into any city of the Samaritans:***

but go rather to the lost sheep of the house of Israel" (Mt.10:5,6). He did not send them to those who did not have a covenant with God, but rather only to those that did. In the New Testament, it is the Christians that have covenant promises of deliverance, healing, and provision, not the world. *(Col.1:13) Who delivered us out of the power of darkness, and translated us into the kingdom of the Son of his love.*

Since we have the promises of deliverance, we can use them for ourselves and those coming to Christ. *(2 Cor.7:1) Having therefore these promises, beloved, let us cleanse ourselves from all defilement of flesh and spirit, perfecting holiness in the fear of God.* Believers are to cleanse self which is synonymous with soul (compare Mt.16:26 with Lk.9:25) of both flesh and spirit, meaning evil spirits. Paul warned Christians not to *"receive a different spirit" (2 Cor.11:4)*. Also we are told, *"neither give place* (Greek: "region") *to the devil" (Epe.4:27)*. Simply, we are not to give any territory in ourselves to the devil or his minions.

(Lk.13:11) And behold, a woman that had a spirit of infirmity eighteen years; and she was bowed together, and could in no wise lift herself up. (16) And ought not this woman, being a daughter of Abraham, whom Satan had bound, lo, [these] eighteen years, to have been loosed from this bond on the day of the sabbath? The condition for deliverance was a child of Abraham, and such are the Christians. *(Gal.3:7) Know therefore that they that are of faith, the same are sons of Abraham.*

Jesus said that He was only sent to the house of Israel. When asked by a Canaanite woman to cast a spirit of infirmity out of her daughter, Jesus said, *"It is not meet to take the children's bread and cast it to the dogs" (Mt.15:22-28)*. From this we can see that the children of God have a covenant right to their Father's bread of deliverance and healing, not the lost. Since Jesus was beginning a New Testament and because of this woman's faith, He accounted her as righteous (Gal.3:6), granting her request. I have been casting out demons since around 1976, and almost all of the subjects were Christians. Most of this time, I have had a gift of discerning of spirits in which I see the demons in people's eyes. I know of no one with this gift, in one of its various forms, who does not believe that Christians can have demons.

We should never cast demons out of lost people without the direction of God because their house is not filled with Christ to defend them against the seven worse demons that will come. *(Mt.12:43) But the unclean spirit, when he is gone out of the man, passeth through waterless places, seeking rest, and findeth it not. (44) Then he saith, I will return into my house whence I came out; and when he is come, he findeth it empty, swept, and garnished. (45) Then goeth he, and taketh with himself seven other spirits more evil than himself, and they enter in and dwell there: and the last state of that man becometh worse than the first. Even so shall it be also unto this evil generation.* We see here that the generation of God's people who received deliverance from Jesus and the disciples later lost it when they did not continue as disciples. The same thing happens to New Testament people who are delivered today. They must continue to walk in the covenant and be filled with the Word and Spirit of God in order to give no place to the devil. If the Lord does direct us to deliver a lost person, it can mean that He plans salvation for this person. Also, deliverance can be used to stop some demon-possessed person from hindering the work of God, just as Paul cast the spirit of divination out of a lost soothsaying maid because she was hindering his ministry (Acts 16:16-18).

Some years ago, my mother, who had never become a Christian, came to stay with us. She had been tormented by what the psychiatrists call dementia, paranoia, manic-depression, etc., for many years. She began to torment our household with things such as running up the phone bill, threatening to keep us awake all night, leaving the refrigerator open all night, seeing things happening in the area when she was not there, claiming ailments that were not there, and falsely accusing; she had general self-will. Though we would bind the demons in her, the results were temporary. I went to God in prayer about this. I reasoned with the Lord that though she had no right to covenant deliverance, she was tormenting our house and we were not under the curse, but the blessings. *(Gal.3:13) <u>Christ redeemed us from the curse</u> of the law, having become a curse for us; for it is written, Cursed is every one that hangeth on a tree: (14) <u>that upon the Gentiles might come the blessing of Abraham</u> in Christ Jesus* .... In light of this, I asked the Lord for permission to cast the demons out of her to deliver us.

That night Jennifer, my youngest daughter, had a dream. She saw my mother's house in the middle of our house; however, her house was three stories tall going up through our roof. Out of the second story was a plank leading out to the street. On the plank were <u>five chickens marching out to the street</u>. I thanked the Lord for His clear direction and permission. The interpretation is that the three stories were the spirit, soul, and body of my mother's spiritual house. The five chickens were five demons. According to Rev.18:2, demons are unclean birds. These chickens were leaving her soul, the second story, meaning we had authority to evict them. The revelation is this: Whenever someone else's spiritual house is under the authority of our house, we have authority over the demons. Jesus used Jairus' faith for his daughter, the centurion's, for his servant, the Canaanite woman's for her daughter, and Peter's for his mother as examples of the rights we have to exercise faith for those under our authority. My mother was also <u>hindering our ministry</u>, which is why Paul delivered the soothsaying maid.

That night my mother, threatening to keep us awake all night, banged on our bedroom door, and I replied, "You will not." Mary and I went to her room and commanded the demons out as their names came to our minds. As I recall the names were dementia, paranoia, manic-depression, self-will or stubbornness, and one more that I cannot remember. Although demons can have individual names, they also answer to the name of the infirmity that they cause. We did not wait around to see any results but went to bed and had a good night's sleep. The next morning we noticed that it was quiet in her room, so we peeked in. We did not see her but noticed the room was in a mess. There were sheets, covers, pillows, and other things all over the floor, like someone had wrestled there all night. We walked into the room, and she came crawling out from under the bed. We immediately saw that this woman was a different woman than the one that I had known for most of my life. She was sweet and submissive and humble. She stayed this way for a while, during which time we preached the Gospel to her. We knew that the house needed to be filled with the things of God or the demons may come back. She always fell back on her religion as an excuse rather than accept the Gospel, so the demons started coming back, although not nearly as bad as before. At this time, she decided to move to an assisted-living facility. Just before she died, she steadfastly told me that she knew Jesus and He was her Savior.

The Old Testament tabernacle or temple symbolizes us. We are the temple of God. We have an outer court (flesh), a holy place (soul), and a holy of holies (spirit). Evil men entered into the outer court and even into the holy place to take hold of the horns of the altar (1 Ki.1:50; 2:28), but only the high priest could enter the holy of holies, anyone else would die. According to this type, demons can enter the flesh and even possess the soul; but only our High Priest Jesus may enter our spirit, unless we have become reprobate (2 Cor.13:5). Demons can oppress the soul (mind, will, and emotions) from without or from within the flesh. They can also possess the soul from without the flesh one moment and recede into the flesh the next, allowing that person to appear normal. This is called by the world schizophrenia.

241

Demons may enter the flesh because the flesh is the enemy of God, Who dwells in your spirit (Rom.8:7; Gal.5:17). I have heard some use the supposed verse, "My spirit will not dwell in an unclean temple," to say that Christians cannot have demons: There is no such verse! Our flesh is so corrupt that it cannot enter the kingdom. *(1 Cor.15:50) Now this I say, brethren, that flesh and blood cannot inherit the kingdom of God; neither doth corruption inherit incorruption.* Since the flesh is not in the kingdom, it may be entered by demon spirits. From this stronghold they may enter the soul.

Demons may enter the soul because the part of the soul that is not sanctified by the Word is of the flesh. *(Lev. 17:11) For the life* (Hebrew: "soul") *of the flesh is in the blood; and I have given it to you upon the altar to make atonement for your souls: for it is the blood that maketh atonement by reason of the life* (soul). Notice in type the flesh has to die for the soul to be free. In any part of the soul (mind, will, emotions) that we have not overcome temptation we are not yet sanctified or made holy. We all have overcome some things that no longer have any influence or temptation in our lives. However, there are other areas we still feel this. It is here that we are open to be used by demons. Every Christian knows this by experience. If we walk in willful disobedience, we invite oppression or possession in that area.

Demons can be passed on from generation to generation just like the nature of sin. *(Ex.34:7) Keeping lovingkindness for thousands, forgiving iniquity and transgression and sin; and that will by no means clear [the guilty], visiting the iniquity of the fathers upon the children, and upon the children's children, upon the third and upon the fourth generation.* We have a friend who adopted three babies, all siblings. H.R.S. would not tell her who the biological parents were. The children all had sweet dispositions and forgiving natures. As these children grew through puberty they became constantly tormented by lying, stealing, fornication, alcohol, and drugs. These were not just temptations of the fallen nature but were compulsive and irresistible, a sure sign of demons.

This greatly troubled the adoptive mother because she had done her best to raise them with the Bible as Christians. Although we had cast demons out of them several times, the effects were not lasting. She decided to try to find out who the biological parents were. She went to the H.R.S. office seeking this information and finally was permitted to look in their files. In this way, she found the mother and invited her and the grandmother for a visit. She was astounded to find that, though she had raised the children from babies, they were manifesting the spirits that were in their biological parents. The grandmother related that they were blood descendants of Jesse James. What we become is not all environment. We inherit much through blood nature, and demons sometimes come along for the ride. *(Lev. 17:11) For the life* (Hebrew: "soul") *of the flesh is in the blood* .... Thank God through repentance and faith in the Gospel we can have a spiritual transfusion of the blood of Jesus. When I wrote this, I contacted our friend who related to me that she has received assurances from the Lord that these children, now grown and gone, will be saved. She knows these troubles have done much to humble her and the children, and she sees signs of repentance in them.

I am not necessarily speaking of this case, but we can prematurely try to deliver someone. God through Paul delivered a rebellious Christian to Satan to bring him to repentance. *(1 Cor.5:5) To deliver such a one unto Satan for the destruction of the flesh, that the spirit may be saved in the day of the Lord Jesus.* For anyone to try to deliver this man from a curse that was ordained of God to crucify his flesh and bring him to repentance would be detrimental. God will for a short time honor the faith of the minister, and the cursed man may get a temporary deliverance. When God has put a curse on someone to teach him or her a lesson, you cannot prematurely, permanently remove it. It will come back, unless they repent. *(1 Tim.1:20) Of whom is Hymenaeus and Alexander; whom I delivered unto Satan, that they might be taught not to blaspheme* (Greek: "to speak against"). For anyone to deliver these two before they repented would have been counterproductive. They first needed someone wise enough to tell them that their problems stemmed from speaking against the kingdom. That is why we need to hear the voice of the Spirit. I have even heard of demons speaking from people saying, "I have a right to be here" or "They want me here." Sometimes this is a lie, but sometimes it is true. You can cast them out, but the demons will go right back if there is a good purpose for them to be there, as in the above verses.

I cast demons out of a woman who was in and out of a mental institution. She was totally delivered and no longer needed medicine. Later, the demons came back, so she came to us and was again delivered. A second time, the demons came back. I began to question her more carefully and found that she could not stop complaining about the way her relatives had treated her. I pointed out to her that Jesus taught that if we do not forgive our fellow servants, the Father will deliver us *"to the tormentors"* or demons until we pay our own debt of sin (Mt.18:34,35). She claimed that she was not unforgiving and that her actions were justified. She was offended that I was blaming her for the problem instead of her relatives. She was obviously defiled by a root of bitterness (Heb.12:15). I told her that the demons would stay until she repented, and as far as I know, they are still there.

In the mission church that I previously mentioned, we cast out many demons from homeless people, drunks, harlots, and drug addicts who had come to the Lord. One drunk by the name of Jim came in during the teaching and was miraculously saved and sobered-up at the same time. He began to stay in the mission. About this time, one of the deacons began to discuss demonology with me. I perceived that he was not fully given over to the Lord. I advised him to get filled with the Holy Spirit before attempting to cast out demons because there was much more power and discernment available to him for this. The very next day the pastor called me and told me that the deacon had gone to the mission to exorcise Jim, who had inexplicably been filled with demons and was exhibiting supernatural strength. The demons in Jim had chased the deacon through the mission and literally put him through the thick plate glass front door, totally shattering it. This left the deacon lying on the front lawn bleeding and screaming for someone to get the demons off him. A newborn Christian happened by and not sure of what to do commanded them to come out in Jesus' Name. The demons came out and an ambulance hauled the deacon to the hospital. This could not have happened if he was right with God.

The pastor then told me that he and his secretary had gone in to see what they could do with Jim and were chased out, too. He asked if I could do something. I told him something to the effect that I could not, but the Lord could. I met them out front, and together we walked through the shattered front door and down the hall to Jim's room. At this point, I walked straight through the open doorway but noticed that the pastor and his secretary stopped just short of the doorway. Just as if I had good sense, I marched toward Jim, who was seated in the other end of a long room. Before I got to him, he jumped up with his hands in the air like claws and a fierce countenance, growling just like a big old bear. Before I had time to think about it, I very loudly and sharply said, "SIT!" Jim's countenance immediately changed as he sat down just like an obedient puppy. I looked around to see two heads looking through the doorway. I do not normally do this, but I commanded the demons to tell me their names. As they told me their names in different voices, I commanded them to come out in Jesus' Name. Some argued, reasoned, or lied as usual, but I stood my ground. One asked if it could enter into the dog. I looked around and saw no dog in the room but later found out there was one in the next room. I told the demon, "No, but you may enter into the nearest cockroach." (There is an insane cockroach out there somewhere!)

One of the demons asked if it could enter into the secretary, who was still standing in the doorway. I again forbade it but later questioned her lifestyle which proved to be a well-founded doubt. The pastor had come next to me by this time and was also commanding demons. When they spoke to him, they seemed to like him, which again made me suspicious, and again it was well-founded. Unknown to others, the pastor and secretary had been intimate. The Lord then spoke to me and said, "The demons entered through the TV set." I asked, "Jim, what were you watching on this set?" By this time, he was able to respond in his own voice and he showed me a video skin flick that he had watched. Men, pornography will destroy your eternal soul. Jim would have ended up in an asylum, if it were left up to the leadership of this church. After casting out nine or ten demons, the Lord said, "There are two more. Leave them." I thought this was strange until the next service when Jim came forward for more deliverance. I had been asking the Lord to give me wisdom concerning this pastor's habit of slaying everyone in the Spirit, although he had no effect on Mary and me. The pastor put his hand on Jim's forehead, and he started to fall. Before I thought about it, I put my hand behind him and stood him back up. I then commanded the demons out, and they obeyed. Later, as I thought on this, I had discernment that the devil wanted Jim unconscious on the floor to hinder his deliverance.

I have seen some slain in the Spirit in my own ministry, but I do not exercise faith for this to happen. Paul was possibly slain in the Spirit on the road to Damascus, but neither Paul nor anyone else was exercising faith to do this. This <u>emphasis</u> is not in Scripture, and we should *"learn not to go beyond the things that are written" (1 Cor.4:6).*

I suspect anything that becomes a <u>habitual</u> show brings glory to such men. This pastor was the serpent I spoke of earlier. He had been a performer in a famous rock band when he "came to the Lord" toting a lot of excess baggage. I asked the Lord to reveal his demons. The next day, two ladies, unknown to each other, from different towns, called me. The Lord told them to tell me that this man had the same spirits as Jim Jones.

Chapter 15
Binding and Loosing What?

Verily I say unto you, <u>what things soever ye shall bind</u> (forbid) *on earth shall be bound* (forbidden) *in heaven; and <u>what things soever ye shall loose</u>* (permit) *on earth shall be loosed* (permitted) *in heaven (Mt.18:18).*

Faith <u>permits</u> the sovereignty of God to be manifest through the body of Christ and <u>forbids</u> the devil. Jesus' condition for receiving His benefits are plain: *"As thou hast believed, [so] be it done unto thee"* and *"According to your faith be it done unto you"* and *"Thy faith hath made thee whole."* As we believe, God's benefits will be given. Unbelief <u>forbids</u> God's benefits because He has made a condition and He cannot lie. Unbelief <u>permits</u> the devil to continue administering the curse. *(Mk.6:5) And he <u>could there do no mighty work</u>, save that he laid his hands upon a few sick folk, and healed them. (6) And he marvelled <u>because of their unbelief</u>.* Even Jesus was <u>forbidden</u> to do mighty works for those who would not believe. Whether we know it or not, we are constantly <u>forbidding</u> or <u>permitting</u> by our thoughts, words, and actions. Since all authority in heaven and earth was given to Jesus and He in turn delegated it to His disciples, where does the devil get his authority? He gets it from our unbelief, words, and disobedience.

(Rev.22:18) I testify unto every man that heareth <u>the words of the prophecy of this book</u>, <u>if any man shall add unto them, God shall add unto him the plagues</u> which are written in this book (19) and <u>if any man shall take away from the words</u> of the book of this prophecy, <u>God shall take away his part from the tree of life</u>, and out of the holy city, which are written in this book. Adding to or taking from God's Word <u>permits</u> the curse by the devil and <u>forbids</u> God's blessings for us or through us. This is by God's design to motivate us to come back into agreement with Him. Adam fell out of agreement with God and fell

under the curse, and God ordained that we would come back into agreement with Him to come out from under the curse. In no way does our disagreement hinder God's sovereignty. It only stops us from cooperating with Him in it and being a vessel for it. *(Lk.19:40) ...If these shall hold their peace, the stones will cry out.* Jesus made it clear that God would find a vessel to use. The only question is will that be you?

We must agree with God's Word in our speech, without adding to or subtracting from, to receive or to administer His benefits. In Hebrews 3:1, Jesus is called the *"High Priest of our confession."* Confession here is the Greek word *homologeo* meaning "to speak the same." In other words, Jesus offers before the Father our vocal agreement with His Word. We make an offering of our confession through Jesus to the Father. *(Heb.13:15) Through him then let us offer up a sacrifice of praise to God continually, that is, the fruit of lips which make confession* (speak the same) *to his name.* Both the Greek and Hebrew words for "name" in Scripture mean "character and authority." If we want the benefits of God consistently, we must continually speak in agreement with the character and authority of Jesus Who is the Word. If we disagree with the character and authority of God's Word, Jesus will deny us the benefits of those promises. Jesus said, *(Mt.10:32) Every one therefore who shall confess me* (speak the same as me) *before men, him will I also confess* (speak the same) *before my Father who is in heaven. (33) But whosoever shall deny me before men, him will I also deny before my Father who is in heaven.*

True believers speak in agreement with the Word and receive Christ's mediation for them to receive its benefits. Many wonder why they do not receive what the Bible promises, while in their mind and actions they disagree with it. *(Rom.10:10) For with the heart man believeth unto righteousness; and with the mouth confession is made unto salvation.* Notice that salvation comes when we believe and speak in agreement with it. Many do not know what the fullness of salvation is. "Salvation" here is the Greek word *soteria* which means "everything that the *soter* or 'savior' provided." We once asked a Greek man what *soteria* meant. He said, "It means all my needs provided for like a little baby." The verb of *soteria* is *sozo*. This Greek word is translated "saved" when speaking of salvation of the soul (Lk.7:50). It is translated "made whole" when speaking of healing (Lk.8:48; Jas.5:15) and deliverance from demon possession (Lk.8:36). It is translated "save" when speaking of salvation from adverse circumstances (Mt.8:25; Jude 1:5). Salvation covers <u>all</u> of the benefits that Christ paid for. We see here that it is not enough to believe only with the heart to have God's benefits. If a person has faith, it will come out of their mouth. *(2 Cor.4:13) But having the same <u>spirit of faith</u>, according to that which is written, <u>I believed, and therefore did I speak</u>; <u>we also believe, and therefore also we speak</u>.* As you can see, faith without works is dead. It is clear that Jesus mediates between the Father and us if our faith is proven in our words.

(Lk.12:8) And I say unto you, Every one who shall <u>confess me</u> before men, him shall the Son of man also <u>confess before the angels</u> of God: (9) but he that <u>denieth me</u> in the presence of men shall be <u>denied in the presence of the angels</u> of God. It is imperative that we say before men what God says in order for these same words to be given to the angels to bring to pass. If we confess the promises of the Word, Jesus gives authority to the angels to administer to us the benefits of God's salvation. *(Heb.1:14) Are they not all <u>ministering spirits, sent forth to do service</u> for the sake of <u>them that shall inherit salvation</u>?* The angels only have authority to administer our salvation when we become the *"voice of His Word." (Ps.103:20) Bless the Lord, ye his angels, that are mighty in strength, <u>that fulfill his word, Hearkening unto the voice of his word</u>.* When the angels hear the Word through us, they have authority from Jesus to fulfill it. When we speak unbelief, fear, and anxiety, we are speaking negative faith, or faith in the curse.

This gives authority to the demons to administer the curse. *(Num.14:28) As I live, saith the Lord, surely <u>as ye have spoken in mine ears, so will I do to you</u>*.

One day, I felt I was going to teach on the importance of right confession the next day. That night I had a very vivid dream. I saw myself fighting in a war to take the land from giants. (Our life spiritually is the land that must be conquered for God. *(1 Cor.3:9) For we are God's fellow-workers: <u>ye are God's husbandry</u>* (Greek: tilled <u>land</u>), *God's building.* In Malachi 3:11,12 the Spirit tells us that if we bear fruit we *"shall be a delightsome <u>land</u>."* The Israelites, who represented the spiritual man, sought to take their Promised Land from the Canaanites, who represented the carnal man. This is our battle, too. *(Gal.5:17) For the flesh lusteth against the Spirit, and the Spirit against the flesh; for these are contrary the one to the other* .... We are in a battle to see who rules in the Promised Land of our life.)

In this battle I had captured one of the enemies and was holding him in a neck lock while walking down a trail. The neck lock was obviously to prevent him from speaking. (The Lord helped me to see that this enemy that I should keep from speaking was my carnal man.) As we walked around a bend, we saw a giant standing by a camp fire. Although I knew he was a giant, he actually was no bigger than I. (A giant can be any enemy or obstacle that we perceive to be greater than us or greater than our ability to take control of our life for God.) As we faced this giant, I momentarily released the neck lock and my enemy spoke to him. He said, "Bigger, bigger, bigger." I knew that my enemy had the ability by speaking to make this giant much bigger. I then turned and karate chopped him in the Adam's apple to keep him from speaking and said, "No. Smaller, smaller, smaller!" (From this you can see that the carnal man has authority, if permitted, to speak about any adverse situation to make it worse. The flesh walks by sight, not by faith. On the other hand, the spiritual man has authority to speak giants such as sins, sicknesses, curses, and needs to make them smaller until they do not exist.)

Have you eyes to see and ears to hear, as Jesus put it? When Joshua (Hebrew: "Jesus") led the Israelites to take the Promised Land they had to <u>conquer the five kings who ruled that land first</u> (Josh.10:3,16). The five kings that rule our lives first are the five carnal senses. The carnal man walks after and is ruled by the carnal senses. Born again senses are formed by the Spirit and the Word. These spiritual senses enable us to walk in the "experience of the Word." *(Heb.5:13) For every one that partaketh of milk is without <u>experience of the word</u> of righteousness; for he is a babe. (14) But <u>solid food</u> is for fullgrown men, [even] those who by reason of use have their <u>senses exercised to discern good and evil</u>.* Babies on milk have unregenerate senses and cannot follow their father. Those who have senses conformed to the Word of righteousness are on solid food, able to walk as Jesus did. *(Jn. 4:34) Jesus saith unto them, My <u>meat</u>* (Greek: "solid food") *is to <u>do the will</u> of him that sent me, and to <u>accomplish</u> his work.* Jesus did not react to what He felt, heard, and saw with His natural senses. He only did what He <u>heard</u> and <u>saw</u> from the Father (Jn.5:19,30). This made Him a reliable representative of the Father because He could not be manipulated by external circumstances, conditions, or lies. *(Gen.21:8) "Abraham made a great feast on the day that Isaac was weaned"* from the milk because now he was not restricted to his mother but could go with his father. Samuel's mother could not give him to the service of the Lord until he was weaned (1 Sam.1:11,22). The Spirit taught through Paul that those who are divided from their brethren through sectarianism (denominationalism) are still on the milk (1 Cor.1:10-14; 3:1-5). They are still bound to their spiritual mother.

(Josh.10:16) And these five kings fled, and hid themselves in the <u>cave</u> at Makkedah. (17) And it was told Joshua, saying, The five kings are found, <u>hidden in the cave</u> at Makkedah. (18)

And Joshua said, Roll great <u>stones unto the mouth of the cave</u>, and set men by it to keep them. In Hebrews 6:4-8, the Spirit teaches that we are *"the <u>land</u> which hath drunk the rain"* of the Spirit and Word in order to bear fruit. The mouth of the cave in our land clearly symbolizes our mouth. Joshua, typifying Jesus, gave command to block the mouth with great <u>stones</u> to stop the five kings from escaping. Jesus is called a stone by Paul (Epe.2:20) and Peter (1 Pet.2:7,8). John called Him the Word (Jn.1:1,14; Rev.19:13). Hence, the stones symbolize the <u>Word</u> of God in our mouth restraining the five senses from speaking. As in my dream, if the carnal man speaks, the giants get bigger. If the spiritual man speaks the Word, the giants get smaller. Jesus taught that if we speak faith the mountains (giants) in our way will be removed (Mk.11:23). Ten of the dozen spies sent to spy out the Promised Land came back saying only what they saw, felt, and heard by their carnal senses – how big the giants were (Num.13:27-33). This *"evil report"* caused the people to believe that the land could not be taken. Because they believed the evil report, they all died in the wilderness.

In like manner, the land of our life cannot be taken over by the spiritual man unless we speak the promises of the Word instead of the negative things our carnal senses show us. We must have senses to <u>taste</u> the Word so that we may <u>see</u>, <u>hear</u>, <u>feel</u>, and <u>smell</u> (discernment) that we were saved, healed, delivered, and provided for in all things at the cross. *(Ps.34:8) Oh <u>taste</u> and <u>see</u> that the Lord is good. (2 Pet.1:3) <u>Seeing</u> that his divine power <u>hath granted</u> unto us <u>all things</u> that pertain unto life and godliness ... (4) whereby he hath granted unto us his precious and exceeding great <u>promises</u>; that through these ye may become partakers of the <u>divine nature</u>, having escaped from the corruption that is in that world by lust. (Rom.10:17) So belief [cometh] of <u>hearing</u>, and <u>hearing by the word</u> of Christ.* We cannot be led of the Spirit while making decisions and speaking according to carnal senses. A brother once called me about a dream. *In his dream, I appeared to him. He spoke to me in the dream and said, "You remind me of someone I read about in Isaiah." Then in the dream, I said to him, "I know those verses." Then I quoted some verses, one of which was Isaiah 11:3. (Isa.11:3) And his delight* (Hebrew: "scent or smell") *shall be in the fear of the Lord; and he shall not judge after the sight of his eyes, neither decide after the hearing of his ears*.

After Joshua's (Jesus') army imprisoned the five kings, they pursued and conquered their armies of carnal men (Josh.10:19,20). As the Lord's army, He will lead us to conquer the carnal senses that we may conquer the carnal man. *(2 Cor.4:16) … Our outward* (carnal) *man is decaying, yet our inward* (spiritual) *man is renewed day by day. (18) while we look not at the things which are seen, but at the things which are not seen: for the things which are seen are temporal; but the things which are not seen are eternal.* While we have spiritual eyes to see the promises which are not yet seen (manifested), the carnal man will be dying and the spiritual man taking his place. *(Rom.6:6) Knowing this, that our old* (carnal) *man was crucified with [him], that the body of sin might be done away, that so we should no longer be in bondage to sin.* If a person had eyes and ears to believe this, what would be in their mouth? They would say with Paul, *"It is no longer I* (the carnal man) *that live, but Christ* (the spiritual man) *liveth in me."* There are promises to cover every need that a person could have, but God's people continue to speak the bad report of what they see with carnal eyes.

When Joshua returned, he commanded his spiritual men to take the kings from the cave and to *"Come near, put your feet upon the necks of these kings. And they came near, and put their feet upon the necks of them"* (Josh.10:24). This again kept the carnal senses from speaking until they were crucified. *(26) And afterward Joshua smote them, and put them to death, and hanged them on five trees: and they were hanging upon the* trees *until the evening. (27) And it came to pass at the time of the going down of the sun, that Joshua commanded, and they took them down off the trees, and cast them into the cave wherein they had hidden themselves, and laid great stones on the mouth of the cave, unto this very day.* Just look at the similarities between this crucifixion and that of Jesus. *(Acts 5:30; 10:39) Jesus, whom ye slew and hanged on a tree.* Jesus' five senses were crucified. Jesus also had to be taken down before sundown which began a high Sabbath (Jn.19:21). Jesus was placed in a cave called a tomb, which was then covered by a great stone (Jn.20:1). The good news is since our carnal man was crucified with Christ, our old senses have already been put to death for us. If we walk in the faith of this, God will manifest it for us.

Joshua also said, *"For thus shall the Lord do to all your enemies against whom ye fight" (Josh.10:25).* The key to victory over all our enemies is conquering the carnal senses with the Word. The Church needs to *"have their senses exercised* (by the Word) *to discern good and evil."* This is what made little David victorious over the giant Goliath. On his way to the battle he *"chose him five smooth stones out of the brook, and put them in the shepherd's bag which he had, even in his wallet; and his sling was in his hand: and he drew near to the Philistine"* *(1 Sam.17:40).* The brook here represented *"the washing of water* with the *word" (Epe.5:26).* The five stones representing David's senses were polished smooth by the water of the Word. (From this you can see that the great stones that blocked the mouth of the cave restraining the five kings represented not just the Word, but the Word manifested in the spiritual senses.) With these born again senses, David knew that he represented the Lord, that he had authority against God's enemies, that with God's power, he was more than a match for the giant and his weapons, and that he could speak the Word of Faith, and it would be done. *(1 Sam.17:45) Then said David to the Philistine, Thou comest to me with a sword, and with a spear, and with a javelin: but I come to thee in the name of the Lord* *of hosts, the God of the armies of Israel, whom <u>thou hast defied</u>. (46) <u>This day will the Lord deliver thee into my hand</u>; and <u>I will smite thee</u>, and <u>take thy head from off thee</u>; and I will give the dead bodies of the host of the Philistines this day unto the birds of the heavens, and to the wild beasts of the earth; that all the earth may know that <u>there is a God in Israel</u>.* Notice also that Godly leadership through the born again senses of one man brought understanding and faith to Israel to conquer the army of the Philistines.

(1 Sam.17:49) And David put his hand in his bag, and took thence a <u>stone</u>, and slang it, and smote the Philistine in his forehead; and the stone sank into his forehead, and he fell upon his face to the earth. Which of the senses is represented by this one stone that killed Goliath? A good case can be made for hearing because David only spoke what he had ears to hear, but I believe his tongue killed Goliath. The tongue not only tastes things to discern if the body will accept them but also speaks those things that the body has accepted. David's senses boldly spoke faith out of his mouth, therefore, it had to happen. After David smote Goliath, he took off his head with Goliath's own sword (1 Sam.17:51), fulfilling those words of faith.

<u>Our confession forbids or permits</u>, and determines who will win the battle in the heavens. Victory in the battle in heaven has nothing to do with the power of the angels or demons, but our authority. One angel will easily bind Satan and cast him into the abyss (Rev.20:1,2). *(Rev.12:7) And there was war in heaven: <u>Michael and his angels</u> [going forth] to war with the dragon; and the <u>dragon warred and his angels</u>; (8) and they prevailed not, neither was their place found any more in heaven* .... Even though the angels and demons carry out the warfare, the saints give authority by the words of their mouth to the winning side. *(11) And <u>they</u>* (saints) *<u>overcame him</u> because of the blood of the Lamb, and <u>because of the word of their testimony</u>; and they loved not their life even unto death.* The saints forbid or permit angels

and demons according to the *"word of their testimony."* This is according to Jesus. *"Verily I say unto you, <u>what things soever ye shall bind</u>* (forbid) *on earth shall be bound* (forbidden) *in heaven; and <u>what things soever ye shall loose</u>* (permit) *on earth shall be loosed* (permitted) *in heaven" (Mt.18:18).* Because of this, we are motivated to agree with the Word even when it is contrary to the sight realm or human sentiment.

The Word of God in us gives authority to the angels to conquer Satan. Many say, "I bind the demons," or "I loose the angels," while they continue to disagree with the Word. This is only hot air. It accomplishes nothing. Neither Jesus nor His disciples made these statements. We do not have to either, just agree with the Word in our everyday thinking, speech, and actions. Demons will be forbidden while angels permitted. I include actions here because we cannot confess Christ while living in willful sin and expect the demons to be forbidden.

It is imperative that we repent, change our mind, in order to cast down Satan's ability to rule us. *(2 Cor.10:4) For the weapons of our warfare are not of the flesh, but mighty before God to the <u>casting down of strongholds</u>, (5) casting down <u>imaginations</u>* (Greek: "reasonings"), *and every high thing that is exalted against the knowledge of God, and <u>bringing every thought into captivity to the obedience of Christ</u>.* If we want to win the battle in the heavens, we must first win it in our mind and with our tongue. *(Pr.18:21) Death and life are in the power of the tongue.*

Chapter 16
Actions Complete Faith

Even so faith, if it have not works, is dead in itself (Jas.2:17).

Faith has no power without works that agree with it. *(Jas.2:14) What doth it profit, my brethren, if a man say he hath faith, but have not works? can that faith save him? (17) Even so faith, if it have not works, is dead in itself.* There are no recorded instances in the Bible where God's people were saved, healed, delivered, or provided for without acting on faith. *(18) Yea, a man will say, Thou hast faith, and I have works: show me thy faith apart from [thy] works, and I by my works will show thee [my] faith.* Many have said that they had faith without seeing the answer, but just as there are no Christians without fruit, we can only prove our faith by corresponding actions. Jesus never said He would judge our faith, but our fruit and our works (Rev.2:5,23,26; 3:1,15). *(22) Thou seest that faith wrought with his works, and by works was faith made perfect.* The most important way that we perfect or complete our faith is with our tongue, but that is not the only way. Peter completed his faith when he stepped out of the boat. The ten lepers completed their faith when they went to show themselves as healed before their healing was manifested. The answer never comes until after the works.

When my wife Mary and I were first coming to the Lord, she was suffering with chronic urinary tract infections. She already had one in-hospital cystiscope, but she continued to have infections that created more scar tissue. The doctor recommended repeating the procedure, but our insurance would not cover it for another month. So he prescribed antibiotics and pain medication and set up a pre-operation visit for when the insurance would cover it. During this time, we discovered in the Word promises of healing and had a Spirit-filled pastor pray over Mary. At first, we saw no immediate change, but then we had a surprising and eye-opening experience.

When Mary was wondering where we might be missing it, the Lord spoke to her very clearly. What He said showed us the key to what was missing in our faith. The Lord said, "If you believe that I <u>have healed you</u>, why are you taking all that medicine?" In other words, "Why are your <u>actions</u> <u>disagreeing</u> with what you say you believe?" Mary did not hesitate but grabbed her medicine and started pouring it into the commode, completing her faith. As she stood there, she was instantly healed! At this point, I am sure many would argue against my theology, but they cannot argue with success, then or now. The Lord was not saying to get rid of your medicine so that you would be healed. That is legalism. That thinking gets people hurt. He was saying that if you *"believe that ye received"* your healing, then your actions will prove it. *"Faith if it have not works is dead in itself ... and I by my works will show thee faith."* You see, <u>faith must come before works</u> as the horse must come before the cart, for *"by works was faith made perfect."* A month later, on the previously set date for the pre-operation visit, the symptoms returned. By this time, we had learned about our right in God and about our enemy. We knew there was an evil intelligence involved in the symptoms returning on that date. We just rebuked the devil and the symptoms left forever. This is where many accept the sickness back and lose the healing.

In the early 1980's, I had a mental vision several times of myself on my motorcycle about to hit a car turned sideways in the road. To avoid it, I stood up on my bike. That is not the normal way for bikers to react to sudden obstructions that cannot be avoided. Usually you end up laying the bike down. These visions were a warning I did not recognize quickly enough. The Lord was dealing with me to obey the speed limit on the interstate. I used to fudge and justify it with the thought that the police would not bother you for a few miles an hour over the limit. God did not agree and gave me a spanking.

As I was approaching the beginning of an overpass at my normal fudging speed, the driver in the car in front of me for some unknown reason slammed on his brakes, turning sideways, just as I had seen in the visions. The car was taking up two lanes between the overpass rails, and all the cars quickly took the third lane, which left me with no choice. I had only a moment to steer the bike away from the driver's door and to stand up, which I believe my mind had been programmed to do by the visions. If I had laid the bike down, I probably would be dead. My bike plowed into the car, and I flew over the hood. I landed on the top of the overpass about 70 feet away. I wish I had observed rather than participated in this spectacle. Considering my flight with no helmet and the hardness of the concrete, I came out miraculously well. I landed on my arm and face and immediately realized that I was blind. Thinking that a vehicle might be coming, I rolled over till I felt the concrete curb. A spirit of praise came over me like I have never experienced. As I lay there praising the Lord, my sight gradually came back. No one came near me until an officer showed up. They probably thought I was a deranged religious fanatic. Fanatic maybe, but not deranged.

There was a rather light moment in this. The officer asked me if I had my seat belt on. I tried to focus on his face to see if he was serious and decided that he was. I said, "I was on the bike. They don't have seat belts." He just turned and walked away. The ambulance came and picked me up. I asked the driver if he would take me home, but he refused. At the hospital, I still had this wonderful uplifted spirit and was witnessing to the nurses and technicians as they x-rayed my arm. Later the doctor came and told me that my arm was broken and would have to be put in a cast. <u>I told him that I did not want a cast because God would heal me</u>. I told him I just wanted to go home. He then wanted to sew up my lower lip, which was split, and my chin, which was gashed to the bone, and I told him the same thing. By that time, Mary had come to the hospital, and she pleaded with me to let him stitch me up because she did not want to look at it. So I relented. Later, at home, those stitches did not hold, so I took them out, and God healed the gash.

I could not walk because my legs and arms were so painful. When I flew over the car one shoe stayed with the bike and the other stayed with me. We figured that one shoe hooked on the bike as I took flight and stretched me out some. It could also have been the whiplash from the sudden stop. When we got home, Mike Burley carried me into the house, and we prayed the prayer of faith. In a few days, I was out hobbling around my neighbor's yard trying to exercise my sore muscles. He had been clearing some trees from his lot. I came across a tree trunk next to a fire. Since I had been helping him before the wreck, I thought, "I should heave that over on the fire and burn it in two so that we can handle it later." My next thought was, "Oh sure, if I do that my arm will be laying on the ground." The next thought was, "If by Jesus' stripes you <u>were healed</u>, then you can pick that up." I believe that thought came from the Lord to remind me to <u>act on what the Word says</u>. By the grace of God, I bent down and picked that trunk up and heaved it on the fire. I immediately noticed that there was no pain in my arm, and I knew that the Lord had manifested my healing. In the Gospels, when they acted on the word of Jesus, the miracle came.

Before Exxon would let me go back to work, I had to be checked out in their infirmary. I told the doctor there that the Lord had healed me, and I was ready to go back to work. He told me, "That is impossible because it takes at least 12 weeks for a break like that to heal." I said, "Doctor, what religion are you?" He said, "Episcopalian." I said, "Don't you Episcopalians believe God heals?" He said, "Yes, we do, but we believe He uses doctors to do it." I said, "Well, He didn't do that this time." He said, "Well, you will have to prove that to me." He sent me to their x-ray department. Later when I was back in his office and he looked at the x-ray, he said, "Something is wrong here." I said, "No doctor, nothing is wrong. Could I do this if I had a broken arm?" I did a few calisthenics for him. Although he was puzzled, he let me go back to work.

My very first job was to stretch cables across the top of a 40-foot wide cooling tower stack to keep it from pulsating as the fan turned inside. Melvin Jenkins, the man working with me, started out pulling the cables with one hand while holding the stack for leverage with the other. I would start a nut when he stretched the cables. He soon tired and could not stretch them far enough, so we switched places. Satan tempted me to fear using the arm at this point, but by the grace of God, I ignored him and acted my faith. It took all my strength with my once broken arm to do this and it surprised Melvin. He said, "Are you sure that arm was broken?" I said, "The x-rays say that it was." Eventually, he was converted through this and other testimonies.

My oldest boys were getting into Motocross racing. For those who do not know, this is dirt bikes with racing engines going around a dirt track with turns, 180° turns, jumps, etc. They were at a local track a few years ago practicing. Corban, my oldest, attempted a long jump but landed wrong, and the bike went one way while he went another. Nathan said that Corban was knocked out temporarily but finally got up and walked to his truck and sat in it. Corban said that he did not remember walking to the truck, but he remembers gaining consciousness while sitting in the truck looking out of the windshield. Corban's arm clearly was broken. The flesh was pushed out in a point about four inches below the right elbow. Nathan did not have a license yet, so he shifted and Corban steered them home. Satan attacks with fear and doubt when you are faced with a sight like this, but you can become hardened to him with your armor so that his fiery darts bounce right off. The best thing to do is to deflect the dart with the shield of faith before it enters and starts a bonfire that you cannot put out. We prayed the prayer of faith over his arm, and in a few days, it improved until he was completely healed. God is absolutely faithful to His Word.

About a year later, Nathan was chasing Corban and Tommy, his cousin, on his motocross bike when he missed a curve and ran off into a creek bed. The boys missed him and retraced their tracks a couple of times looking for him. As they passed the place where Nathan wrecked, a lady who was riding down the creek bed on a four-wheeler motioned to them. She pointed out Nathan, who was knocked out lying on the edge of the creek. They put Nathan in the back of Tommy's truck and hurried him to the hospital in Jay, Florida and then called us. When I contacted the hospital they said that Nathan's arm appeared broken, he was talking irrationally, and they thought that his brain was swelling. Because of this they had already sent him to Baptist Hospital in Pensacola because they did not have an M.R.I. machine. I went there and found Nathan in the Emergency Room. His arm appeared broken within a few inches of where his brother's was the year before. The bone had not come through the skin, but it had pushed the flesh up an inch and a half. He kept repeating the same questions every few minutes. We prayed concerning the condition of his soul/mind. Then I asked him if he wanted to believe God for healing. Probably because that was the only way of healing he had ever known, he said yes. So we prayed the prayer of faith. Since we knew from the Word and experience that faith without corresponding action is useless, when the nurse walked in we told her we were ready to go home. She objected on the grounds that he could die with brain swelling and that his arm appeared broken. <u>I assured her that we had prayed and everything would be fine.</u>

She hurried off to get a doctor who tried to warn us of the same things and finally gave up. They brought some papers in for us to sign, absolving the hospital of all liability. Nathan hobbled out to the car, leaning upon my shoulder.

By the next morning he was thinking, eating, walking, and looking much better. He had taken a shower by himself and the arm had gone down considerably. That afternoon a Children and Families Services worker showed up at the door. She said, "You don't look surprised to see me." I said, "No ma'am, but you are welcome." She asked me if I had anything against doctors. I said, "Not at all, but <u>I believe that God consistently heals the sick when they believe Him</u>." She told us that the report she had received accused us of "medical neglect." She wanted to see Nathan, so we called him in. She looked him over and asked him a few questions, which he answered to her satisfaction. When she was through she said, "Well, I do not see any reason to go any further with this. He seems to be doing pretty good, but since we were called-out this will stay in the record for five years." With that she left, and we have never seen the C.F.S. again. Nathan quickly returned to normal. Glory to God! He enabled us to believe and to act on His Word and saved us from the C.F.S.

Before we came to know the Lord, Mary was in labor a day and a half with our first child Deborah. It was a terribly drawn out affair. Deborah was breach but both the doctor and we hoped she would turn without a C-section. The doctor would give Mary pain medication with the side-effect that she had trouble pushing the baby, so they put her on the drip to counteract the pain medication. We went back and forth like this a few times. At the last few minutes after we decided to give up and do a C-section, the baby turned and was born normally. Had God not done this we might not have done what He wanted next.

Not long after this, we turned to the Lord and discovered faith. We were seeing God do wonderful things and believed from then forward that He could do anything. When our next child was on the way we felt that the Lord wanted us to have him at home. (I say him because Mary had a dream and saw Corban with his distinguishing characteristics.) Others tried to give me books on the subject of childbirth, but I felt not to count on my own wisdom but God's. I did learn how to tie the cord. When it was time for him to be born, not having had sonograms, we did not know that Corban was breach. You can imagine the shock when that little toe came out and I said, "What is that?" As we realized what was happening we prayed fervently. We felt a strong sense of the Lord's presence.

Don't laugh now! Then I commanded that baby to "come out of there in the name of Jesus," which he soon did. Our boy was born a "footling breach" as the medical profession calls it. That is one foot up, one foot down, and wrong end up. We did not know at the time how rare this was. As doctors have told me since, it just does not happen because they always do a C-section. *(Jer.32:27) Behold, I am the Lord, the God of all flesh: is there anything too hard for me?* Corban looked just like he did in Mary's dream.

Because Mary's and my own blood were not compatible, Corban was born jaundiced. We prayed over him and thanked God for healing him. Then we turned our attentions to getting a birth certificate. We called the public health unit, and the lady wanted to know if we had problems getting to the hospital. When we told her that we had not planned to go, she said they would send someone right out to give us a birth certificate.

The nurse who came out took one look at Corban's yellow body and said, "Sir, you need to get this baby to the hospital for a blood transfusion. He has blood poisoning." Faith was completed in our actions. I said, "No, ma'am, we prayed for him, and he will be just fine. Jesus said, '*All things whatsoever ye pray and ask for, believe that ye receive them, and ye shall have them.*'" She was polite and did not argue, but she left. We really did not know her intentions but in a little while when she came back, Corban was totally healed. Glory to God! The nurse said, "That just does not happen without a transfusion." She was amazed but glad.

Nathan was born 15-1/2 months later. He was seven weeks premature and was a tiny 4 lb. 3 oz. We prayed for him, put him in his bed and put a light bulb close over him for warmth. When we called the health unit the same lady answered the phone. She said, "Is that you again?" Guess what? She sent the same nurse out, who brought another nurse with her. The first thing she asked was, "May we see the baby that was born the year before last?" We said, "Sure." They went in to look at Corban, who was sleeping soundly. She said quietly to the other nurse, "This is the baby that I was telling you about." It was obvious to Mary and me that Corban's healing had become a testimony to them. When they looked at Nathan, our newborn, it seemed that they were not worried about him. It was as though they had gained a little faith themselves. Nathan outgrew full-term children who were born at the same time. Thanks to the Lord!

During Mary's next pregnancy she fell down the front steps and landed very hard on her rump. Not long after that, to our great disappointment, our baby was born dead. I examined and found that the baby's skull was crushed, probably by the pelvic cradle when Mary fell. I asked the Lord if He wanted to raise this baby up, but I felt that He said, "No." In all of our questioning the Lord, Mary and I were reminded of the same thing. I had asked the Lord when we first came to Him, that if He foresaw that any of our children would grow up and be lost, that He would take them as infants to be with Him. *(Eccl.6:3) If a man beget a hundred children, and live many years, so that the days of his years are many, but <u>his soul be not filled with good</u>, and moreover he have no burial; I say, that <u>an untimely birth is better</u> than he: (4) for it cometh in vanity, and departeth in darkness, and the name thereof is covered with darkness; (5) moreover it hath not seen the sun nor known it; <u>this hath rest rather than the other</u>.* We were comforted to understand that our baby had entered God's rest. This cannot be said of the overwhelming majority of babies, who grow up to rebel against the Lord. Considering the alternative, we are thankful. We trust the Lord to work all things together for our good. Abortion is a terrible sin, but if these ungodly parents raised these babies up, most would turn against God and be lost. God is sovereign even in this. As I have already shared with you, our youngest two children were also born at home. We are not trying to set a precedent for anyone else, but we do believe this knowledge will help some in the wilderness experience about to come.

From some of these testimonies, some could erroneously conclude that faith always works very quickly and that if you do not get an answer quickly you have done something wrong or God has not heard. The overwhelming majority of answers to prayer will come after a trial of our faith. This trial is a result of being faced with the need and at the same time being faced with the promise of the Word that this need is met. The wilderness trial for Israel was just like this, and our trials are no different. God promised Abraham a seed, but he was tried first. *(Rom.4:18) Who in hope believed against hope, to the end that he might become a father of many nations, according to that which had been spoken, So shall thy seed be. (19) And without being weakened in faith he considered his own body now as good as dead (he being about a hundred years old), and the deadness of Sarah's womb; (20) yet, looking unto the promise of God, he wavered not through unbelief, but waxed strong through faith, giving glory to God.* Abraham was 75 when God told him, *"I will make of thee a great nation"* (Gen.12:2,4). He had to wait 25 more years as he and Sarah both continued to age. God waited until Abraham and Sarah gave up trying by their own natural efforts, which produced Ishmael, to bring the promise to pass. Abraham did not permit what he saw and experienced to destroy his faith in God's promise, therefore, he received.

267

If in our trial we are double-minded, we cannot receive. *(Jas.1:5) But if any of you lacketh wisdom, let him ask of God, who giveth to all liberally and upbraideth not; and it shall be given him. (6) But let him ask in faith, nothing doubting: for he that doubteth is like the surge of the sea driven by the wind and tossed. (7) For let not that man think that he shall receive anything of the Lord; (8) a double minded man, unstable in all his ways.* Since this is true, what hope do we who have been double-minded have? Just before Isaac was conceived, Abraham and Sarah both laughed in unbelief that they could bring forth a son (Gen.17:17; 18:12,15). However, God leaves this point out of the glorious report of Abraham's faith in the above account. Why? Abraham and Sarah obviously repented and walked in faith again. God no longer remembered their sin and left it out of the Romans 4 account. *(Isa.43:25) I, even I, am he that blotteth out thy transgressions for mine own sake; and I will not remember thy sins.* Thank God!

We are in a battle for what God says is ours in Christ, which is where our heavenly places are. *(Epe.1:3) Blessed [be] the God and Father of our Lord Jesus Christ, who hath blessed us with every spiritual blessing in the heavenly [places] in Christ.* Christ's resurrection gave us the position of being already seated in the abundant provision of those same heavenly places. *(Epe.2:6) And raised us up with him, and made us to sit with him in the heavenly [places], in Christ Jesus.* What we have by position becomes manifestly ours as we fight unbelief by faith. God gave to Israel the land of the promises (Josh.1:2); but then they had to take it with the sword, which represents the Word (Heb.4:12). Paul goes on to say that we must protect our mind and heart and use the sword of the Word in a battle to take that position (Epe.6:10-18). *(Epe.6:12) For our wrestling is not against flesh and blood, but against the principalities, against the powers, against the world-rulers of this darkness, against the spiritual [hosts] of wickedness in the heavenly [places].* Demonic hosts seek to keep us from our inheritance by every form of lie, religion, and manipulation. By faith in the promises, we must violently take from them what is ours. *(Mt.11:12) And from the days of John the Baptist until now the kingdom of <u>heaven</u> <u>suffereth violence</u>, and men of violence <u>take it by force</u>.* We must *"fight the good fight of the faith"* in order to take from Satan what God says is ours. We *"confess the good confession"* by faith that we have eternal life and we are the righteousness of God in Christ, etc. In so doing, we *"lay hold on"* these promises. *(1 Tim.6:11) But thou, O man of God, flee these things; and <u>follow after righteousness</u>, godliness, faith, love, patience, meekness. (12) <u>Fight the good fight of the faith</u>, <u>lay hold on the life eternal</u>, whereunto thou wast called* (Greek: "invited"), *and didst <u>confess the good confession</u> in the sight of many witnesses.*

We win this battle as we believe we are who God says we are, we can do what God says we can do, and we have what God says we have.

Chapter 17
Methods and God's Glory

But <u>God chose</u> the <u>foolish</u> things of the world, that he might put to shame them that are wise; and God chose the <u>weak</u> things of the world, that he might put to shame the things that are strong; and the <u>base</u> things of the world, and the things that are <u>despised</u>, did God choose [yea] and the <u>things that are not</u>, that he might bring to naught the things that are: that <u>no flesh should glory before God</u> (1 Cor.1:27-29).

God's methods will always be considered foolish, weak, base, and despised by the world and the worldly church. I inherited from my father a chronic weakness in nasal, sinus, and inner ear infections. By the time I came to the Lord, my eardrums had burst many times because of these infections. I dreaded this because it was very painful. My hearing was impaired due to scars on my eardrums. Also, as did my father, I carried nasal spray with me almost year-round to open up my sinuses. This had destroyed the lining in my nose, which made the problem worse. Because of this, I started using saltwater as a nasal spray, which did not work as well. Penicillin became useless and vitamin C, too.

Shortly after I came to the Lord I discovered that I did not have to seek healing any more because 2,000 years ago I was healed by Jesus' stripes. <u>I threw my nasal spray and my vitamin C away by faith</u>. My nose and sinuses have not stopped up since, even when I have had a cold. I have had no more burst eardrums, either. This testimony has been given to many who also came to faith and were healed. At the end of all of my works to save myself by man's methods, God gave me faith to see His works. God's method was faith in Him combined with my own weakness. He said, *"my power is made perfect in weakness" (2 Cor.12:9)*. Faith is foolish, weak, and base to the world but it brings God's power.

Before I knew the Lord, I applied for a job at Exxon. Their physical showed that I had hearing loss from scarred eardrums and a non-functional heart murmur, which I had from childhood. They almost did not hire me. A few years later after I discovered the Lord and His method, they called me in for another physical. There was no sign of hearing loss or heart murmur. My poor attendance record caused by sickness also made a complete turnaround. Worldly methods failed me, but faith in the promises brought the most awesome deliverance. Glory to God!

Recently, I watched a report on antibacterial soaps on the national news. They reported that the net effect was that they were not wiping out bacteria, but making it resistant. What did penicillin do but make antibiotic-resistant bacteria for which there is no medical cure on the horizon? Poisons on the crops to try to destroy the curse go into the water supply and cause a multitude of diseases. Read your toothpaste tube; fluoride is a deadly poison. The *Journal of the American Medical Association* Vol. 284 July 26, 2000, reports that doctors are the third leading cause of death in the U.S., causing 250,000 deaths every year from iatrogenic causes! Iatrogenic is defined as induced in a patient by a physician's activity, manner, or therapy, used especially of a complication of treatment. If this is what their organization admits, what is the truth? The numbers are much higher. If, as some believe, this is God's preferred method of healing today, He is surely making a lot of mistakes. I have a good doctor friend named John Farmer, who prefers to not use drugs. He has told me how he prays for patients who will believe, with results. The problem is that most are not interested in deliverance from their curse if it takes repentance and faith so he does what he can.

My mother took a drug for years. One day she was reading an article by *Reader's Digest* on the side-effects of medicines. The side-effects of the drug she was on were breast cancer and glaucoma, and she had them both. That was a terrible trade.

271

My father's favorite doctor told him after an examination, "One thing I am sure of, you are not going to die of a heart attack. You have the heart of a much younger man." About a month later, he had a serious heart attack. I became convinced it was because of a drug he was taking to put oxygen into his blood because he lost a lung to smoking. Two close friends took a drug that had a side-effect of damaging their kidneys. Their doctors admitted this in both cases. Man shifts the curse around and sometimes multiplies it, but he cannot deliver by his own efforts. If he could, then Jesus' death was for naught. I believe it is God's purpose that we understand that there is no permanent deliverance from the curse except God's deliverance through Jesus Christ. The world's deliverance is a deception, because, ultimately, their gods fail them. God wants us to see through that.

We have been told that God now uses modern methods for delivering us from the curse. God's method is always free. It is salvation by grace, which is the unmerited, unpaid for, favor of God. Neither Jesus nor His disciples charged anything for healing, deliverance, or any other form of salvation. The world's method always costs. The poor often go untreated until they die. In God's kingdom, <u>all</u> are treated on condition of faith. God desires to use the same method He used in Scripture, the Word of Faith, because it is the only one that does not give glory to man. For instance, if a Christian receives a recovery from some disease while under the care of doctors and medicine, everyone wants to know what the medicine was or who the doctor was. God will not share His glory with another. I am not condemning those who use doctors or medicine. I am offering the good news that Jesus has already healed you almost 2,000 years ago. All we have to do is read the New Testament once to find out that God did not use the methods of man. In the coming wilderness we will need to understand this.

272

Soon God's people will not be able to buy or sell with the world. Then all will be forced into a wilderness experience where there will be no idolatry with the gods of this world. For the people of God there will be a great lack of doctors, medicine, lawyers, bankers, psychiatrists, insurance, public assistance of all types, food, clean water, and everything else. Then we will see God's power in man's weakness (2 Cor.12:9,10). The church's methods of obtaining provision today are the same as the world's methods and are therefore acceptable to the world.

God has a peculiar method for ministering deliverance from the curse that costs nothing, gives no glory to man, and proves His sovereignty. *(1 Cor.1:28) And the base things of the world, and the things that are despised, did <u>God choose</u>, [yea] and <u>the things that are not, that he might bring to naught the things that are:</u> (29) that no flesh should glory before God*. We see here that God chose to use something that does not exist in the physical realm in order to destroy the things that do. The *"things that are not"* are the promises in the Word that we do not see fulfilled. The *"things that are"* are the cursed things of sin, sickness, and lack, which God wants to *"bring to naught."* For instance, if you are sick, that is a <u>thing that is</u>; but *"by whose stripes ye were healed"* is a thing that <u>is not</u> in the physical realm. God chose faith in this promise that <u>is not</u> in order to bring to naught the sickness. Jesus and the disciples used God's method for dealing with the curse by *"<u>calling the things that are not, as though they were</u>" (Rom.4:17)*. They just commanded it done according to the promises. <u>They did not choose the things that are</u>, like doctors, medicine, psychiatrists, and such to <u>bring to naught the things that are</u>, like sickness, torment, poverty, and such. The things that appear in this cursed realm are the things that are. *(Heb.11:3) By faith we understand that the <u>worlds have been framed by the word of God</u>, so that <u>what is seen hath not been made out of things which appear</u>*.

God's method is to use the Word and not the physical things that appear, just as in the Gospels and Acts. In anointing with oil, it is obviously not the oil but the faith that heals. Oil is just a symbol of the Holy Spirit. Paul's handkerchief did not heal; it was the power from his faith (Acts 19:12). Some might think that <u>once</u> Jesus also used things such as when He made clay with His spit to heal a blind man in John 9:6,7. It was not the clay that healed his eyes, but the washing it out of his eyes; clay symbolizes the Adamic nature and the things that are (Job 10:9; 33:6; Isa.29:16; 45:9) just as man was made from clay.

In other words, our eyes must be cleansed of seeing through eyes of clay. We need the spiritual eyes to see the promise as done by faith. *(2 Pet.1:3)* <u>*Seeing that his divine power*</u> <u>*hath granted*</u> *unto us all things that pertain unto life* (Greek: *zoe*, "God's life") *and godliness* .... To have spiritual eyes, we must see that Jesus has already given us His life and blessings. We need to be cleansed of fleshly eyes that keep us from God's blessings. *The* <u>*natural man*</u> (of clay) <u>*receiveth not the things of the Spirit*</u> *of God, for they are foolishness unto him, and he cannot know them because they are spiritually judged* (Greek: "examined" or "seen") *(1 Cor.2:14).* By the way, the spit from Jesus mouth symbolizes that which comes out of the mouth of the Lord that gives life to man, the Word or manna (Dt.8:3; Jn.1:1-3; 6:33,51).

I once knew a preacher who said, "The reason Paul did all those miracles was because Luke the physician was with him." Wrong! Not in one verse do we see Luke using physician skills, which could never result in a miracle. The Greek word *Iatros* is falsely translated "physician" and just means "healer." *Iatros* is also used of Jesus as "healer." Translators put their modern ideas here. "Physician" means "one who practices medicine," which Jesus and the apostles never did. The term used for drugs or medicine in the Greek is *pharmakia* (English: "pharmacy") and is translated "witchcraft" or "sorcery," which Paul called a work of the flesh in Galatians 5:20. The nations are deceived with *pharmakia* (Rev.18:23). Luke was a healer in the same way Jesus and the other disciples were.

It should seem strange to these people that Jesus and his disciples did not use "the things that are" to administer healing or deliverance. If Paul's handkerchief had the power to heal, why could it not heal before he touched it? It only acted as a medium to carry the healing anointing to the sick by faith. I have prayed over handkerchiefs, water, or <u>people</u> as mediums and seen healings. A brother, whose wife was very sick, came into our meeting. He was very troubled and on the edge of tears about this. The brother was not yet convinced that he needed to be filled with the Holy Spirit. Asking the Lord in my thoughts what to do, it came to me to pray over him to impart healing power to him, which we did. Then I said, "Now brother, go lay hands on your wife, and she will be healed." He was not convinced that healing was our right today, but he went home to lay hands on his wife. When he did, she was healed, and he came back excited. You see, it is not the medium; it is the healing power manifested through it, or in this case him, by faith. Jesus imparted authority to the disciples to heal before they received the Holy Spirit.

So how do we use God's method of *"the things that are not"*? By *"calling the things that are not as though they were" (Rom.4:17)*. In other words, agree with the promise and call it done. God chooses to use *"the things that are not, that he might bring to naught the things that are: <u>that no flesh should glory before God</u>."(1 Cor.1:28,29)*. God does not desire to use man's inventions so that only He can brag. God's salvation is not by our works. It is by getting our eyes off the problem and on the promise. 2 Corinthians 4:17,18 teaches that our affliction will be temporary if *"we look not at the things which are seen, but at the things which are not seen."* When the Israelites got their eyes off the snake bite (curse) and on the serpent on the pole (Christ who became our curse [Jn.3:14]), they were healed (Num.21:4-9).

As we saw, Paul's "thorn in the flesh" had nothing to do with sickness but a demon that was bringing him into humbling circumstances where he was weak to save himself so God's power was present to save him. His advice to Timothy puts a question in some concerning the use of remedies. In the text we can see that sin is the subject before and after the verse in question. *(1 Tim. 5:22) Lay hands hastily on no man, neither be partaker of other men's sins: keep thyself pure. (23) Be no longer a drinker of water, but use a little wine for thy stomach's sake and thine often infirmities* (Greek: *asthenia;* meaning "weaknesses"). *(24) Some men's sins are evident, going before unto judgment; and some men also they follow after. (25) In like manner also there are good works that are evident; and such as are otherwise cannot be hid.*

The word sometimes translated "infirmities" is actually "weaknesses" and is clearly seen in other texts where the same word is correctly translated. *(1 Cor.1:25) … The weakness of God is stronger than men.* Now we know that God is not infirm or sick so this word has to be "weakness." *(2 Cor.13:4) For he was crucified through weakness, yet he liveth through the power of God. For we also are weak in him, but we shall live with him through the power of God toward you.* We know that Jesus Christ was not crucified through infirmity, but weakness because He would not defend Himself when He was brought before Pilate and the Jewish leaders. Timothy had spiritual weaknesses for which the only cure was the spiritual wine of the nature of Jesus. The stomach or belly was spiritually considered the seat of rulership for the carnal man. It represented being driven by the lusts (Greek: "desires") of the flesh, driven by sin. *(Phl.3:19) Whose end is perdition, whose god is the belly, and [whose] glory is in their shame, who mind earthly things.* Peter called those who returned to their sins, *"the sow that was washed to wallowing in the mire."* The sow best identifies those who are servants to their flesh appetites.

On the other hand, wine was considered the cure for bondage to sin. Wine represents the blood of Jesus. *(Mt.26:27) And he* took a cup (of wine), *and gave thanks, and gave to them, saying, Drink ye all of it; (28) for this is my blood of the covenant, which is poured out for many unto remission of sins. (29) But I say unto you, I shall not drink henceforth of this fruit of the vine, until that day when I drink it new with you in my Father's kingdom.* Through our own blood we have inherited the lusts of the sinful flesh and through Jesus' pure blood that nature is destroyed. *(Lev.17:11) For the life of the flesh is in the blood; and I have given it to you upon the altar to make atonement for your souls: for it is the blood that maketh atonement by reason of the life.* His blood is in us to the extent that we repent and partake of the life of His Word. *(Jn.6:53) Jesus therefore said unto them, Verily, verily, I say unto you, Except ye eat the flesh of the Son of man and drink his blood* (wine), *ye have not life in yourselves. (54) He that eateth my flesh and drinketh my blood hath eternal life: and I will raise him up at the last day.* Partaking of the blood or wine is a matter of walking in His Word by faith in His blood that was given to us. *(1 Jn.1:7) But if we walk in the light, as he is in the light, we have fellowship one with another, and the blood of Jesus his Son cleanseth us from all sin.*

The combined fruitful faith that resides in the true body of Christ is the answer to the question of why Isaiah commanded a cake of figs for Hezekiah's boil. *(Isa.38:21) Now Isaiah had said, Let them take a cake of figs, and lay it for a plaster upon the boil, and he shall recover.* The figs here represent the Body of Christ or Israel as in Jesus' warnings about bearing fruit. *(Lk.13:6) And he spake this parable; A certain man had a fig tree planted in his vineyard; and he came seeking fruit thereon, and found none. (7) And he said unto the vinedresser, Behold, these three years I come seeking fruit on this fig tree, and find none: cut it down; why doth it also cumber the ground? (Rev.6:13) and the stars of the heaven* (Abraham's seed) *fell unto the earth, as a fig tree casteth her unripe figs when she is shaken of a great wind.* Jesus identified the righteous as being under the fig tree when He saw Nathaniel there as an Israelite without guile (Jn.1:47-50). Notice that in the verse before the "cake of figs" was laid on the boil, faith was expressed to God by the body for Hezekiah's healing as the saints in the "house of Jehovah" were praising God for this. It was the figs' faith that sucked the poison out of the boil. *(Isa.38:20) Jehovah is [ready] to save me: Therefore we will sing my songs with stringed instruments All the days of our life in the house of Jehovah.* The cake of figs was a natural parable that represented a spiritual happening just as in Jesus' parables of planting wheat and corn, etc.

Chapter 18
Assurance Versus Insurance

For thou, O Lord, art my refuge! (Ps.91:9)

This confession of faith and the deliverance that comes of it is merely acting on what the Word says. I received a revelation years ago in Louisiana before it was a law to have any form of auto insurance. The Lord began to spiritually reason with me. It occurred to me that God is sovereign over what we call "accidents." *(Jn.3:27) A man can receive nothing, except it have been given him from heaven;* therefore, an "accident" could not come without God sending it. Since He said that if we prayed believing we would receive, then I could ask Him to keep my vehicles, and He would. I thought, "Why would I need insurance if I believed the assurance?" *(Ps.91:9) For thou, O Lord, art my refuge!* (Notice the good confession and its resulting benefit.) *Thou hast made the Most High thy habitation; (10) There shall no evil befall thee, Neither shall any plague come nigh thy tent (11) For he will give his angels charge over thee, To keep thee in all thy ways. (12) They shall bear thee up in their hands, Lest thou dash thy foot against a stone.* Notice that when we abide in Christ by faith, angels keep us from "accidents." An exception to this can be a Job experience to show hidden faults (Job 32:1,2). As in Job's case, God strictly controls the chastening and later restores what is taken. To Job was restored twice as much as he had and without insurance. God desires to be our security. *(Ps.119:22) Be surety* (Hebrew: "to give or be security") *for thy servant for good. (Heb.7:22) By so much also hath Jesus become the surety of a better covenant.* God and His promises are the believers' assurance of provision and protection.

After seeing what the Lord was saying to me, I dropped my auto insurance. Then I called my life insurance man, and he came over. I told him that I would not need insurance anymore because God would be my <u>assurance</u>. He was a good Lutheran man who sincerely tried to reason with this fanatic, but to no avail. The week after I did this, I drove to a Stop-N-Go mart and went in. While I was walking down an aisle, I heard a crash that shook the store windows. I looked up to see that my car had been in a wreck without me! I went out and found a heavy old Buick's front end wrapped around the back corner of my Datsun station wagon. The driver backed the car up a foot or so, and we both stood there speechless. The hood, grill and bumper of his car were notched back about six inches as if he had hit a big oak tree. Here is the good part. Datsun station wagons were tin boxes and could be dented with an elbow. This tank hit my car on the left rear <u>wrap-around, plastic tail lens</u>! I reached out and with my thumbnail scraped a piece of paint from his hood off the plastic lens, and we stood there for a moment looking at this miracle. There was not a scratch, dent, or crack on my car anywhere. Awesome God! He made my wimpy car, which should have been totaled, invincible to this old tank of a car. The assurance of God saved me from any need of insurance.

The man said, "I think my brakes went out," and then he mumbled, "They sure make 'em better than they used to." As I was thinking about how ludicrous that statement was, he got in his car and left. Suddenly it hit me that I missed the best chance in the entire world to witness to someone. I jumped into my car and caught him at the next red light. I grabbed some tracts out of the glove box and hurried to his door. I said, "Sir, that was a miracle." He said, "It had to be." I said, "I didn't have any insurance on my car and I was trusting God to keep it and He did." The light turned green and we parted company. Since then I have never had any insurance that covers our family, vehicles, or home other than what the law demands. We now, by law, have to have P.I.P., which covers our injuries, and P.D., which covers the other guy's vehicle.

That first wreck, or lack thereof, was an awesome testimony, but we did not plunder Egypt as we did with later wrecks. Since then, God has not always protected our vehicles or bodies, but in every case, it was to our advantage, for He healed our bodies and blessed us financially. During this time, though we sued no one, the other guy's insurance blessed us with money for the following: to repair a motorcycle with money leftover in my pocket for a new one; to repair a Toyota pickup that needed painting anyway, with $1,500 left in my pocket; to buy two cars, one new; to buy our home; to enable us to buy and give cars to others; to enable us to give our home away; and to buy a travel trailer for a homeless woman and her son. Besides all that and more, we have not spent God's money on many years' worth of insurance. I can hear someone say, "But Dave, what if …?" What if what? God almighty fell off His throne? *(Rom.10:11) For the scripture saith, Whosoever believeth on him shall not be put to shame. (Jer.17:7) Blessed is the man that trusteth in the Lord, and whose trust the Lord is.* By the grace of God, it has been almost 18 years since we have had a wreck. Praise God!

One day, in that same Datsun station wagon, I was driving along rather frustrated because I had had three flats on relatively new tires. Most people would be complaining to the manufacturer, but I believed God was in control, so I was complaining to the Lord. A little frustrated I said, "Lord, can't you keep my tires?" He said to me very clearly, "Don't you believe I can keep your tires?" I replied in my ignorance, "Yes, I believe you can keep them." He replied, "Then why do you keep putting that spare back there?" To be honest, I put the spare in the trunk because it was traditional and I had not questioned it, but also, the underlying reason was in case God didn't keep my tires. (I'm not trying to make a new doctrine on spares, just share a lesson God gave to me.) Fear and unbelief insulates us from any possibility of lack, loss, or threat.

Since we are trusting in insurances besides the Lord, we usually end up needing them. Jesus sent out His disciples in a way that would make them dependent on living by faith. He sent them without their own provision so that in their weakness His power could be proven. *(Mt.10:9) Get you no gold, nor silver, nor brass in your purses; (10) no wallet for [your] journey, neither two coats, nor shoes, nor staff: for the laborer is worthy of his food.* Later Jesus wanted to see what they learned from this experience of depending on God's supply. *(Lk.22:35) And he said unto them, When I sent you forth without purse, and wallet, and shoes, lacked ye anything? And they said, nothing.* In the wilderness of man's supply, God's provision was evident. God starts His works when we finish ours. His power is made perfect in our weakness. That was my experience with these tires. <u>I threw out my spare and never had another flat</u> on that car, and the neighbors who used to borrow it, quit. The moral of that story is if you prepare for a rainy day, it will come. With the next car, I had the same experience, no flats. When I decided after many years to give it to a mission, I put the keys and title into the hand of the pastor in my living room. We walked outside, and the car was on a flat. God made His point. As long as I owned the car, putting my trust in Him, there was never a flat. In other words, trusting in God takes away the need for insurances.

Men serve insurance companies, H.M.O.s, banks and store up their treasures on earth for the security they think it gives them. *(Mt.6:19) Lay not up for yourselves treasures upon the earth, where moth and rust consume, and where thieves break through and steal.* Y2K revealed the paranoia and lack of trust in those who stored up their treasures on earth contrary to our Lord's command. Quite a few that I showed these principles to went home to give their store away and found it full of bugs just as Jesus said, *"thieves break through and steal."* Jesus told of a man who found peace in the insurance of storing up his goods in greater barns (Lk.12:18). He said to himself, *(19) "Soul,* *thou hast <u>much goods laid up for many years; take thine ease,</u> eat, drink, be merry."* His misplaced trust brought judgment. *(20) But God said unto him, Thou foolish one, this night is <u>thy soul required</u>* (Greek: "they require thy soul") *of thee; and the things which thou hast prepared, whose shall they be? (21) So is he that <u>layeth up treasure for himself</u>, and is not rich toward God.* Notice that it was his stored up treasures that required his soul. Jesus promised the unfailing kingdom provisions to those who would store up their treasures in heaven by giving. *(32) Fear not, little flock; for it is your Father's good pleasure to <u>give you the kingdom</u>. (33) Sell that which ye have, and <u>give alms</u>; make for yourselves purses which wax not old* (not storing up), *<u>a treasure in the heavens that faileth not</u>, where no thief draweth near, neither moth destroyeth.* As long as we are on this earth, we can draw on our heavenly bank account if we have deposited by giving to the needs of others. *"Give and it <u>shall be</u> given unto thee."* If we have stored up on earth instead, the promise is that it will be stolen by thieves of one kind or another. Our heart will be on our treasures, falsely thinking them to be our security. *(34) For where your treasure is, there <u>will</u> your heart be also.*

I am told that Psalms 118:8 is the center verse in the Bible. I am sure that it is central to God's heart. *"It is better to take refuge in the Lord than to put confidence in man." (Jer.17:5) Thus saith the Lord: <u>Cursed is the man that trusteth in man</u>, and maketh flesh his arm, and whose <u>heart departeth from the Lord</u>.* As we can see, the insurances themselves bring the curse that they are thought to relieve. God is offended with those who call themselves believers yet trust in man's strength and insurances. This is a heart that departs from the Lord. In 2 Chronicles 16:1-6, Asa, king of Judah, put his trust in the worldly king of Syria for insurance against his enemies. This offended God who sent judgment. *(16:7) And at that time Hanani the seer came to Asa king of Judah, and said unto him, <u>Because thou hast relied on the king of Syria, and hast not relied</u>*

283

on the Lord thy God, therefore is the host of the king of Syria escaped out of thy hand. (8) Were not the Ethiopians and the Lubim a huge host, with chariots and horsemen exceeding many? yet, <u>because thou didst rely on the Lord</u>, he delivered them into thy hand. (9) For the eyes of the Lord run to and fro throughout the whole earth, <u>to show himself strong</u> in the behalf of them whose <u>heart is perfect toward him</u>. Herein thou hast done foolishly; for from henceforth thou shalt have wars. God is eager to show signs and wonders to those who trust in Him with a perfect heart. You would think that Asa would have learned this lesson, but his trust in man cost him his life as it does for so many. *(12) And in the thirty and ninth year of his reign Asa was diseased in his feet; his disease was exceeding great: yet <u>in his disease he sought not to the Lord, but to the physicians</u>. (13) And Asa slept with his fathers ....*

Christians justify their misplaced trust in man's insurances not realizing that this brings the judgment in the first place. Melvin Jenkins and I were about to go to work on a large crude oil pump for Exxon. Process department had blocked it out of line and drained it, or so we thought. What we did not know was that the pressure gauge read "0" because it was broken and the drain valve though open was stopped up, so there was a little pressure still in the pump. We took the bolts out of the head plate to remove it, but it was stuck. I stood up and took about four steps away to get something to break it loose when I heard a "pop" sound and turned around to see Melvin drenched with black crude from head to foot. As he opened his eyes, he sarcastically looked at me and said, "Dave, you did this to me." Well I could not contain myself and busted out laughing. The thought of me stepping away in the nick of time so that Melvin could get plastered was too much for me. Attempting to sound serious, he said, "Dave, you're never going to do this to me again." I said, "Melvin, you had better watch those self-confident statements. You know God is listening." Then he repeated his statement and said, "Bring me up to the shower house. I have a spare set of clothes up there." I said, "<u>Oh, now I know why you got it instead of me</u>." He said, "Why?" I said, "<u>Because I don't have a spare set of clothes, and God knew it</u>." He looked at me inquisitively. I explained that <u>planning for a catastrophe is the same as having faith for it</u>. It also proves that you do not believe that God will protect or provide. Later that day, we were working on another pump. Melvin was next to me as we used an impact gun to take off some bolts. Suddenly slurry squirted down one of the open bolt holes and hit Melvin in the middle of his chest, leaving me untouched. He looked at me in unbelief. I playfully said, "Melvin, I told you God doesn't like those self-confident statements," but we both knew that God was speaking in this. We could not remember when this had happened to us before, much less twice in one day.

Chapter 19
God's Sovereign Supply

Knowing that the proving of your faith worketh patience. And let patience have its perfect work, that you may be perfect and entire, lacking nothing (Jas.1:3,4).

The children of Israel angered God and spoke against Him in their wilderness trials. In Psalms 78:19-22, they said, *"Can God prepare a table in the wilderness?"* The answer was, *(20) "Behold, <u>he smote the rock so that waters gushed out</u> and streams overflowed."* If He can get a stream out of a rock, He can supply our needs anywhere, anyhow, and we are foolish to question Him. That did not stop them. They said, *(21) "Can He give bread also?"* God was angry when He heard this, and His wrath was kindled. These so-called believers *(22) "<u>Believed not in God, and trusted not in His salvation</u>."* You see, Friends, God wants us to believe for salvation, which in this case means God's supply, every day. If He can pay Peter's taxes out of a fish's mouth or bring water out of a rock, He can meet our needs in any kind of lack. They provoked God with their evil heart of unbelief when all they had to do was mix faith with His promises of provision (Heb.3:6; 4:3).

Early in our discipleship, we began to walk by faith for God to be our supplier so that when we went from part-time to full-time ministry it was natural to continue these methods. We have never "<u>taken</u> up <u>offerings</u> (an oxymoron)," told people our needs, preached "gimmee" sermons, borrowed money, taken government benefits, or worked at a secular job. I am not saying this to brag, but to show God's power to provide without these methods. I also had to go this way to be qualified to teach on this subject. The Apostle Paul said, *(Rom.15:18) "For <u>I will not dare to speak of any things save those which Christ wrought through me</u>, for the obedience of the Gentiles, by word and deed, (19) in the power of signs and* *wonders, in the power of the Holy Spirit."* Years ago the Lord told me, "I am sending you through a wilderness so that you can tell my people that I still supply in the wilderness." As you can imagine, this lifestyle put us in many situations to prove His promises. The Lord wanted me to be able to speak from experience about His sovereignty to *"supply your every need, according to His riches in glory,"* without resorting to the legalistic manipulations that "Christendom" normally resorts to. He said, *"Freely ye received, freely give."* We have received only freewill offerings sent from God through those that He spoke to. I would not have traded these wilderness experiences for anything, for they have totally impressed me with my Father. We have worked diligently in the Lord's service, and He said the *"laborer is worthy of his hire."* My pay comes from Him. This also keeps us free from the manipulations of man.

There is an advantage to knowing that God has sent you. Always seek to be in His Will. About two years after being sent to Pensacola, we had a wonderful experience. We had run out of all food in the house. My wife asked me what we should do. I told her, "Let's set the table by faith." So we did, and the seven of us sat down with empty plates. I prayed a simple little prayer, the only kind I know. I am sure God put this prayer in my heart. I said, "Lord you sent us here, and we are asking you to fill our plates or fill our tummies." In a moment, my oldest son said something that I had never heard out of him before. He said, "Dad, I'm full, I don't need to eat," and he got up. I started looking around at the rest, and they started agreeing with him. I was so surprised listening to them that it was a minute or so before I noticed that I was full and not hungry either. Praise God! God can put food in you that you did not eat. His name is *Jehovah Jireh* meaning "I am Provider"!

Now I do not want you to think that we have always lived on the edge of disaster because God has supplied abundantly. However, when we were in that place of weakness, God's power was made perfect! My children were forced to fast only once in their lives, and that instance ended in a miracle. I did not start out with the faith that I have today. It was kind of mechanical rather than natural. *(Mk.11:24) Therefore I say unto you, All things whatsoever ye pray and ask for, believe that ye receive them, and ye shall have them.* I would go through these steps: I pray; I believe I have received; I accept no other thought. Eventually, it becomes natural to trust in God and not have to work so hard to keep your mind straight. The proving of faith through tribulation works patience, and patience will have its perfect work so that you lack nothing (Jas. 1:2-4).

In another instance, when we once again were running out of food, Mary made a large pot of spaghetti. We blessed the food and ate our fill, which was about two-thirds of the spaghetti. The next day I was standing by the stove when Mary pulled the pot from the refrigerator to heat it up. When she took off the lid, we both looked in the pot and then at each other. I said, "This pot was down to here yesterday," motioning with my finger on the side of the pot. She said, "Yes, I know," and we were awed at the power and goodness of the Lord. What we had eaten the day before had been replaced. Our sovereign God multiplies food. Like the wilderness trial, there is no place that God cannot provide.

My youngest child Jennifer was complaining to Mary in the washroom that her brother Nathan had taken the only bag of potato chips camping. Mary gently pushed her out telling her to go ask the Lord for some. As she did this, the doorbell rang. Jennifer yelled, "It's here! It's here already!" Mary came out and hushed her because she did not know who was at the door. It was a neighbor returning a pan because Mary had given them corn bread in it a few days before. He handed the pan, which had tin foil over it, to Jennifer. When she took off the foil, guess what was inside. Yes, chips! The man lived two blocks behind us. He was coming with the chips before Jennifer complained to Mary. Our sovereign God answered before she called.

Jennifer told Mary that her little wading pool was broken and she wanted another one. Mary sent her to me. She came to me with a catalog in hand. I said, "Jenny, you know where we get things from. Let's ask the Lord." We agreed that God would send her a pool. About a week later, a lady who lived about four blocks away came to our door. She said she was looking for two little boys who had cut her grass before. Nathan recognized her voice and came to the door. When she saw him, she said, "Oh, I see I have found the right house. I would like to make a deal with you. I have a swimming pool I would like to give to you if you could cut my grass a couple of times." The boys agreed. The pool was a 3-foot tall by 12-foot diameter above-ground type with a sand filter, ladder, and vacuum. It was new, still in the box. She had bought it about eight months before to use as an exercise pool but had changed her mind. Sovereign God has pools around the corner just waiting for you to pray.

Once, in our own private wilderness, I decided to grow tomatoes. The bugs and the birds made war on me, and the harvest was a total flop. The Lord then told me that He did not call me to raise tomatoes and to be about the work that He did call me to do. Within a few days, a lady who knew nothing of this was picking tomatoes at a local farm when she thought to pick some for us. She brought us two large bags of the prettiest tomatoes I have ever seen. When I compared them to my little cherries, God's point hit home. The Lord did not need my help.

Mary and I agreed in prayer one morning for meat, mayonnaise and cheese. No one knew of this. That night a lady was going out of town and brought us a gallon of mayonnaise and a turkey that she did not want to go to waste. Then another couple brought the cheese. We can be specific with God. He will prepare a table in the wilderness.

My children wanted to go camping in the woods not far from our house. Making excuses, I told them that the only thing I did not like about that place was that there was no wood for a fire and we could not cut down someone else's trees. God made me eat those unbelieving words. God will supply your needs anywhere! After we set up the tent, I sent the children out to find wood. They came back with rotten limbs and bark off a tree, nothing very usable. There was a fallen tree next to our tent but we did not have any way to cut it up. As I thought on this situation, I walked in a straight line about 20 to 30 feet away from our tent. I noticed a small hump in the leaves on the ground and casually kicked it. There was something hard underneath. I raked the leaves back to find a pillowcase and within it was God's provision! A fairly new Husqvarna chainsaw, the very kind I liked! I thought, "Wouldn't it be awesome if this cranked?" Of course it did, for God had put it there for us. It had been there for a while because the leaves on top looked very natural. Oh, the sovereignty of God, to put in my mind to walk straight to His predestined provision! We cut up that fallen tree and left some for the next guy. I repented for doubting God's provision in that wilderness.

My boys told me that a boy they knew camped in those woods all the time and that he had probably stolen that saw. So I called the police and gave it to them. They said that if no one claimed it within 90 days, I could have it. Even though I did not have a lot of use for it, I claimed it after the 90 days. Just after that, I had a utility bill due, with no money in my hand yet to pay it. The Lord reminded me of the saw. I called a local small engine shop. I told the man I had found the saw but before I could even ask if he knew anyone who needed it, he said, "You bring that saw over here right now, and I'll give you $100 for it." I got the money and went straight to pay the bill just before it was overdue. God saved me twice with that saw. That is the only time I ever sold something to pay a bill. Thank you Father!

Once when traveling and ministering, we noticed a cloud of smoke coming out the rear of our car, which had relatively few miles on it. I checked the oil and found that the car had suddenly started drinking it to the extent of using two quarts in about 50 miles. I checked the normal things and finding them all right concluded that I had broken some rings. We did not have the time nor the money to stop and get the engine overhauled. After several stops to put more oil in, I commanded the rings to be repaired in the name of Jesus. This time the car went much farther before needing oil, and after that it stopped using it entirely. Glory to God! His power was once again made perfect in our weakness as we walked by faith. *(Phl.4:19) And my God shall supply <u>every need</u> of yours according to his riches in glory in Christ Jesus.*

One day on my way to the mailbox, I remembered I had received less than the needed offering that month. Had I stopped and calculated it would have been about $200. As I walked, I asked the Lord to put it in the mailbox. He answers before we call, doesn't He? The answer had to be coming for two or three days before I prayed. Sure enough there was a $200 money order in the mailbox, from an anonymous source. Although offerings in the mail are not very common to our ministry, God had once again come through in time.

There have been times when we needed larger sums of money. Since we did not store up our treasures on earth, and our purses waxed not old, meaning we did not save up money, then we needed manna from heaven. We prayed once to change out the windows of our house and to buy our oldest daughter Deborah a good car. Within a month, we had our answer; $16,000 was coming our way from a completely unexpected source. God has never failed us, no matter what the need.

One reason that there is such an emphasis in Christian circles on investing, buying, selling, and storing is because there is so little understanding of God's true economy of <u>giving</u> and <u>receiving</u>. Jesus said that the last days would be like it was in Lot's day when they <u>bought and sold</u> and God destroyed them (Lk.17:28-30). *(Mt.21:12) And Jesus entered into the temple of God, and cast* *out all them that <u>sold</u> and <u>bought</u>* …. What do you suppose Jesus had against buying and selling among His people? I believe He detested that it had replaced giving and receiving in the nature of His people. Jesus commanded us to *"<u>give and it shall be given unto you</u>, good measure, pressed down, shaken together, running over, shall they give into your bosom" (Lk.6:38).* He promised a reward for giving but none for selling. An opportunity to give is an opportunity to receive it back multiplied. There are times when we need more cash than what we have. In order to be eligible for this multiplication we have to give, not save or invest. Several times I have sent out to someone else the money that I needed for bills only to receive it back from another source multiplied, sometimes on the same day. Curt Bryan is a brother who has always given sacrificially to our ministry. He has given testimony several times that he has written checks to pay his own bills without the money in the bank to cover it, believing God to have the money there in time. In his business his customers are walk-ins, so income is hard to predict. Whenever he has stepped out by faith in this way, God has always come through. A sudden rush of customers would come in, or a generous tip would be given to him.

(2 Cor.9:6) He that soweth sparingly shall reap also sparingly, and he that soweth bountifully shall reap also bountifully. An opportunity to give can also be an opportunity to sit on, or eat the seed. We can only reap to the extent we sow. God multiplies it back not to make us rich but to be channels of His blessing to the needy. He multiplies our seed for sowing, not hoarding. *(10) And he that <u>supplieth seed to the sower</u> and bread for food, shall supply and <u>multiply your seed for sowing</u>, and increase the fruits of your righteousness.* God's promise to those who are faithful in giving is here. *(8) And God is able to make <u>all grace abound unto you, that you having always all sufficiency in everything may abound unto every good work</u>."* This is one of the most powerful, all-encompassing promises

of provision in all of the Scriptures. On the other hand, he that sits on or eats his seed will have to invest, buy, sell, and store with the world because he is disobedient and has no faith. This is where the merchants of Babylon are. They make *"Father's house a house of merchandise" (Jn.2:16)* when they peddle the Word for salaries like the world. Peddling things such as books, tapes, trinkets, chicken dinners, and tours is the way of the world and for those who have an impoverished God. They make *"merchandise of the word of God"* (2 Cor.2:17 [in Greek]). Why would anyone who believed that *"God shall supply every need" (Phl.4:19)* stoop to this? When God sends, He supplies. Without God's supernatural supply, people have to resort to other tactics to support "their own" ministry.

Another tactic is to put God's people under the law to support them when the Scripture clearly states that our giving is *"not of necessity." (2 Cor. 9:7) Let each man do according as he has purposed in his heart* (not according to law)*; not grudgingly, or of necessity* (not according to law)*, for God loveth a cheerful giver.* In the New Testament, God wants an offering from the heart from those born of His Spirit. God made the Old Testament Law with natural Israel, not the Church. If a doctrine, like tithing, is not in the New Testament then it was never made with us! Jesus, rebuking those under the Old Testament, said, *"Woe unto you scribes and Pharisees, hypocrites! for ye tithe mint and anise and cummin* (even their seasoning)*, and have left undone the weightier matters of the law, Justice and mercy, and faith: but these you ought to have done* (past tense) *and not to have left the other undone" (Mt.23:23)*. Jesus clearly said here that tithing was of the Law, and is in the past. Some say tithing was before the Law. Yes, circumcision and animal sacrifice were before the Law too, but they were included in the law, and we are not under law to do them anymore, either. Paul also said tithing was of the Law. *(Heb.7:5) And they indeed of the sons of Levi that receive the priest's office have commandment to take tithes of the people according to the*

293

law .... There is <u>no New Testament command or request to</u> <u>tithe</u> because we are no longer stewards of ten percent but one hundred percent.

In the Old Testament, they were ninety percent owners and ten percent stewards. Jesus taught that we must renounce ownership of the other ninety percent or we cannot be His disciples. *(Lk.4:33) So therefore whosoever he be of you that renounceth not <u>all that he hath</u>, he cannot be my disciple.* "All" here means "<u>all possessions</u>, rights, and will." In the New Testament, either we are stewards of all or we are thieves. The widow who gave the two mites got Jesus' attention, but all the rich Pharisees who tithed did not. That is because God counts the sacrifice and what you have left, not the amount you give. That widow sowed bountifully, not according to the Law. According to 2 Corinthians 9:8, she received *"all grace"* and *"all sufficiency"* for that. When you give, obey the New Testament commands, not the Law, and you will be blessed. None of the great promises above are for those under the Law. When we disobey a New Testament command to obey a law, we have to keep the whole law in order to be justified. *(Gal.3:10) For <u>as many as are of the</u>* <u>*works of the law are under a curse*</u>*: for it is written, Cursed is every one who continueth not in <u>all things that are written in</u>* <u>*the book of the law*</u>*, to do them.*

We are severed from Christ when we hear and obey the law instead of Him. *(Gal.5:4) Ye are <u>severed</u>* <u>*from Christ*</u>*, ye who would be <u>justified by the law</u>; ye are <u>fallen away from grace</u>.* Notice these commands. *(1 Jn.3:17) But whoso hath the world's goods, and <u>beholdeth</u>* <u>*his brother in need*</u>*, and shutteth up his compassion from him, how doth the love of God abide in him? (Lk.6:30) Give to <u>every</u>* <u>*one that asketh thee*</u> .... Many ignore the Lord's commands and pass up the needy in order to keep the law of *"bring ye the whole tithe into the storehouse."* Of course, every religion tells its people that they are the New Testament storehouse. Wrong! The storehouse was in the temple (Mk.12:41;

1 Ki.7:51), and God's people are the temple. Jesus will ask when He returns what we did for the least of His brethren (Mt.25:40), not what we did to support legalistic religious kingdoms. Many will be rejected because they were disobedient. *(Mt.25:44) ... Lord, when saw we thee hungry, or athirst, or a stranger, or naked, or sick, or in prison, and did not minister unto thee? (45) ... Verily I say unto you, Inasmuch as ye did it not unto one of these least, ye did it not unto me. (46) And these shall go away into eternal punishment: but the righteous into eternal life.* All the beautiful buildings will burn, but the temple made without hands will be forever. Support it.

Chapter 20
Spiritual or Carnal Dominion?

If any man [is] for captivity, into captivity he goeth: If any man shall kill with the sword, with the sword must he be killed (Rev.13:10).

Jesus exercised dominion in His kingdom, not the kind of dominion that some want and false religious leaders have, that glorifies man. Jesus rejected the offer by Satan to be a worldly king with carnal dominion. The Pharisees and Sadducees had a carnal dominion over the people of God. Jesus commanded the people not to do what they do but to obey them because they sit in the seat of Moses. They were given governmental authority much the way they are today in the church. Jesus exercised dominion over the curse and over Satan's kingdom. He was destroying the works of Satan in the lives of His people. Jesus had spiritual authority, and the people followed him willingly because they were drawn of the Father, not because they were under the condemnation of the Law. Spiritual authority was necessary to be spiritually and physically fed, healed, and delivered.

The apostate religious leaders had no authority like that then, nor do they now. Even though the disciples did not resist their carnal authority, they did resist their attempting to exercise spiritual authority when it was important. They said, *"We must obey God rather than men."* When Peter tried to enforce his carnal authority with the sword, Jesus said, *All they that take the sword shall perish with the sword (Mt.26:52).* Then to show that His spiritual authority can when necessary dominate the carnal realm, Jesus said, *(Mt.26:53) Or thinkest thou that I cannot beseech my Father, and he shall even now send me more than twelve legions of angels?*

Anyone who has an angel much less 12 legions would not need a puny sword for defense. One angel killed 185,000 men to defend Zion. Jesus then makes the point that if He calls the angels to defend His flesh, how would it be crucified? *(54) How then should the scriptures be fulfilled that thus it must be?* This is a good principle for us who also must be crucified. According to type, crucifixion <u>does not necessitate the physical death of the body, but the old nature.</u> *(Rom.12:1) ... Present your <u>bodies</u> a <u>living</u> sacrifice* .... The body is dead, meaning that it no longer has a will and rights of its own but is devoted to the service of God. In type, just as Jesus sacrificed His literal flesh, we sacrifice the flesh of the old man while we live.

We are told that those who try to defend the body by physical force will be killed for their lack of faith. *(Rev.13:10) If any man [is] for captivity, into captivity he goeth: <u>if any man shall kill with the sword, with the sword must he be killed</u>. Here is the patience and the faith of the saints*. It is also clear here that if a person needs captivity to fulfill in some way their own crucifixion, the sword will not save them. In fact, it will be judgment to them. *(Jn.18:36) Jesus answered, My kingdom is not of this world: <u>if my kingdom were of this world, then would my servants fight</u>, that I should not be delivered to the Jews* .... Those who wrestle with flesh and blood in disobedience to the Word are not fighting for God's kingdom but the world and the flesh. They are attempting to exercise carnal dominion.

Jesus exercised dominion to save God's creation. He did not exercise dominion over people who wanted to put to death His flesh. That is a type for us. We go through many things in order to put to death our flesh. That is what the world was created for, to bring us into sanctification through the death of the old man, the flesh. Even while the world around us is spiritually putting us on our cross by insults, injuries, persecutions, slander, etc., we have to cooperate with them by turning the other cheek. We have authority to save, heal, deliver, provide, AND DIE TO SELF. Exercising our dominion is God exercising His sovereignty through us. Jesus exercised dominion, but He resisted not the evil by turning the other cheek. While the world was crucifying Him, even before He came to the natural cross, His spiritual man was exercising dominion and delivering His people from the curse. We can get mixed up on when to exercise this dominion and when not. We do not have authority to save the old man. We do not want to keep our old life; we want our new life. Jesus said that unless we lose our life, we would not gain our life. So this authority to exercise dominion that God has given us is the same as Jesus had.

This dominion is not to get rich, but it is to have all we need to do God's Will. God gave me my house and car free in order to do His Will. *(Phl.4:19) My God shall supply every __need__ of yours according to His riches in glory in Christ Jesus.* Dominion is not to live after the lusts of the flesh, in a false, worldly prosperity that encourages and empowers the flesh to live. *(1 Tim.6:8) But __having food and covering we shall be therewith content__. (9) But they that are minded to be __rich fall into a temptation and a snare__ and __many foolish and hurtful lusts, such as drown men in destruction__ and perdition.* Here is a promise to those who are not content but love the things of the world. They will be overcome by lusts, and it will be as impossible for them to enter the kingdom as it would be for a camel to go through the eye of a needle (Mt.19:24-26).

Jesus exercised dominion over His flesh when He was going to the cross. He said, *"Not my will but thine be done."* He gave them authority to crucify His flesh. In the garden, when Jesus spoke to those who came to take Him, *"they went backward, and fell to the ground,"* showing that He could stop them if He wanted to save His life or until it was time to go to the cross. He said in John 10:18, *"No one taketh it away from me, but I lay it down of myself."* A couple of times, He passed through their midst, apparently translated, because it was not His time to die (Lk.4:30). He had been given authority to save God's people, who believed, and to destroy Satan's kingdom. Our flesh (the carnal man) is part of Satan's kingdom (Rom.8:7). The book of Esther is not only literally true but also a prophetic parable. Haman (the beast) had been given authority by the king (the Lord) to destroy the people of God while Esther (the bride) had been given authority to save the people of God. The beast and the bride were given opposing authority at the same time by the same king. In type, the beast was given authority to crucify the old man, the carnal nature, and the bride was given authority to bring to life the spiritual man. The king's authority could not be annulled in anything, just as our Lord's authority. Ultimately, the house of the beast was given unto the bride to have authority over it (Esth.8:1).

The time will come when God will no longer offer grace to the Gentiles but will return it to Israel. He will permit Christians, at that time, to exercise authority over the people who are trying to kill them. Fire from the Witnesses' mouths destroying their enemies, smiting the earth with every plague, and stopping the rain for 3-1/2 years, are examples (Rev.11:5,6). From there to the end authority will be manifested to destroy the beast's kingdom until this world becomes God's kingdom and He takes control (Rev.11:15). Personal control differs from control by proxy. God runs everything but He must use vessels of dishonor now (Rom.9:21-24). The time is coming when He will take control in and through His saints who believe. This dominion is ours as spiritual children of Jesus Christ, but we will grow into it by grace.

Dominion starts here in the training grounds but continues for eternity. Here the Lord teaches us how to be rulers under Him over His creation. *(1 Cor.6:1) Dare any of you, having a matter against his neighbor, go to law before the unrighteous, and not before the saints? (2) Or know ye not that the <u>saints shall judge the world</u>? and if the <u>world is judged by you</u>, are ye unworthy to judge the smallest matters? (3) Know ye not that we shall judge angels? How much more things that pertain to this life? (4) <u>If then ye have to judge things pertaining to this life</u>,* *do ye set them to judge who are of no account in the church? (5) I say this to move you to shame ....* If we have authority to judge angels in the next life, how much more do we have authority to judge things in this life?

Jesus taught His disciples to pray like this: *"Thy kingdom come, thy will be done, on earth as it is in heaven."* The Lord pointed out to me that this is a command that God is putting in our mouth. Some would object that this puts us in the place of commanding God. *(Isa.45:11) Thus saith the Lord, the Holy One of Israel, and his Maker: Ask me of the <u>things that are to come</u>; <u>concerning my sons</u>, and <u>concerning the work of my hands, command ye me</u>.* In effect, what we command when led by the Spirit, He carries out.

In Acts 3:6, Peter commands the lame beggar, *"<u>What I have, that give I thee</u>. In the name of Jesus Christ of Nazareth* (we represent Him), *walk."* Peter had authority to represent Jesus and to command the curse. When the lame man walked and bystanders were tempted to credit Peter, he said, *"Why fasten ye your eyes on us, as though by our own power or godliness we had made him to walk?" (Acts 3:12)* God's power fulfills what we command in obedience to Him. Our work here is to manifest God's kingdom here on the earth.

At the last trump, it will be said *(Rev.11:15) ... the kingdom of the world has become the kingdom of our Lord and of his Christ ....* Through whom did God bring this to pass? The Bible gives credit to the saints. *(Dan.7:26) The judgment shall be set and <u>they</u>* (the saints) *<u>shall take away his</u>* (the beast) *<u>dominion to consume and destroy it unto the end</u>. (27) And the kingdom, and the dominion, and the greatness of the kingdoms under the whole heaven shall be given unto the people of the saints of the Most High.* The saints, by God's grace, shall exercise dominion to end the beast's dominion.

Chapter 21
Holiness and Dominion

Holding a form of godliness, but having denied the power thereof: from these also turn away (2 Tim.3:5).

God gave dominion unto Samson even in his ignorance. What was the secret of Samson's power? Judges tells us that the secret was his long hair, and as soon as he lost his long hair he lost his power. Samson was not a big, muscle-bound man. In Judges 16:17, he told Delilah, *"If I be shaven, then my strength will go from me, and I shall become weak, and be like any other man."* His enemies wanted to know the <u>secret</u> of his power. They were not asking, "How did you get such big muscles?" That did not occur to them. It is not because of our great ability, or power, or wisdom, or even sinlessness, but through what Jesus did at the cross that we have this authority to reign over sin and its curse. Samson reigned over the enemies of God's people. When Samson lost his submission to God, he lost his dominion. In 1 Corinthians 11:3-16, the <u>long hair</u> was given unto the woman as <u>a sign of submission to her husband</u>. Who is our husband? The Lord is our husband. The one who took the Nazarite vow, as Samson did, could not cut his hair as a sign of submission. The point is that this great dominion was given to Samson, and he lost it because he lost his hair, a sign of his submission to the Lord.

Nazarites were <u>separated</u> from the world by their submission unto the Lord signified by their long hair. *(Num.6:5) All the days of his vow of <u>separation</u> there shall <u>no razor come upon his head</u>: until the days be fulfilled, in which he <u>separateth himself unto the Lord</u>, he shall <u>be holy</u>; he shall let the locks of the <u>hair of his head grow long</u>.* This separation by submission is the meaning of holiness. How did Samson lose his holiness and power? *(Jdg.16:19) And she* (Delilah) *made him <u>sleep upon her knees</u>; and she called for a man, and <u>shaved off the seven</u>*

locks of his head; and she began to afflict him, and his strength went from him. Samson went to sleep, spiritually meaning he no longer had his eyes open to the light of the truth. He submitted his head or mind in the lap of the harlot Delilah and lost his hair (submission, separation, holiness) and consequently his power or dominion. The moral of that story is that we should not let the harlot have our mind for then we will have no power of dominion. The religious systems of man, the harlot, have deprived God's people of their power because they are not submitted to the Word of God. *(2 Tim.3:5) Holding a form of godliness, but having denied the power thereof: from these also turn away.*

The "bride" in the Song of Solomon was a prophetic parable of the sojourning of the Bride today who temporarily lost her submission. *(S. of Sol. 5:7) The watchmen* (ministers) *that go about the city found me, They smote me, they wounded me; The keepers of the walls* (denominations or sects) *took away my mantle* (Hebrew: "veil") *from me.* The watchmen are identified by the Lord as shepherds (Hebrew: "pastors") in Isaiah 56:10-12. These pastors, in trying to keep the Bride within their sectarian walls, smote her and took away her veil, which is also a sign of submission to her husband, the Lord. *(1 Cor.11:3) ... The head of the woman is the man ... (5) But every woman praying or prophesying with her head unveiled dishonoreth her head ... (10) for this cause ought the woman to have [a sign of] authority on her head ... (13) Judge ye in yourselves: is it seemly that a woman pray unto God unveiled?* False shepherds have made the people of God submissive to religions rather than Christ.

In a true type to our day, the Bride in vain sought her beloved first in the broad ways of Babylonish religion. *(S. of Sol. 3:2) [I said], I will rise now, and go about the city* (Babylon)*; In the streets and in the broad ways I will seek him whom my soul loveth: I sought him, but I found him not.* She sought Him from the false shepherds whose loyalty was to themselves and their own kingdom. *(3) The watchmen that go about the city found* *me; [To whom I said], Saw ye him whom my soul loveth?* It was not until she was delivered from them that she found the one whom her soul sought. *(4) It was but a little that I <u>passed from them</u>, When <u>I found him</u> whom my soul loveth: I held him, and would not let him go,* (In her excitement she wanted to share Him with those among whom she was first conceived and birthed.) *Until I had <u>brought him into my mother's house</u>, And into the chamber of her that <u>conceived me</u>.* The other daughters of that corporate mother did not share her excitement for her peculiar beloved. *(5:9) <u>What is thy beloved more than [another] beloved</u>, O thou fairest among women? What is thy beloved more than [another] beloved, That thou dost so adjure us?* Because of her not being content with *"another Jesus,"* she was not defiled with the religions of these other daughters and was chosen by her Lord. *(6:9) My dove, my <u>undefiled</u>, is [but] one; She is the <u>only one of her mother</u>; She is the <u>choice one of her that bare her</u>. The <u>daughters saw her</u>, and called her blessed.* She regained her dominion when she became <u>undefiled</u> with the women representing the false religious systems. Those who bear fruit will walk in the holiness of her steps, not being defiled with the seed (word) of the men, for they are spiritual virgins. *(Rev.14:4) These are they that were <u>not defiled with women</u>; for they are <u>virgins</u>. These [are] they that <u>follow the Lamb</u> whithersoever he goeth. These were purchased from among men, [to be] the <u>firstfruits</u> unto God and unto the Lamb.* The sects of Christianity have become defiled with what Paul warned in 2 Corinthians 11:4, *"Another Jesus, whom we did not preach, or [if] ye receive a different spirit, which ye did not receive, or a different Gospel, which ye did not accept."* *(2 Cor.6:17) Wherefore Come ye out from among them, and <u>be ye separate</u>, saith the Lord, And touch <u>no unclean</u> thing; And I will receive you.* Only the Word is the truth that sets free. *(2 Cor.7:1) Having therefore these promises, beloved, let us <u>cleanse ourselves from all defilement</u> of flesh and spirit, perfecting <u>holiness</u> in the fear of God.*

303

Jesus calls His sheep out of the fold of apostate religion to *"follow the Lamb whithersoever he goeth." (Jn.10:3) ... He calleth his own sheep by name, and leadeth them out. (4) When he hath put forth all his own, he goeth before them, and the sheep follow him: for they know his voice. (5) And a stranger will they not follow, but will flee from him: for they know not the voice of strangers.* This little flock that follows the Lord in rest is what the bride sought for. *(S. of Sol.1:7) Tell me, O thou whom my soul loveth, Where thou feedest [thy flock], Where thou makest [it] to rest at noon: For why should I be as one that is veiled beside the flocks of thy companions?* The veil in this case represents the blindness and bondage of submission to religion. *(2 Cor.3:15) But unto this day, whensoever Moses is read, a veil lieth upon their heart. (16) But whensoever it shall turn to the Lord, the veil is taken away. (17) Now the Lord is the Spirit: and where the Spirit of the Lord is, [there] is liberty. (18) But we all, with unveiled face beholding as in a mirror the glory of the Lord, are transformed into the same image from glory to glory ....* As we can see, those who are unveiled of the legalism of religion see the Lord and come into His likeness.

The beloved Lord's answer to *"Where thou feedest [thy flock]?"* was *(S.of Sol.1:8) If thou know not, O thou fairest among women, Go thy way forth by the footsteps of the flock, And feed thy kids beside the shepherds' tents.* In Jesus' day it was not possible to feed His Church, meaning "called-out ones," in the apostate sects of Judaism, so He fed them *"beside the shepherds' tents."* Likewise, because the Church has greatly apostatized in our day, Jesus is feeding the flock of freedom, rest, and truth, outside the shepherds' tents. This brought reproach to the bride and Jesus. *(6) ... My mother's sons were incensed against me ....* Those who take up their cross to follow Jesus are commanded to accept this same reproach. *(Heb. 13:11) For the bodies of those beasts whose blood is brought into the holy place by the high priest [as an offering] for sin, are burned without the camp.*

(12) Wherefore Jesus also, that he might sanctify the people through his own blood, suffered without the gate. (13) Let us therefore go forth unto him without the camp, bearing his reproach.

Moses, in a true type of Christ, led his people out of the camp of the rebellious apostates. *(Ex.33:7) Now Moses used to take the tent and to pitch it without the camp, afar off from the camp; and he called it, The tent of meeting. And it came to pass, that every one that sought the Lord went out unto the tent of meeting, which was without the camp.* It is in these days that thundering judgments will put the fear of God in those in the camp to come out and meet with the "called-out ones" in the true mountain of God's kingdom. *(Ex. 19:15) And he said unto the people, Be ready against the third day: come not near a woman* (apostate sect). *(16) And it came to pass on the third day, when it was morning* (the beginning of the third millennium since the last Adam – where we are now [2 Pet.3:8], *that there were thunders and lightnings, and a thick cloud upon the mount, and the voice of a trumpet exceeding loud; and all the people that were in the camp trembled. (17) And Moses brought forth the people out of the camp to meet God; and they stood at the nether part of the mount.*

If you have discovered that you have been following man's religions and decide to repent, God will restore your dominion. In bondage to the Philistines, Samson repented and his hair began to grow. His dominion returned and he brought down their false temple upon their heads. *(Jdg.16:30) And Samson said, Let me die with the Philistines. And he bowed himself with all his might; and the house fell upon the lords, and upon all the people that were therein. So the dead that he slew at his death were more than they that he slew in his life.* Likewise, as we die to self, we increase in dominion over our enemies.

Few who ever exercised dominion in the earth for God were manifestly perfect, including Samson. He refused the dominion

305

of the Lord over himself, and he ultimately lost the dominion that he had over the earth. It is not necessary for God to take away the promises of dominion from the rebellious. Their own heart will not have the faith to partake of it. *(1 Jn.3:21) Beloved if our heart condemn us not, we have boldness towards God, and whatsoever we ask, we receive of him, because we keep his commandments and do the things that are pleasing in his sight.* If we do not serve God, our own heart will condemn us and we will have no faith to exercise dominion. He is still not speaking of manifestly perfect people here, but He does expect us to be disciples, walking in the light that we have. In this way, we are perfect by faith until we manifest perfection. The baby Christian has little knowledge of good and evil, but he is innocent in God's eyes if he is doing what he knows to do. Baby Christians have dominion over sin and the curse, but not over God's people.

Years ago, I had a dream instructing me about the way in which God promotes some to leadership positions over His people. I am making no claims for myself with this dream, merely pointing out principles. *In this dream, there were two mountains.* (The first mountain represents the kingdom of the world, Babylon, and the second mountain represents the kingdom of God, Mount Zion.) *I was driving a car down the first steep mountain.* (This represents humbling ourselves to the Word [Isa.40:4], becoming as a child [Mt.18:4], and losing our carnal life in this world [Mt.16:25,26] *The road that descended this mountain had a trench going down the center of it to the bottom. My car had one set of tires on one side of the trench while the other set was on the other side. I could not turn right or left without falling into the trench and, of course, halting my progress.* (Joshua received instructions similar to this for taking the Promised Land. *(Josh.1:7) Only be strong and very courageous, to observe to do according to all the law, which Moses my servant commanded thee; turn not from it to the right hand or to the left that thou mayest have good success whithersoever thou goest.* Turning to the right or to the left symbolizes getting off the narrow road of Scripture. It will stop us from exercising authority to take our promised land, which symbolizes living on the promises.)

At the bottom of this hill, I got out of the car. I sensed that I had many enemies. (The more we humble ourselves to God's Word the more enemies we will have, both in the carnal church and the world, just as our Lord.) *Then I found hidden under a bush some tools like hammers, screwdrivers, and wrenches, which were drenched in oil.* (The burning bush is where Moses received authority to deliver God's people from bondage. Tools bind and loose, as does God's authority given to His disciples (Mt.18:18). The promises of the Word are the binding and loosing keys to the kingdom of God that were given to disciples. The oil signifies the power of the Holy Spirit. In other words, if we stay in the straight and narrow way, we will receive authority to bind and loose for God.) *From there, I turned to the right* (The sheep are set on the right [Mt.25:33]) *and went up a steep mountain.* (Going down the first mountain entitles us to go up the next. Being humbled in the estimation of the world makes us great in the estimation of the kingdom. The last shall be first and the least shall be greatest. *(Isa.40:3) ... Prepare ye in the wilderness the way of the Lord ... (4) Every valley shall be exalted, and every mountain and hill shall be made low ....* The way of the Lord is that those who are humble in the world shall be promoted on God's mountain, but those who are exalted in the worldly mountain will have to come down.) *(Jas.4:10) Humble yourselves in the sight of the Lord, and he shall exalt you.*

Reaching the top of the mountain, I went through the door of an immense palace. (Jn.10:2) But he that entereth in by the door is the shepherd of the sheep. (7) Jesus therefore said unto them again, Verily, verily, I say unto you, I am the door of the sheep. (Jesus is the only Shepherd of the sheep. He uses vessels that come to the sheep only through Him, the door. This palace represents the New Jerusalem on Mount Zion, the city that rules over God's people.) Old Jerusalem ruled over God's physical letter people just as New Jerusalem rules over God's spiritual New Testament people. Paul declared that we <u>have come</u> to this spiritual city. He showed us that it is not a physical city that can be touched. *(Heb.12:18) For ye are <u>not come unto [a mount]</u> <u>that might be touched</u> … (22) but <u>ye are come unto mount Zion</u>, and unto the city of the living God, the heavenly Jerusalem … (23) to the general assembly and <u>church of the firstborn</u>* …. (Jesus' called-out ones come to this mountain. Our journey is to come to this mountain, climb it, and enter the throne room through the door.)

Then I saw Jesus, the Son of David, sitting on the throne of David. I walked over and <u>sat down next to him</u>, and we talked. (The throne is the place of dominion that the bride has next to her king.) *(Rev.3:21) <u>He that overcometh, I will give to him to sit down</u> <u>with me in my throne</u>, as I also overcame, and sat down with my Father in his throne.* All who overcome the stubbornness of their evil heart to abide in the Name of Jesus will come to this throne. *(Jer.3:17) At that time they shall call <u>Jerusalem</u> the <u>throne</u> of the Lord; and <u>all the nations</u>* (of the Gentile Church) *shall be gathered unto it, <u>to the name of the Lord</u>, to Jerusalem: neither shall they walk any more after the <u>stubbornness of their</u> <u>evil heart</u>.* (All who overcome the first mountain of the world will live on the second mountain of the kingdom of God. These act in *"the name of the Lord"* because they are seated in the throne of authority with Jesus. This position has been given to all who are born again, but many have turned to the right or left and do not take their rightful position by abiding in Christ.) *(Epe.2:5) Even when we were dead through our trespasses, made us alive together with Christ (by grace have ye been saved), (6) and raised us up with him, and <u>made us to sit with</u> <u>him in the heavenly [places], in Christ Jesus</u>.*

As I talked with Jesus, I heard a noise behind me and turned to see some men trying to climb up into the throne room through a rear window. Jesus said, "Don't worry about them; they can't come in here." (Obviously, the position of authority may be usurped in Babylon but not in Zion, God's mountain and kingdom.) *(Jn.10:1) He that entereth <u>not by the door</u> into the fold of the sheep, but <u>climbeth up some other way</u>, the same is a <u>thief and a robber</u>.* Jesus, speaking of the apostate ministers of His day said, *"All that came before me are <u>thieves and robbers</u>" (Jn.10:8)*; and so it is today. Many have <u>stolen the position</u> of authority by not going down the road of humbling themselves to the Word and entering through the door of Christ. They have <u>robbed</u> the sheep of gifted mentors. They have <u>robbed</u> the sheep of Christ, for ministers can only pass on what they are. Religion has historically made the same mistake. They mistake education in a sect of Christianity to be God's authority and commission. The disciples were perceived to be unlearned and ignorant by the religious leaders (Acts 4:13). However, the religious leaders knew that the disciples had been with Jesus by their gifts. Faith, fruit, maturity, submission to the Lord, and personal knowledge of the Lord and His ways must be passed on to the sheep. Ministers cannot pass on what they do not possess themselves. The daughter harlots (Rev.17:5) are still mass producing hirelings (Jn.10:12,13; Isa.56:9-12); but Jesus comes to lead His sheep out of the Babylonish sheepfolds of men (Jn.10:3,4) so that, unhindered by the traditions of men, they may run after Him. A man must be an elder in experience and maturity in the Word to be promoted as a bishop (overseer) over God's people (1 Tim.3:1-7; Titus 1:5-9).

A friend dreamed about Christians as babies with beards, showing they had been with the Lord for many years but were still immature. God's people have loved the world so He has given them immature apostate leaders to tell them what they want to hear. *(Isa.3:4) And I will give <u>children to be their princes</u>, and <u>babes shall rule over them</u>. (5) And the people shall be oppressed, every one by another, and every one by his* neighbor: <u>*the child shall behave himself proudly against the old*</u> <u>*man*</u>*, and the base against the honorable.* Choose the man with the gift over the man with the title. *(2 Tim.4:3) For the time will come when they will not endure the sound doctrine; but, having itching ears, will* <u>*heap to themselves teachers after their*</u> <u>*own lusts; (4) and will* </u><u>*turn away their ears from the truth*</u>*, and turn aside unto* <u>*fables*</u>*.*

Chapter 22
Start Now

For he saith, At an acceptable time I <u>hearkened</u> unto thee, And in <u>a day of salvation did I succor</u> (help) <u>thee</u>: behold, <u>now is the acceptable time</u>; behold, <u>now is the day</u> of salvation (2 Cor.6:2).

Everyone is waiting on the Lord to move. He hearkened and, in a day of salvation, He saved us. <u>Now</u> is our acceptable time to act on that salvation. <u>Now</u> is our day of salvation from the entire curse. Jesus conquered the devil and his kingdom in His day. *(Jn.12:31) Now is the judgment of this world: <u>now shall the prince of this world be cast out</u>. (16:33) ... In the world ye have tribulation: but be of good cheer; <u>I have overcome the world</u>.* In other words, be happy because of the good news that this wicked world <u>has been</u> conquered. It is now under the feet of the true body of Christ. *(Epe.1:22) And he put <u>all</u> things in subjection <u>under his feet</u>, and gave him to be head over all things to the church, (23) which is <u>his body</u>, the fulness of him that filleth all in all.*

What is needed now is for those who believe to act on the authority of the Word, <u>using God's power</u> to manifest what happened at the cross. *(Rom.8:13) For if ye live after the flesh, ye must die; but <u>if by the Spirit ye</u> put to death the deeds of the body, ye shall live.* Notice that we act by the power of the Spirit. The Spirit's power is available to all who act on the Word. *(2 Cor.7:1) Having therefore these promises, beloved, <u>let us cleanse ourselves from all defilement of flesh and spirit, perfecting holiness in the fear of God</u>.* Jesus made it plain that we are not to be waiting on His coming in the harvest to accomplish His work. *(Jn.4:35) Say not ye, There are yet four months, and [then] cometh the harvest? behold, I say unto you, Lift up your eyes, and look on the fields, that they are white already unto harvest.*

(36) He that reapeth receiveth wages, and gathereth fruit unto life eternal ....

It is really easy for us to just depend upon the world and the world's way of doing things, but wilderness times are coming that will make this impossible. *"The righteous shall live by faith,"* which is a radical departure from the normal, everyday "Christian" life. We should learn to do things with our faith for no other reason than to grow in the authority and experience of righteous living. You can start in areas that you may think make no difference, except that the Lord wants to train every one of us to be vessels to bring salvation, deliverance, healing, and provision to ourselves and those who believe. When we use our faith, we learn that God honors His Word, and we will begin to step out a little more. Each success is laying a foundation for following successes so that you know you can reach out your faith to command the provision of God. The day will come when your experience will save lives, as it has for me.

I share with you here some of my early experiences, not to glory in self, but Christ; *for we have nothing that we did not receive from Him (1 Cor.4:7).* As a young Christian, I asked the Lord to take me by the hand and to teach me how to be His disciple. I truly felt that He walked with me to teach me. I had been studying faith and was eager to exercise it. Don Robertson, the man who witnessed to me, and I were going water skiing. We started my car to hitch up the boat and noticed a noise under the hood. We opened it and found that the alternator shaft was wobbling because a bearing had gone out. Don said, "What are we going to do?" I said, "Let's command it to be fixed and go skiing by faith." Don agreed, so we put our fingers on the noisy alternator and commanded it to be healed in the name of Jesus. We slammed the hood, hooked up the boat, and took off for Old River, which was about an hour's drive. By this time, it had started to cloud up and lightning in the direction we were going. Then I realized that this was another good opportunity to see God's wondrous works. I said to Don, "Let's point our fingers at those clouds and tell them to get out of our way." We spoke the command together. As we drove, the clouds parted. We could see clouds out both side windows and blue sky out the windshield for several miles in front of our car. We rejoiced in the Lord!

When we reached False River, on the way to Old River, we had to slow down because of the settlement. It was then that we noticed that there was no noise coming from under the hood. Don said, "Stop the car! I want to see this!" We opened the hood, and that alternator was running perfectly true and smooth with no noise. Glory to God, I never did change that alternator! We had to go left toward Old River, so we were turning into the clouds that had parted. We repeated our demand and the clouds parted in a perpendicular direction, ruling out natural wind currents. God was making a point. We had a beautiful, sunny day for skiing but we could see the clouds in almost every direction. Some would think that it is unimportant to Almighty God whether we had a nice day for skiing or not. It is important to Him for our training, experience, and sometimes just for our enjoyment.

Once, on my way to pick up my daughter, Deborah, from church kindergarten, my car died about three blocks from the school. I cranked the car until the battery died. Not wanting to be late, I started walking. The sky was dark with black rolling clouds and immediately the bottom fell out of those clouds. A voice in my head said, "Why don't you command that rain to stop?" I lifted my hand and swung it horizontally at those clouds and said, "STOP, in the name of Jesus." The rain stopped as though I had taken a knife and cut it off across the sky. Encouraged, I picked up Deborah and told her the story as we walked back. I said, "If God can do that, He can also start that car. When we get there we are going to lay our hands on the dash and command it to start in Jesus' name." We got in, laid our hands on the dash and said, "START, in the name of Jesus." I turned the key and held it on. At first the battery had built up a little so it spun over pretty well, but the longer I held it, the weaker it got. The starter spun over until it would spin no more, and still I held the key on. After a moment of holding the key on with a dead battery, it suddenly started like it had two batteries in it. I know that the Lord did it that way so that I would know it was of Him. Looking back, I was so pumped up from the Lord cutting off the rain that I am surprised every car in the city did not start when we gave the command. Glory to God! He takes us by the hand and encourages us along the way.

I hope this has blessed you. Go with God.

Acknowledgments

First and foremost, I thank my Father who works in us to will and to do of His good pleasure and without whom we are nothing and can do nothing. I thank Him also that His continued grace will grant you to understand this work and benefit from it. Please ask God and agree with me to this end.

I would like to give thanks to God for April Fields, whom He sent to me to make up for what I am, as a writer, sadly lacking. She worked tirelessly at her own expense for no other reason than the love of God's people. She designed the cover of this book. She has made me look good. She is also helping me with another book. Thank God.

I thank God for Bill Rowe who bought a transcribing machine and put in long hours at his own expense to transcribe many teaching cassettes on the Sovereignty of God. These were the foundation for this book. He did it for the love of you the reader. God bless him.

I thank God for my friend Doug McDuffee who prodded me for a couple of years to make a book from those cassettes. At the time I was not impressed to do it. Then, when in a moment of time I became impressed, I saw Doug's efforts as confirmation of God's will.

I thank God for the brothers and sisters who have contributed toward the publishing of this book. I will not reveal your names "that thine alms may be in secret: and thy Father who seeth in secret shall recompense thee."

I thank God for my son Justin, who helped me day and night with his computer skills. God prepared him just in time to help me with this book. God bless him. I thank God for my wife Mary, who worked tirelessly on the galley. Please pray for her and my children that they will be vessels of honor.

God bless JoAnn Booker, Dwora Jawer and Brad Moyers, who proofread the manuscript for the love of you the reader. And last but not least, God bless Jamie Hughs for formatting the manuscript.

Your servant in Christ,
Dave Eells

Author's End Notes

I have been told that I should supply a picture and biography for this book. Honestly, the thought makes me uncomfortable. If this is an important part of Christian authorship then you have the wrong book. I assure you I am not an eminent theologian. The important question is, has the Holy Spirit found a willing vessel?

When the disciples were interrogated by the theologians, the Scripture says in Acts 4:13, *"Now when they beheld the boldness of Peter and John, and had perceived that they were unlearned and ignorant men, they marveled; and they took knowledge of them, that they had been with Jesus."* When you read this book, I believe that you will see that I am qualified for the same reasons to be used by the Lord, for His *"power is made perfect in weakness."*

Once, as I was teaching a group of seminary students, one of them asked me why I had not attended their college. I said, "If I had attended your college, I would have been limited to study from the best that your denomination has to offer. If I desire to study what men have to say about the Word, I can go to the Christian bookstore and study the best that history has to offer." Another then asked, "How do you then discipline yourself to study? We have to study in order to give answers." I said, "Yes, but only the answers that they want to hear. For me it is a gift. It is my desire to study. I do not have to be under a law."

When I came to the Lord, having never been a studious person, those who knew me were shocked because all I wanted to do was study the Word. A little later I studied the writings of the reformers, early church fathers and a few modern teachers. Soon that fad passed and I stuck with the Word and the Holy Spirit, finding them immeasurably superior.

May God bless you in your search for truth.

Your servant in Christ,
David Eells

ALSO COMING SOON

HIDDEN MANNA FOR THE END TIMES is for the purpose of giving insight into hidden revelations of the last days. Solidly proven from Scripture, Words of Knowledge and Wisdom, the author brings explosive revelations that are clearly explained to the reader. This will prepare God's people to recognize the signs for the times to come.

SUBJECT MATTER:

Beginning Revelation • First Key to Hidden Manna • When Do We Go? • Second Key to Hidden Manna • Man-child and Woman • Caught Up To The Throne • Maturity and Harvests • Prepare For a Wilderness Blessing • Son of Perdition • Two Witnesses • Who is the Antichrist Beast? • Beast Covenant and Abomination • Mark and Image of the Beast • False Prophet and Religious Harlot • Fall of the United States • Fall of the World • Fall of the Fruitless

More of David's teachings
audios, videos, books, radio programs, & chatroom programs
can be found at:
www.americaslastdays.com